To: Dad ♡♡♡

Hope you enjoy the book

Lots of love,

Nic..

7/30/09

# THE REASON FOR GOD

# THE REASON FOR GOD

*Belief in an age of scepticism*

Timothy Keller

HODDER &
STOUGHTON

First published by Penguin Group (USA) Inc. in 2008

First published in Great Britain in 2008 by Hodder & Stoughton
An Hachette Livre UK company.

4

A CIP catalogue record for this title is available from the British Library

ISBN 978 0 340 97932 7
Trade paperback ISBN 978 0 340 97947 1

Offset by Avon DataSet Ltd, Bidford on Avon, Warwickshire

Printed and bound in Great Britain by Clays Ltd, St Ives plc

Hodder & Stoughton policy is to use papers that are natural, renewable and
recyclable products and made from wood grown in sustainable forests. The
logging and manufacturing processes are expected to conform to the
environmental regulations of the country of origin.

Hodder & Stoughton
338 Euston Road
London NW1 3BH

www.hodder.co.uk

*To Kathy, the Valiant*

# Contents

# Contents

# INTRODUCTION

*I find your lack of faith – disturbing.*
—Darth Vader

## The Enemies Are Both Right

There is a great gulf today between what is popularly known as liberalism and conservatism. Each side demands that you not only disagree with but disdain the other as (at best) crazy or (at worst) evil. This is particularly true when religion is the point at issue. Progressives cry out that fundamentalism is growing rapidly and non-belief is stigmatised. They point out that politics has turned toward the right, supported by mega-churches and mobilised orthodox believers. Conservatives endlessly denounce what they see as an increasingly sceptical and relativistic society. Major universities, media companies and elite institutions are heavily secular, they say, and they control the culture.

Which is it? Is scepticism or faith on the ascendancy in the world today? The answer is Yes. The enemies are both right. Scepticism, fear and anger towards traditional religion are growing in power and influence. But at the same time, robust, orthodox belief in the traditional faiths is growing as well.

The non-churchgoing population in the United States and Europe is steadily increasing.[1] The number of Americans answering 'no religious preference' to poll questions has skyrocketed, having doubled or even tripled in the last decade.[2] A century ago most US universities shifted from a formally Christian foundation to an overtly secular one.[3] As a result, those with traditional religious beliefs have little foothold in any of the institutions of cultural power. But even as more and more people identify themselves as having 'no religious preference', certain churches with supposedly obsolete beliefs in an infallible Bible and miracles are growing in the United States and exploding in Africa, Latin America and Asia. Even in much of Europe, there is some growth in church attendance.[4] And despite the secularism of most universities and colleges, religious faith is growing in some corners of academia. It is estimated that 10 to 25 per cent of all the teachers and professors of philosophy in America are orthodox Christians, up from less than 1 per cent just thirty years ago.[5] Prominent academic Stanley Fish may have had an eye on that trend when he reported, 'When Jacques Derrida died [in November 2004] I was called by a reporter who wanted to know what would succeed high theory and the triumvirate of race, gender, and class as the center of intellectual energy in the academy. I answered like a shot: religion.'[6]

In short, the world is polarising over religion. It is getting both more religious and less religious at the same time. There was once a confident belief that secular European countries were the harbingers for the rest of the world. Religion, it was thought, would thin out from its more robust, supernaturalist forms or die out altogether. But the theory that technological advancement brings inevitable secularisation is now being scrapped or radically rethought.[7] Even Europe may not face a secular future, with Christianity growing modestly and Islam growing exponentially.

# The Two Camps

I speak from an unusual vantage point on this two-edged phenomenon. I was raised in a mainline Lutheran church in eastern Pennsylvania. When I reached my teens in the early 1960s, the time came for me to attend confirmation class, a two-year course that covered Christian beliefs, practices and history. Its aim was to bring young people into a fuller understanding of the faith, so they could publicly commit to it. My teacher for the first year was a retired minister. He was quite traditional and conservative, speaking often of the danger of hell and the need for great faith. In the second year of the course, however, the instructor was a new, young cleric just out of seminary. He was a social activist and was filled with deep doubts about traditional Christian doctrine. It was almost like being instructed in two different religions. In the first year, we stood before a holy, just God whose wrath could only be turned aside at great effort and cost. In the second year, we heard of a spirit of love in the universe, who mainly required that we work for human rights and the liberation of the oppressed. The main question I wanted to ask our instructors was, 'Which one of you is lying?' But fourteen-year-olds are not so bold, and I just kept my mouth shut.

My family later found its way to a more conservative church in a small Methodist denomination. For several years this strengthened what could be called the 'Hellfire Layer' of my religious formation, although the pastor and people there were personally as gentle as could be. Then I went off to one of those fine, liberal, smaller universities in the Northeast, which quickly began to throw water on the hellfire in my imagination.

The history and philosophy departments were socially radicalised and were heavily influenced by the neo-Marxist critical theory of the Frankfurt School. In 1968, this was heady stuff. The social activism was particularly attractive, and the critique of American bourgeoisie society was compelling, but its philosophical underpinnings were confusing to me. I seemed to see two camps before me, and there was something radically wrong with both of them. The people most passionate about social justice were moral relativists, while the morally upright didn't seem to care about the oppression going on all over the world. I was emotionally drawn to the former path – what young person wouldn't be? Liberate the oppressed and sleep with who you wanted! But I kept asking the question, 'If morality is relative, why isn't social justice as well?' This seemed to be a blatant inconsistency in my professors and their followers. Yet now I saw the stark contradiction in the traditional churches. How could I turn back to the kind of orthodox Christianity that supported segregation in the South and apartheid in South Africa? Christianity began to seem very unreal to me, though I was unable to discern a viable alternative way of life and thought.

I didn't know it at the time, but this spiritual 'unreality' stemmed from three barriers that lay across my path. During my college years, these three barriers eroded and my faith became vital and life-affecting. The first barrier was an intellectual one. I was confronted with a host of tough questions about Christianity: 'What about other religions? What about evil and suffering? How could a loving God judge and punish? Why believe anything at all?' I began to read books and arguments on both sides of these issues and slowly but surely, Christianity began to make more and more sense. The rest of this book lays out why I still think so.

The second barrier was an interior, personal one. As a child, the plausibility of a faith can rest on the authority of others, but when we reach adulthood there is a need for personal, firsthand experience as well. While I had 'said my prayers' for years, and while I sometimes had that inspirational, aesthetic sense of wonder at the sight of a sea or mountain, I had never experienced God's presence personally. This required not so much knowledge of techniques for prayer, but a process in which I came to grips with my own needs, flaws and problems. It was painful, and was, as is typical, triggered by disappointments and failures. It would take another, different kind of book to go into them. But it needs to be said that faith-journeys are never simply intellectual exercises.

The third barrier was a social one. I desperately needed to find a 'third camp', a group of Christians who had a concern for justice in the world but who grounded it in the nature of God rather than in their own subjective feelings. When I found that 'band of brothers' – and sisters (just as important!) – things began to change for me. These three barriers did not come down quickly or in any set order. Rather, they were intertwined and dependent on one another. I did not work through them in any methodical way. It's only in hindsight that I see how the three factors worked together. Because I was always looking for that third camp, I became interested in shaping and initiating new Christian communities. That meant the ministry, so I entered it just a few years after college.

## The View from Manhattan

In the late 1980s, my wife, Kathy, and I moved to Manhattan with our three young sons to begin a new church for a largely non-churchgoing population. During the research phase I was told by almost everyone that it was a fool's errand. Church meant moderate or conservative; the city was liberal and edgy. Church meant families; New York City was filled with young singles and 'non-traditional' households. Church most of all meant belief, but Manhattan was the land of sceptics, critics and cynics. The middle class, the conventional market for a church, was fleeing the city because of crime and rising costs. That left the sophisticated and hip, the wealthy and the poor. Most of these people just laugh at the idea of church, I was told. Congregations in the city were dwindling, most struggling to even maintain their buildings.

Many of my early contacts said that the few congregations that had maintained a following had done so by adapting traditional Christian teaching to the more pluralistic ethos of the city. 'Don't tell people they *have* to believe in Jesus – that's considered narrow-minded here.' They were incredulous when I explained that the beliefs of the new church would be the orthodox, historic tenets of Christianity – the infallibility of the Bible, the deity of Christ, the necessity of spiritual regeneration (the new birth) – all doctrines considered hopelessly dated by the majority of New Yorkers. Nobody ever said forget about it 'fuggedaboutit' out loud, but it always hung in the air.

Nevertheless, we launched Redeemer Presbyterian Church, and by the end of 2007 it had grown to more than 5,000 attendees and had spawned more than a dozen daughter congregations in the immediate metropolitan area. The church is quite multiethnic and young (average age about thirty) and is more than two-thirds single. Meanwhile, dozens of other similarly orthodox-believing congregations have sprung up in Manhattan and hundreds of others throughout the four other boroughs. One survey showed that in the last several years more than a hundred churches had been started in New York City by Christians from Africa alone. We were as stunned by this as anyone.

New York isn't alone. In the autumn of 2006 *The Economist* ran a story with the subtitle 'Christianity is collapsing everywhere but London'. The crux of the article was that despite the fact that church attendance and profession of the Christian faith was plummeting across Britain and Europe, many young professionals (and new immigrants) in London were flocking to evangelical churches.[8] That is exactly what I've seen here.

This leads to a strange conclusion. We have come to a cultural moment in which both sceptics and believers feel their existence is threatened because both secular scepticism and religious faith are on the rise in significant, powerful ways. We have neither the Western Christendom of the past nor the secular, religionless society that was predicted for the future. We have something else entirely.

## A Divided Culture

Three generations ago, most people inherited rather than chose their religious faith. The great majority of people belonged to one of the historic, mainline Protestant churches or the Roman Catholic Church. Today, however, the now-dubbed 'old-line' Protestant churches of cultural, inherited faith are ageing and losing members rapidly. People are opting instead for a non-religious life, for a non-institutional, personally constructed spirituality, or for orthodox, high-commitment religious groups that expect members to have a conversion experience. Therefore the population is paradoxically growing both more religious and less religious at once.

Because doubt and belief are each on the rise, our political and public discourse on matters of faith and morality has become deadlocked and deeply divided. The culture wars are taking a toll. Emotions and rhetoric are intense, even hysterical. Those who believe in God and Christianity are out to 'impose their beliefs on the rest of us' and 'turn back the clock' to a less enlightened time. Those who don't believe are 'enemies of truth' and 'purveyors of relativism and permissiveness'. We don't reason with the other side; we only denounce.

We have an impasse between the strengthening forces of doubt and belief, and this won't be solved simply by calling for more civility and dialogue. Arguments depend on having commonly held reference points that both sides can hold each other to. When fundamental understandings of reality conflict, it is hard to find anything to which to appeal. The title of Alasdair MacIntyre's book, *Whose Justice? Which Rationality?* says it all. Our problems are not going away soon.

How can we find a way forward?

First, each side should accept that *both* religious belief *and* scepticism are on the rise. Atheist author Sam Harris and Religious Right leader Pat Robertson should each admit the fact that his particular tribe is strong and increasing in influence. This would eliminate the self-talk that is rampant in each camp, namely that it will soon be extinct, overrun by the opposition. Nothing like that is imminently possible. If we stopped saying such things to ourselves it might make everyone more civil and generous towards opposing views.

Such an admission is not only reassuring, but also humbling. There are still many of a secular turn of mind who confidently say orthodox faith is vainly trying to 'resist the tide of history', though there is no historical evidence that religion is dying out at all. Religious believers should also be much less dismissive of secular scepticism. Christians should reflect on the fact that such large sectors of our formerly largely Christian societies have turned their backs on faith. Surely that should lead to self-examination. The time for making elegant dismissive gestures towards the other side is past. Something more is now required. But what?

## A Second Look at Doubt

I want to make a proposal that I have seen bear much fruit in the lives of young New Yorkers over the years. I recommend that each side look at *doubt* in a radically new way.

Let's begin with believers. A faith without some doubts is like a human body without any antibodies in it. People who blithely go through life too busy or indifferent to ask hard questions about why they believe as they do will find themselves defenceless against either the experience of tragedy or the probing questions of a smart sceptic. A person's faith can collapse almost overnight if she has failed over the years to listen patiently to her own doubts, which should only be discarded after long reflection.

Believers should acknowledge and wrestle with doubts – not only their own but their friends' and neighbours'. It is no longer sufficient to hold beliefs just because you inherited them. Only if you struggle long and hard with objections to your faith will you be able to provide grounds for your beliefs to sceptics, including yourself, that are plausible rather than ridiculous or offensive. And, just as important for our current situation, such a process will lead you, even after you come to a position of strong faith, to respect and understand those who doubt.

But even as believers should learn to look for reasons behind their faith, sceptics must learn to look for a type of faith hidden within their reasoning. All doubts, however sceptical and cynical they may seem, are really a set of alternate beliefs.[9] You cannot doubt Belief A except from a position of faith in Belief B. For example, if you doubt Christianity because 'There can't be just *one* true religion', you must recognise that this statement is itself an act of faith. No one can prove it empirically, and it is not a universal truth that everyone accepts. If you went to the Middle East and said, 'There can't be just one true religion,' nearly everyone would say, 'Why not?' The reason you doubt Christianity's Belief A is because you hold unprovable Belief B. Every doubt, therefore, is based on a leap of faith.

Some people say, 'I don't believe in Christianity because I can't accept the existence of moral absolutes. Everyone should determine moral truth for him- or herself.' Is that a statement they can prove to someone who doesn't share it? No, it is a leap of faith, a deep belief that individual rights operate not only in the political sphere but also in the moral. There is no empirical proof for such a position. So the doubt (of moral absolutes) is a leap.

Some will respond to all this, 'My doubts are not based on a leap of faith. I have no beliefs about God one way or another. I simply feel no need for God and I am not interested in thinking about it.' But hidden beneath this feeling is the very modern belief that the existence of God is a matter of indifference unless it intersects with my emotional needs. The speaker is betting his or her life that no God exists who would hold you accountable for your beliefs and behaviour if you didn't feel the need for him. That may be true or it may not be true, but, again, it is quite a leap of faith.[10]

The only way to doubt Christianity rightly and fairly is to discern the alternative belief under each of your doubts and then to ask yourself what reasons you have for believing it. How do you know your belief is true? It would be inconsistent to require more justification for Christian belief than you do for your own, but that is frequently what happens. In fairness you must doubt your doubts. My thesis is that if you come to recognise the beliefs on which your doubts about Christianity are based, and if you seek as much proof for those beliefs as you seek from Christians for theirs – you will discover that your doubts are not as solid as they first appeared.

I commend two processes to my readers. I urge sceptics to wrestle with the unexamined 'blind faith' on which scepticism is based, and to see how hard it is to justify those beliefs to those who do not share them. I also urge believers to wrestle with their personal and culture's objections to the faith. At the end of each process, even if you remain the sceptic or believer you have been, you will hold your own position with both greater clarity and greater humility. Then there will be an understanding, sympathy, and respect for the other side that did not exist before. Believers and non-believers will rise to the level of disagreement rather than simply denouncing one another. This happens when each side has learned to represent the other's argument in its strongest and most positive form. Only then is it safe and fair to disagree with it. That achieves civility in a pluralistic society, which is no small thing.

## A Spiritual Third Way?

The rest of this book is a distillation of the many conversations I've had with doubters over the years. In both my preaching and personal interactions I've tried to respectfully help sceptics look at their own faith-foundations while at the same time laying bare my own to their strongest criticisms. In the first half of this volume we will review the seven biggest objections and doubts about Christianity I've heard from people over the years. I will respectfully discern the alternative beliefs beneath each of them. Then in the second half of the book we will examine the reasons underlying Christian beliefs.

Respectful dialogue between entrenched traditional conservative and secular liberal people is a great good, and I hope this book will promote it. But my experience as a pastor in New York has given me another incentive to write this volume. As soon as I arrived in New York I realised that the faith and doubt situation was not what the experts thought it was. Older white people who ran the cultural business of the city definitely were quite secular. But among the increasingly multiethnic younger professionals and the working-class immigrants there was a lush, category-defying variety of strong religious beliefs. And Christianity, in particular, was growing rapidly among them.

I think these younger Christians are the vanguard of some major new religious, social and political arrangements that could make the older form of culture wars obsolete. After they wrestle with doubts and objections to Christianity many come out on the other side with an orthodox faith that doesn't fit the current categories of liberal Democrat or conservative Republican. Many see both sides in the 'culture war' making individual freedom and personal happiness the ultimate value rather than God and the common good. Liberals' individualism comes out in their views of abortion, sex and marriage. Conservatives' individualism comes out in their deep distrust of the public sector and in their understanding of poverty as simply a failure of personal responsibility. The new, fast-spreading multiethnic orthodox Christianity in the cities is much more concerned about the poor and social justice than Republicans have been, and at the same time much more concerned about upholding classic Christian moral and sexual ethics than Democrats have been.

While the first half of the book lays out a pathway that many of these Christians have taken through doubt, the second half of the book is a more positive exposition of the faith they are living out in the world. Here are three people at the church now.

June was a graduate of an Ivy League university, living and working in Manhattan. She became so obsessed with her physical image that she developed eating disorders and substance addictions. She came to see that she was heading for self-destruction, but she also realised that she had no particular reason to stop being reckless with her life. After all, what did her life mean? Why not be self-destructive? She turned to church and sought an understanding of God's mercy and an experience of his reality. She saw a counsellor at the church who helped her draw a connection between the mercy of God and her seemingly inexhaustible need for acceptance. Finally, she had the confidence to seek an encounter with God himself. Though she can't pinpoint one moment, she came to feel, for the first time, 'unconditionally loved as a true daughter of God'. Gradually she received freedom from her self-destructive behaviour.

Jeffrey was a New York City musician, raised in a conservative Jewish home. Both his father and mother suffered terribly with cancer, his mother succumbing to it. Because of a variety of physical ailments from his youth, he took up the practice of Chinese healing arts, along with Taoist and Buddhist meditation, and became extremely focused on physical wellness. He was in no state of 'spiritual need' when a friend began taking him to Redeemer. He liked the sermons 'until that Jesus business came around at the end' at which point he'd stop listening. Soon, however, he became somewhat jealous of his Christian friends' joy and hope for the future, which he had not encountered before. Then he began listening to the ends of the sermons and realising they posed an intellectual challenge that he had not wanted to face. Finally, to his surprise, during his times of meditation he discovered his 'moments of normally pure quiet and stillness were constantly interrupted by visions of Jesus on the cross'. He began to pray to the Christian God, and soon he realised that his dominant life narrative had been the escape and total avoidance of suffering. Now he saw how futile such a life goal was. When he understood that Jesus had surrendered his physical health and life to save the world – and him – it moved him deeply. He saw a way to get the courage to face the inevitable suffering of the future, and to know there would be a path through it. He embraced the gospel of Jesus Christ.

Kelly was an Ivy League atheist. As a twelve-year-old, Kelly watched her grandfather die of cancer and her two-year-old sister undergo surgery, chemotherapy, and radiation therapy for a brain tumor. By the time she was an undergraduate at Columbia University, she had lost hope that life had any meaning to it. Several of her Christian friends at college spoke to her of their faith, but she was 'rocky soil for the seeds' of their testimonies. However, when her sister had a stroke and was paralysed at the age of fourteen, it moved her not to give up on God but to begin more deliberate searching. By then she was living and working in the city. She met her future husband, Kevin, also a Columbia graduate and an atheist, who was working on Wall Street with J. P. Morgan. Their doubts about God were very stubborn, and yet they had doubts about their doubts, and so they began attending Redeemer. Their pilgrimage towards faith was slow and painstaking. One of the things that kept them on the trail, however, was the large number of believing Christians they met who were every bit as sophisticated and smart as anyone else they'd met in the city. Finally, they were not only convinced of Christianity's intellectual credibility, but were attracted by its vision for life. Kelly wrote, 'As an atheist I thought I lived a moral, community-oriented, concerned-with-social-justice kind of life, but Christianity had an even higher standard – down to our thoughts and the state of our hearts. I accepted God's forgiveness and invited him into my life.' Kevin wrote, 'While sitting in a coffee shop reading C. S. Lewis's *Mere Christianity,* I put down the book and wrote in my notebook "the evidence surrounding the claims of Christianity is simply overwhelming". I realised that my

Introduction

achievements were ultimately unsatisfying, the approval of
man is fleeting, that a *carpe diem* life lived solely for ad-
venture is just a form of narcissism and idolatry. And so I
became a believer in Christ.'[11]

## Jesus and Our Doubts

Kelly's account recalls how, as a struggler with doubt and faith, the
passage about Thomas in the New Testament was a comfort to her.
There Jesus modelled a view of doubt more nuanced than those of either modern sceptics or modern believers. When Jesus confronted
'doubting Thomas' he challenged him not to acquiesce in doubt
('believe!') and yet responded to his request for more evidence. In another incident, Jesus meets a man who confesses that he is filled with
doubts (Mark 9:24), who says to Jesus, 'Help thou my unbelief' –
help me with my doubts! In response to this honest admission, Jesus
blesses him and heals his son. Whether you consider yourself a believer
or a sceptic, I invite you to seek the same kind of honesty and to grow
in an understanding of the nature of your own doubts. The result will
exceed anything you can imagine.

**PART 1**

# THE LEAP OF DOUBT

# ONE

## THERE CAN'T BE JUST *ONE* TRUE RELIGION

*'How could there be just one true faith?' asked Blair, a twenty-four-year-old woman living in Manhattan. 'It's arrogant to say your religion is superior and try to convert everyone else to it. Surely all the religions are equally good and valid for meeting the needs of their particular followers.'*

*'Religious exclusivity is not just narrow – it's dangerous,' added Geoff, a twenty-something British man also living in New York City. 'Religion has led to untold strife, division, and conflict. It may be the greatest enemy of peace in the world. If Christians continue to insist that they have 'the truth' – and if other religions do this as well – the world will never know peace.'[1]*

DURING my nearly two decades in New York City, I've had numerous opportunities to ask people, 'What is your biggest problem with Christianity? What troubles you the most about its beliefs or how it is practised?' One of the most frequent answers I have heard over the years can be summed up in one word: *exclusivity*.

I was once invited to be the Christian representative in a panel discussion at a local college along with a Jewish rabbi and a Muslim imam. The panellists were asked to discuss the differences among religions. The conversation was courteous, intelligent and respectful in tone. Each speaker affirmed that there were significant, irreconcilable differences between the major faiths. A case in point was the person of Jesus. We all agreed on the statement: 'If Christians are right about Jesus being God, then Muslims and Jews fail in a serious way to love God as God really is, but if Muslims and Jews are right that Jesus is not God but rather a teacher or prophet, then Christians fail in a serious way to love God as God really is.' The bottom line was – we couldn't all be equally right about the nature of God.

Several of the students were quite disturbed by this. One student insisted that what mattered was to believe in God and to be a loving person yourself. To insist that one faith has a better grasp of the truth than others was intolerant. Another student looked at us clerics and said in his frustration, 'We will *never* come to know peace on earth if religious leaders keep on making such exclusive claims!'

It is widely believed that one of the main barriers to world peace is religion, and especially the major traditional religions with their exclusive claims to superiority. It may surprise you that though I am a Christian minister I agree with this. Religion, generally speaking, tends to create a slippery slope in the heart. Each religion informs its followers that they have 'the truth', and this naturally leads them to feel superior to those with differing beliefs. Also, a religion tells its followers that they are saved and connected to God by devotedly performing that truth. This moves them to separate from those who are less devoted and pure in life. Therefore, it is easy for one religious group to stereotype and caricature other ones. Once this situation exists it can easily spiral down into the marginalisation of others or even to active oppression, abuse, or violence against them.

Once we recognise how religion erodes peace on earth, what can we do about it? There are three approaches that civic and cultural leaders around the world are using to address the divisiveness of religion. There are calls to outlaw religion, condemn religion or at least to radically privatise it.[2] Many people are investing great hope in them. Unfortunately, I don't believe any of them will be effective. Indeed, I'm afraid they will only aggravate the situation.

## 1. Outlaw religion

One way to deal with the divisiveness of religion has been to control or even forbid it with a heavy hand. There were several massive efforts to do this in the twentieth century. Soviet Russia, Communist China, the Khmer Rouge and (in a different way) Nazi Germany were all determined to tightly control religious practice in an effort to stop it from dividing society or eroding the power of the state. The result, however, was not more peace and harmony, but more oppression. The tragic irony of the situation is brought out by Alister McGrath in his history of atheism:

> *The 20th century gave rise to one of the greatest and most distressing paradoxes of human history: that the greatest intolerance and violence of that century were practised by those who believed that religion caused intolerance and violence.*[3]

Going hand in hand with such efforts was a widespread belief in the late nineteenth and early twentieth century that religion would weaken and die out as the human race became more technologically advanced. This view saw religion as playing a role in human evolution. We once needed religion to help us cope with a very frightening, incomprehensible world. But as we become more scientifically sophisticated and more able to understand and control our own environment, our need for religion would diminish, it was thought.[4]

But this has not happened, and this 'secularisation thesis' is now largely discredited.[5] Virtually all major religions are growing in number of adherents. Christianity's growth, especially in the developing world, has been explosive. There are now six times more Anglicans in Nigeria alone than there are in all of the United States. There are more Presbyterians in Ghana than in the United States and Scotland combined. Korea has gone from 1 per cent to 40 per cent Christian in a hundred years, and experts believe the same thing is going to happen in China. If there are half a billion Chinese Christians fifty years from now, that will change the course of human history.[6] In most cases, the Christianity that is growing is not the more secularised, belief-thin versions predicted by the sociologists. Rather, it is a robust supernaturalist kind of faith, with belief in miracles, scriptural authority and personal conversion.

Because of the vitality of religious faith in the world, efforts to suppress or control it often serve only to make it stronger. When the Chinese Communists expelled Western missionaries after the Second World War, they thought they were killing off Christianity in China. Instead, this move only served to make the leadership of the Chinese church more indigenous and therefore to strengthen it.

Religion is not just a temporary thing that helped us adapt to our environment. Rather it is a permanent and central aspect of the human condition. This is a bitter pill for secular, non-religious people to swallow. Everyone wants to think that they are in the mainstream, that they are not extremists. But robust religious beliefs dominate the world. There is no reason to expect that to change.

## 2. Condemn religion

Religion is not going away and its power cannot be diminished by government control. But can't we – via education and argument – find ways to socially discourage religions that claim to have 'the truth' and that try to convert others to their beliefs? Couldn't we find ways to urge all of our citizens, whatever their religious beliefs, to admit that each religion or faith is just one of many equally valid paths to God and ways to live in the world?

This approach creates an environment in which it is considered unenlightened and outrageous to make exclusive religious claims, even in personal conversations. It does so by stating and restating certain axioms that eventually achieve the status of common sense. Those who deviate from them are stigmatised as foolish or danger-ous. Unlike the first strategy, this approach to the divisiveness of religion is having some effect. It cannot ultimately succeed, how-ever, because at its heart is a fatal inconsistency, even perhaps a hy-pocrisy, that will eventually lead to the collapse of this way of thinking. What follows are several of these axioms and the prob-lems with each.

### *'All major religions are equally valid and basically teach the same thing.'*

This assertion is so common that one journalist recently wrote that anyone who believed that 'there are inferior religions' is a right-wing extremist.[7] Do we really want to say that the Branch Davidi-ans or religions requiring child sacrifice are not inferior to any other faith? The great majority of people would almost certainly agree that they are.

Most people who assert the equality of religions have in mind the major world faiths, not splinter sects. This was the form of the objection I got from the student the night I was on the panel. He contended that doctrinal differences between Judaism, Islam, Christianity, Buddhism and Hinduism were superficial and insignificant, that they all believed in the same God. But when I asked him who that God was, he described him as an all-loving Spirit in the universe. The problem with this position is its inconsistency. It insists that doctrine is unimportant, but at the same time assumes doctrinal beliefs about the nature of God that are at loggerheads with those of all the major faiths. Buddhism doesn't believe in a personal God at all. Judaism, Christianity and Islam believe in a God who holds people accountable for their beliefs and practices and whose attributes could not all be reduced to love. Ironically, the insistence that doctrines do not matter is really a doctrine itself. It holds a specific view of God, which is touted as superior and more enlightened than the beliefs of most major religions. So the proponents of this view do the very thing they forbid in others.

### 'Each religion sees part of spiritual truth, but none can see the whole truth.'

Sometimes this point is illustrated with the story of the blind men and the elephant. Several blind men were walking along and came upon an elephant that allowed them to touch and feel it. 'This creature is long and flexible like a snake' said the first blind man, holding the elephant's trunk. 'Not at all – it is thick and round like a tree trunk,' said the second blind man, feeling the elephant's leg. 'No, it is large and flat,' said the third blind man, touching the elephant's side. Each blind man could feel only part of the elephant – none could envisage the entire elephant. In the same way, it is argued, the religions of the world each have a grasp on part of the truth about spiritual reality, but none can see the whole elephant or claim to have a comprehensive vision of the truth.

This illustration backfires on its users. The story is told from the point of view of someone who is not blind. How could you know that each blind man only sees part of the elephant unless *you* claim to be able to see the whole elephant?

> *There is an appearance of humility in the protestation that the truth is much greater than any one of us can grasp, but if this is used to invalidate all claims to discern the truth it is in fact an arrogant claim to a kind of knowledge which is superior to [all others] . . . We have to ask: 'What is the [absolute] vantage ground from which you claim to be able to relativize all the absolute claims these different scriptures make?*[8]

How could you possibly know that no religion can see the whole truth unless you yourself have the superior, comprehensive knowledge of spiritual reality you just claimed that none of the religions have?

### *'Religious belief is too culturally and historically conditioned to be "truth".'*

When I first came to New York City nearly twenty years ago, I more often heard the objection that all religions are equally true. Now, however, I'm more likely to be told that all religions are equally false. The objection goes like this: 'All moral and spiritual claims are the product of our particular historical and cultural moment, and therefore no one should claim they can know the Truth, since no one can judge whether one assertion about spiritual and moral reality is truer than another.' The sociologist Peter L. Berger reveals the serious inconsistency in this common assumption.

In his book *A Rumor of Angels* Berger recounts how the twentieth century had uncovered 'the sociology of knowledge', namely that people believe what they do largely because they are socially conditioned to do so. We like to think that we think for ourselves, but it is not that simple. We think like the people we most admire and need. Everyone belongs to a community that reinforces the plausibility of some beliefs and discourages others. Berger notes that many have concluded from this fact that, because we are all locked into our historical and cultural locations, it is impossible to judge the rightness or wrongness of competing beliefs.

Berger goes on, however, to point out that absolute relativism can only exist if the relativists exempt themselves from their own razor.[9] If you infer from the social conditionedness of all belief that 'no belief can be held as universally true for everyone,' that itself is a comprehensive claim about everyone that is the product of social conditions – so it cannot be true, on its own terms. 'Relativity relativizes itself,' says Berger, so we can't have relativism 'all the way down'.[10] Our cultural biases make weighing competing truth-claims harder, yes. The social conditionedness of belief is a fact, but it cannot be used to argue that all truth is completely relative or else the very argument refutes itself. Berger concludes that we cannot avoid weighing spiritual and religious claims by hiding behind the cliché that 'there's no way to know the Truth'. We must still do the hard work of asking: which affirmations about God, human nature and spiritual reality are true and which are false? We will have to base our life on *some* answer to that question.

The philosopher Alvin Plantinga has his own version of Berger's argument. People often say to him, 'If you were born in Morocco, you wouldn't even be a Christian, but rather a Muslim.' He responds:

*Suppose we concede that if I had been born of Muslim parents in Morocco rather than Christian parents in Michigan, my beliefs*

*would have been quite different. [But] the same goes for the*
*pluralist. . . . If the pluralist had been born in [Morocco] he prob-*
*ably wouldn't be a pluralist. Does it follow that . . . his pluralist*
*beliefs are produced in him by an unreliable belief-producing*
*process?*[11]

Plantinga and Berger make the same point. You can't say, 'All
claims about religions are historically conditioned except the one I
am making right now.' If you insist that no one can determine
which beliefs are right and wrong, why should we believe what you
are saying? The reality is that we all make truth-claims of some sort
and it is very hard to weigh them responsibly, but we have no alternative but to try to do so.

### *'It is arrogant to insist your religion is right and to convert others to it.'*

The noted religion scholar John Hick has written that once you
become aware that there are many other equally intelligent and
good people in the world who hold different beliefs from you and
that you will not be able to convince them otherwise, then it is arrogant for you to continue to try to convert them or to hold your
view to be the superior truth.[12]

Once again there is an inherent contradiction. Most people in
the world don't hold to John Hick's view that all religions are
equally valid, and many of them are equally as good and intelligent as he is, and unlikely to change their views. That would make
the statement 'all religious claims to have a better view of things
are arrogant and wrong' to be, on its own terms, arrogant and
wrong.

Many say that it is ethnocentric to claim that our religion is
superior to others. Yet isn't that very statement ethnocentric? Most

non-Western cultures have no problem saying that their culture and religion is best. The idea that it is wrong to do so is deeply rooted in Western traditions of self-criticism and individualism. To charge others with the 'sin' of ethnocentrism is really a way of saying, 'Our culture's approach to other cultures is superior to yours.' We are then doing the very thing we forbid others to do.[13] The historian C. John Sommerville has pointed out that 'a religion can be judged only on the basis of another religion'. You can't evaluate a religion except on the basis of some ethical criteria that in the end amounts to your own religious stance.[14]

By now the fatal flaw in this approach to religion in general and to Christianity in particular should be obvious. Sceptics believe that *any* exclusive claims to a superior knowledge of spiritual reality cannot be true. But this objection is itself a religious belief. It assumes God is unknowable, or that God is loving but not wrathful, or that God is an impersonal force rather than a person who speaks in Scripture. All of these are unprovable faith assumptions. In addition, their proponents believe they have a superior way to view things. They believe the world would be a better place if everyone dropped the traditional religions' views of God and truth and adopted theirs. Therefore, their view is also an 'exclusive' claim about the nature of spiritual reality. If all such views are to be discouraged, this one should be as well. If it is not narrow to hold this view, then there is nothing inherently narrow about holding to traditional religious beliefs.

Mark Lilla, a professor at the University of Chicago, spoke to a bright young student at Wharton Business School who, to Lilla's bafflement, had gone forward at a Billy Graham crusade to give his life to Christ. Lilla writes:

*I wanted to cast doubt on the step he was about to take, to help him see there are other ways to live, other ways to seek knowledge,*

*love . . . even self-transformation. I wanted to convince him his*
*dignity depended on maintaining a free, skeptical attitude to-*
*wards doctrine. I wanted . . . to save him . . .*

*Doubt, like faith, has to be learned. It is a skill. But the curi-*
*ous thing about skepticism is that its adherents, ancient and*
*modern, have so often been proselytizers. In reading them, I've*
*often wanted to ask: 'Why do you care?' Their skepticism offers*
*no good answer to that question. And I don't have one for my-*
*self.*[15]

Lilla's wise self-knowledge reveals his doubts about Christianity
to be a learned, alternative faith. He believes that the individual's
dignity as a human being rests on doctrinal scepticism – which
is, of course, an article of faith. As he admits, he can't avoid
believing that it would be better for people if they adopted
his beliefs about reality and human dignity rather than Billy
Graham's.

It is no more narrow to claim that one religion is right than to
claim that one way to think about all religions (namely that all are
equal) is right. We are all exclusive in our beliefs about religion, but
in different ways.

## 3. Keep religion completely private

Another approach to the divisiveness of religion is to allow that
people may privately believe their faith is the truth and may
'evangelise' for their faith, but that religious beliefs should be
kept out of the public sphere. Influential thinkers such as John
Rawls and Robert Audi have argued that, in public political discussions, we may not argue for a moral position unless it has a secular, non-religious grounding. Rawls is well known for insisting

that what he calls 'comprehensive' religious views be excluded from public discourse.[16] Recently a large array of scientists and philosophers signed 'A Declaration in Defense of Science and Secularism', which called on the leaders of our government 'not to permit legislation or executive action to be influenced by religious beliefs'.[17] The signatories included Peter Singer, E. O. Wilson, and Daniel C. Dennett. The philosopher Richard Rorty, for example, has argued that religious faith must remain a strictly private affair and must never be brought into discussions of public policy. To ever use an argument grounded in a religious belief is simply a 'conversation stopper', with which the non-believer cannot engage.[18]

To those who complain that this approach discriminates against religion, Rorty and others retort that this policy is simply pragmatic.[19] They are not ideologically opposed to religion per se, nor are they seeking to control religious beliefs, so long as they are kept in the private sphere. However, in the public square it is divisive and time-consuming to argue constantly over religion. Religion-based positions are seen as sectarian and controversial, while secular reasoning for moral positions are seen as universal and available to all. Therefore, public discourse should be secular, never religious. Without reference to any divine revelation or confessional tradition, we should work together on the great problems of our time – such as AIDS, poverty, education, and so on. We should keep our religious views to ourselves and unite around policies that 'work' best for the most people.

However, Stephen L. Carter of Yale responds that it is impossible to leave religious views behind when we do any kind of moral reasoning at all.

*Efforts to craft a public square from which religious conversation is absent, no matter how thoughtfully worked out, will always in the end say to those of organized religion that they alone, unlike everybody else, must enter public dialogue only after leaving behind that part of themselves that they may consider the most vital.*[20]

How can Carter make such a claim? Let's begin by asking what religion is. Some say it is a form of belief in God. But that would not fit Zen Buddhism, which does not really believe in God at all. Some say it is belief in the supernatural. But that does not fit Hinduism, which does not believe in a supernatural realm beyond the material world, but only a spiritual reality within the empirical. What is religion then? It is a set of beliefs that explain what life is all about, who we are, and the most important things that human beings should spend their time doing. For example, some think that this material world is all there is, that we are here by accident and when we die we just rot, and therefore the important thing is to choose to do what makes you happy and not let others impose their beliefs on you. Notice that though this is not an explicit, 'organised' religion, it contains a master narrative, an account about the meaning of life along with a recommendation for how to live based on that account of things.

Some call this a 'worldview' while others call it a 'narrative identity'. In either case it is a set of faith-assumptions about the nature of things. It is an implicit religion. Broadly understood, faith in some view of the world and human nature informs everyone's life. Everyone lives and operates out of some narrative identity, whether it is thought out and reflected upon or not. All who say 'You ought to do this' or 'You shouldn't do that' reason out of such an implicit moral and religious position. Pragmatists say that we should leave our deeper worldviews behind and find consensus about 'what works' – but our view of what works is determined by (to use a Wendell Berry title) what we think

15

people are for. Any picture of happy human life that 'works' is necessarily informed by deep-seated beliefs about the purpose of human life.[21] Even the most secular pragmatists come to the table with deep commitments and narrative accounts of what it means to be human.

Rorty insists that religion-based beliefs are conversation stoppers. But all of our most fundamental convictions about things are beliefs that are nearly impossible to justify to those who don't share them. Secular concepts such as 'self-realisation' and 'autonomy' are impossible to prove and are 'conversation stoppers' just as much as appeals to the Bible.[22]

Statements that seem to be common sense to the speakers are nonetheless often profoundly religious in nature. Imagine that Ms A argues that all the safety nets for the poor should be removed, in the name of 'survival of the fittest'. Ms B might respond, 'The poor have the right to a decent standard of living – they are human beings like the rest of us!' Ms A could then come back with the fact that many bioethicists today think the concept of 'human' is artificial and impossible to define. She might continue that there is no possibility of treating all living organisms as ends rather than means and that some always have to die that others may live. That is simply the way nature works. If Ms B counters with a pragmatic argument, that we should help the poor simply because it makes society work better, Ms A could come up with many similar pragmatic arguments about why letting some of the poor just die would be even more efficient. Now Ms B would be getting angry. She would respond heatedly that starving the poor is simply unethical, but Ms A could retort, 'Who says ethics must be the same for everyone?' Ms B would finally exclaim: 'I wouldn't want to live in a society like the one you are describing!'

In this interchange Ms B has tried to follow John Rawls and find universally accessible, 'neutral and objective' arguments that would convince everyone that we must not starve the poor. She has failed because there are none. In the end Ms B affirms the equality and dignity of human individuals simply because she believes it is true and right. She takes as an article of faith that people are more valuable than rocks or trees – though she can't prove such a belief scientifically. Her public policy proposals are ultimately based on a religious stance.[23]

This leads a legal theorist, Michael J. Perry, to conclude that it is 'quixotic, in any event, to attempt to construct an airtight barrier between religiously grounded moral discourse . . . and [secular] discourse in public political argument'.[24] Rorty and others argue that religious argument is too controversial, but Perry retorts in *Under God? Religious Faith and Liberal Democracy* that secular grounds for moral positions are no less controversial than religious grounds, and a very strong case can be made that all moral positions are at least implicitly religious. Ironically, insisting that religious reasoning be excluded from the public square is itself a controversial 'sectarian' point of view.[25]

When you come out into the public square it is impossible to leave your convictions about ultimate values behind. Let's take marriage and divorce laws as a case study. Is it possible to craft laws that we all agree 'work' apart from particular worldview commitments? I don't believe so. Your views of what is right will be based on what you think the purpose of marriage is. If you think marriage is mainly for the rearing of children to benefit the whole society, then you will make divorce very difficult. If you think the purpose of marriage is more primarily for the happiness and emotional fulfilment of the adults who enter it, you will make divorce much easier. The former view is grounded in a view of human flourishing and well-being in which the family is more important than the individual, as is seen in the moral traditions of Confucianism, Judaism and Christianity. The latter approach is a more individualistic view of human nature based on the Enlightenment's understanding of things. The divorce laws you think 'work' will depend on prior beliefs about what it means to be happy and fully human.[26] There is no objective, universal consensus about what that is. Although many continue to call for the exclusion of religious views from the public square, increasing numbers of thinkers, both religious and secular, are admitting that such a call is itself religious.[27]

## Christianity Can Save the World

I've argued against the effectiveness of all the main efforts to address the divisiveness of religion in our world today. Yet I strongly sympathise with their purpose. Religion can certainly be one of the major threats to world peace. At the beginning of the chapter I outlined the 'slippery slope' that every religion tends to set up in the human heart. This slippery slope leads all too easily to oppression. However, within Christianity – robust, orthodox Christianity – there are rich resources that can make its followers agents for peace on earth. Christianity has within itself remarkable power to explain and expunge the divisive tendencies within the human heart.

Christianity provides a firm basis for respecting people of other faiths. Jesus assumes that non-believers in the culture around them will gladly recognise much Christian behaviour as 'good' (Matthew 5:16; cf. 1 Peter 2:12). That assumes some overlap between the Christian constellation of values and those of any particular culture[28] and of any other religion.[29] Why would this overlap exist? Christians believe that all human beings are made in the image of

God, capable of goodness and wisdom. The biblical doctrine of the universal image of God, therefore, leads Christians to expect non-believers will be better than any of their mistaken beliefs could make them. The biblical doctrine of universal sinfulness also leads Christians to expect believers will be worse in practice than their orthodox beliefs should make them. So there will be plenty of ground for respectful co-operation.

Christianity not only leads its members to believe people of other faiths have goodness and wisdom to offer, it also leads them to expect that many will live lives morally superior to their own. Most people in our culture believe that, if there is a God, we can relate to him and go to heaven through leading a good life. Let's call this the 'moral improvement' view. Christianity teaches the very opposite. In the Christian understanding, Jesus does not tell us how to live so we can merit salvation. Rather, he comes to forgive and save us through his life and death in our place. God's grace does not come to people who morally outperform others, but to those who admit their failure to perform and who acknowledge their need for a Saviour.

Christians, then, should expect to find non-believers who are much nicer, kinder, wiser and better than they are. Why? Christian believers are not accepted by God because of their moral performance, wisdom or virtue, but because of Christ's work on their behalf. Most religions and philosophies of life assume that one's spiritual status depends on your religious attainments. This naturally leads adherents to feel superior to those who don't believe and behave as they do. The Christian gospel, in any case, should not have that effect.

It is common to say that 'fundamentalism' leads to violence, yet as we have seen, all of us have fundamental, unprovable faith-commitments that we think are superior to those of others. The real question, then, is *which fundamentals will lead their believers to be the most loving and receptive to those with whom they differ?* Which set of unavoidably exclusive beliefs will lead us to humble, peace-loving behaviour?

One of the paradoxes of history is the relationship between the beliefs and the practices of the early Christians as compared to those of the culture around them.

The Graeco-Roman world's religious views were open and seemingly tolerant – everyone had his or her own God. The practices of the culture were quite brutal, however. The Graeco-Roman world was highly stratified economically, with a huge distance between the rich and poor. By contrast, Christians insisted that there was only one true God, the dying Saviour Jesus Christ. Their lives and practices were, however, remarkably welcoming to those that the culture marginalised. The early Christians mixed people from different races and classes in ways that seemed scandalous to those around them. The Graeco-Roman world tended to despise the poor, but Christians gave generously not only to their own poor but to those of other faiths. In broader society, women had very low status, being subjected to high levels of female infanticide, forced marriages and lack of economic equality. Christianity afforded women much greater security and equality than had previously existed in the ancient classical world.[30] During the terrible urban plagues of the first two centuries, Christians cared for all the sick and dying in the city, often at the cost of their lives.[31]

Why would such an exclusive belief system lead to behaviour that was so open to others? It was because Christians had within their belief system the strongest possible resource for practising sacrificial service, generosity and peace-making. At the very heart of their view of reality was a man who died for his enemies, praying for their forgiveness. Reflection on this could only lead to a radically different way of dealing with those who were different from them. It meant they could not act in violence and oppression toward their opponents.

We cannot skip lightly over the fact that there have been injustices done by the church in the name of Christ, yet who can deny that the force of Christians' most fundamental beliefs can be a powerful impetus for peace-making in our troubled world?

# TWO

# How Could a Good God
# Allow Suffering?

*'I just don't believe the God of Christianity exists,' said Hillary, an English undergraduate. 'God allows terrible suffering in the world. So he might be either all-powerful but not good enough to end evil and suffering, or else he might be all-good but not powerful enough to end evil and suffering. Either way the all-good, all-powerful God of the Bible couldn't exist.'[1]*

*'This isn't a philosophical issue to me,' added Rob, Hillary's boyfriend. 'This is personal. I won't believe in a God who allows suffering, even if he, she or it exists. Maybe God exists. Maybe not. But if he does, he can't be trusted.'*

FOR many people it is not the exclusivity of Christianity that poses the biggest problem, it is the presence of evil and suffering in the world. Some find unjust suffering to be a philosophical problem, calling into question the very existence of God. For others it is an intensely personal issue. They don't care about the abstract question of whether God exists or not—they refuse to trust or believe in any God who allows history and life to proceed as it has.

In December 2004, a massive tsunami killed more than 250,000 people around the rim of the Indian Ocean. Over the following weeks, newspapers and magazines were full of letters and articles asking 'Where was God?' One reporter wrote: 'If God is God, he's not good. If God is good, he's not God. You can't have it both ways, especially after the Indian Ocean catastrophe.'[2] Despite the confident assertion of the columnist, the effort to demonstrate that evil disproves the existence of God 'is now acknowledged on (almost) all sides to be completely bankrupt'.[3] Why?

## Evil and Suffering Isn't Evidence *Against* God

Philosopher J. L. Mackie makes this case against God in his book *The Miracle of Theism* (Oxford, 1982). He states it this way: If a good and powerful God exists, he would not allow pointless evil, but because there *is* much unjustifiable, pointless evil in the world, the traditional good and powerful God could not exist. Some other god or no god may exist, but not the traditional God.[4] Many other philosophers have identified a major flaw in this reasoning. Tucked away within the assertion that the world is filled with pointless evil is a hidden premise, namely, that if evil appears pointless to me, then it must *be* pointless.

This reasoning is, of course, fallacious. Just because you can't see or imagine a good reason why God might allow something to happen doesn't mean there can't be one. Again we see lurking within supposedly hard-nosed scepticism an enormous faith in one's own cognitive faculties. If our minds can't plumb the depths of the universe for good answers to suffering, well, then, there can't be any! This is blind faith of a high order.

The fallacy at the heart of this argument has been illustrated by the 'no-see-ums' illustration of Alvin Plantinga. If you look into your kennel for a St Bernard, and you don't see one, it is reasonable to assume that there is no St Bernard in your kennel. But if you look into your kennel for a 'no-see-um' (an extremely small insect with a bite out of all proportion to its size) and you don't see any, it is not reasonable to assume they aren't there. Because, after all, no one can see 'em. Many assume that if there were good reasons for the existence of evil, they would be accessible to our minds, more like St Bernards than like no-see-ums, but why should that be the case?[5]

This argument against God doesn't hold up, not only to logic but also to experience. As a pastor, I've often preached on the story of Joseph in Genesis. Joseph was an arrogant young man who was hated by his brothers. In their anger at him, they imprisoned him in a pit and then sold him into a life of slavery and misery in Egypt. Doubtless Joseph prayed to God to help him escape, but no help was forthcoming, and into slavery he went. Though he experienced years of bondage and misery, Joseph's character was refined and strengthened by his trials. Eventually he rose up to become a prime minister of Egypt who saved thousands of lives and even his own family from starvation. If God had not allowed Joseph's years of suffering, he never would have been such a powerful agent for social justice and spiritual healing.

Whenever I preach on this text, I hear from many people who identify with that narrative. Many people have to admit that most of what they really needed for success in life came to them through their most difficult and painful experiences. Some look back on an illness and recognise that it was an irreplaceable season of personal and spiritual growth for them. I have survived a bout with cancer and my wife has suffered with Crohn's disease for years, and we would both attest to this.

I knew a man in my first parish who had lost most of his eyesight after he was shot in the face during a drug deal gone bad. He told me that he had been an extremely selfish and cruel person, but he had always blamed his constant legal and relational problems on others. The loss of his sight had devastated him, but it had also profoundly humbled him. 'As my physical eyes were closed, my spiritual eyes were opened, as it were. I finally saw how I'd been treating people. I changed, and now for the first time in my life I have friends, real friends. It was a terrible price to pay, and yet I must say it was worth it. I finally have what makes life worthwhile.'

Though none of these people are grateful for the tragedies themselves, they would not trade the insight, character and strength they had gained from them for anything. With time and perspective most of us can see good reasons for at least *some* of the tragedy and pain that occurs in life. Why couldn't it be possible that, from God's vantage point, there are good reasons for all of them?

If you have a God great and transcendent enough to be mad at because he hasn't stopped evil and suffering in the world, then you have (at the same moment) a God great and transcendent enough to have good reasons for allowing it to continue that you can't know. Indeed, you can't have it both ways.

## Evil and Suffering May Be (If Anything) Evidence *for* God

Horrendous, inexplicable suffering, though it cannot disprove God, is nonetheless a problem for the believer in the Bible. However, it is perhaps an even greater problem for non-believers. C. S. Lewis described how he had originally rejected the idea of God because of the cruelty of life. Then he came to realise that evil was even

25

more problematic for his new atheism. In the end, he realised that suffering provided a better argument for God's existence than one against it.

> My argument against God was that the universe seemed so cruel and unjust. But how had I got this idea of 'just' and 'unjust'? . . . What was I comparing this universe with when I called it unjust? . . . Of course I could have given up my idea of justice by saying it was nothing but a private idea of my own. But if I did that, then my argument against God collapsed too – for the argument depended on saying that the world was really unjust, not simply that it did not happen to please my private fancies. . . . Consequently atheism turns out to be too simple.[6]

Lewis recognised that modern objections to God are based on a sense of fair play and justice. People, we believe, *ought* not to suffer, be excluded, die of hunger or oppression. But the evolutionary mechanism of natural selection *depends* on death, destruction and violence of the strong against the weak – these things are all perfectly natural. On what basis, then, does the atheist judge the natural world to be horribly wrong, unfair and unjust? The non-believer in God doesn't have a good basis for being outraged at injustice, which, as Lewis points out, was the reason for objecting to God in the first place. If you are *sure* that this natural world is unjust and filled with evil, you are assuming the reality of some extra-natural (or supernatural) standard by which to make your judgement. The philosopher Alvin Plantinga said it like this:

> Could there really be any such thing as horrifying wickedness [if there were no God and we just evolved]? I don't see how. There

*can be such a thing only if there is a way that rational creatures are* supposed *to live, obliged* to live. . . . *A [secular] way of looking at the world has no place for genuine moral obligation of any sort . . . and thus no way to say there is such a thing as genuine and appalling wickedness. Accordingly, if you think there really* is *such a thing as horrifying wickedness (. . . and not just an illusion of some sort), then you have a powerful . . . argument [for the reality of God].*[7]

In short, the problem of tragedy, suffering and injustice is a problem for everyone. It is at least as big a problem for non-belief in God as for belief. It is therefore a mistake, though an understandable one, to think that if you abandon belief in God it somehow makes the problem of evil easier to handle.

A woman in my church once confronted me about sermon illustrations in which evil events turned out for the good. She had lost a husband in an act of violence during a robbery. She also had several children with severe mental and emotional problems. She insisted that for every one story in which evil turns out for good there are one hundred in which there is no conceivable silver lining. In the same way, much of the discussion so far in this chapter may sound cold and irrelevant to a real-life sufferer. 'So what if suffering and evil doesn't logically disprove God?' such a person might say. 'I'm still angry. All this philosophising does *not* get the Christian God "off the hook" for the world's evil and suffering!' In response the philosopher Peter Kreeft points out that the Christian God came to earth to deliberately put himself *on* the hook of human suffering. In Jesus Christ, God experienced the greatest depths of pain. Therefore, though Christianity does not provide the reason for each experience of pain, it provides deep resources for actually facing suffering with hope and courage rather than bitterness and despair.

## Comparing Jesus to the Martyrs

The Gospel narratives all show that Jesus did not face his approaching death with anything like the aplomb and fearlessness that was widely expected in a spiritual hero. The well-known Maccabean martyrs, who suffered under the Syrian rule of Antiochus Epiphanes, were the paradigms for spiritual courage in the face of persecution. They were famous for speaking defiantly and confidently of God even as they were having limbs cut off. Contrast that with the demeanour of Jesus, who is depicted as profoundly shaken by his impending doom. '. . . He began to be deeply distressed and troubled' saying, 'My soul is overwhelmed with sorrow to the point of death' (Mark 14:33-34). Luke describes Jesus before his death as being in 'agony' and describes a man with all the signs of being in physical shock (Luke 22:44). Matthew, Mark and Luke all show Jesus trying to avoid death, asking the Father if there isn't some way out of it ('If it be your will . . . take this cup from me' – Mark 14:36; Luke 22:42). Finally, on the cross itself, Jesus does not, as the Maccabean martyrs, confidently call onlookers to be faithful to God. Rather, he cries out that God has forsaken him (Matthew 27:46).

On the cross, Jesus suffered a three-hour-long death by slow suffocation and blood loss. As terribly painful as that was, there have been far more excruciating and horrible deaths that martyrs have faced with far greater confidence and calmness. Two famous examples are Hugh Latimer and Nicholas Ridley, who were burned at the stake at Oxford in 1555 for their Protestant convictions. As the flames leapt up, Latimer was heard to say calmly, 'Be of good comfort, Mr Ridley, and play the man! We shall this day light such a candle by God's grace, in England, as I trust never shall be put out.'

Why was Jesus so much more overwhelmed by his death than others have been, even more than his own followers?

## The Suffering of God

To understand Jesus's suffering at the end of the Gospels, we must remember how he is introduced at their beginning. The Gospel writer John, in his first chapter, introduces us to the mysterious but crucial concept of God as tri-personal. The Son of God was not created but took part in creation and has lived throughout all eternity 'in the bosom of the Father' (John 1:18) – that is, in a relationship of absolute intimacy and love. But at the end of his life he was cut off from the Father.

There may be no greater inner agony than the loss of a relationship we desperately want. If a mild acquaintance turns on you, condemns and criticises you, and says she never wants to see you again, it is painful. If someone you're dating does the same thing, it is qualitatively more painful. But if your spouse does this to you, or if one of your parents does this to you when you're still a child, the psychological damage is infinitely worse.

We cannot fathom, however, what it would be like to lose not just spousal love or parental love that has lasted several years, but the infinite love of the Father that Jesus had from all eternity. Jesus' sufferings would have been eternally unbearable. Christian theology has always recognised that Jesus bore, as the substitute in our place, the endless exclusion from God that the human race has merited. In the Garden of Gethsemane, even the beginning and foretaste of this experience began to put Jesus into a state of shock. New Testament scholar Bill Lane writes: 'Jesus came to be with the Father for an interlude before his betrayal, but found hell rather

29

than heaven opened before him, and he staggered.'[8] On the cross, Jesus's cry of dereliction – 'My God, my God, why have you forsaken me?' – is a deeply relational statement. Lane writes: 'The cry has a ruthless authenticity . . . Jesus did not die renouncing God. Even in the inferno of abandonment he did not surrender his faith in God but expressed his anguished prayer in a cry of affirmation, "My God, my God".'[9] Jesus still uses the language of intimacy – 'my God' – even as he experiences infinite separation from the Father.

## Redemption and Suffering

The death of Jesus was qualitatively different from any other death. The physical pain was nothing compared to the spiritual experience of cosmic abandonment.[10] Christianity alone among the world religions claims that God became uniquely and fully human in Jesus Christ and therefore knows firsthand despair, rejection, loneliness, poverty, bereavement, torture and imprisonment. On the cross he went beyond even the worst human suffering and experienced cosmic rejection and pain that exceeds ours as infinitely as his knowledge and power exceeds ours. In his death, God suffers in love, identifying with the abandoned and godforsaken.[11] Why did he do it? The Bible says that Jesus came on a rescue mission for creation. He had to pay for our sins so that some day he can end evil and suffering without ending us.

Let's see where this has brought us. If we again ask the question: 'Why does God allow evil and suffering to continue?' and we look at the cross of Jesus, we still do not know what the answer is. However, we now know what the answer isn't. It can't be that he doesn't love us. It can't be that he is indifferent or detached from our condition. God takes our misery and suffering *so* seriously that he was willing to take it on himself. Albert Camus understood this when he wrote:

> *[Christ] the god-man suffers too, with patience. Evil and death can no longer be entirely imputed to him since he suffers and dies. The night on Golgotha is so important in the history of man only because, in its shadows, the divinity ostensibly abandoned its traditional privilege, and lived through to the end, despair included, the agony of death. Thus is explained the 'Lama sabachthani' and the frightful doubt of Christ in agony.*[12]

So, if we embrace the Christian teaching that Jesus is God and that he went to the cross, then we have deep consolation and strength to face the brutal realities of life on earth. We can know that God is truly *Immanuel* – God *with* us – even in our worst sufferings.

## Resurrection and Suffering

I think we need something more than knowing God is with us in our difficulties. We also need hope that our suffering is 'not in vain'. Have you ever noticed how desperate the families of lost loved ones are to say that? They work to reform laws or change social conditions that led to the death. They need to believe that the death of their loved ones has led to new life, that the injustice has led to greater justice.

For the one who suffers, the Christian faith provides as a resource not just its teaching on the cross but also the fact of the resurrection. The Bible teaches that the future is not an immaterial 'paradise' but a new heaven and a new earth. In Revelation 21, we do not see human beings being taken out of this world into heaven, but rather heaven coming down and cleansing, renewing and perfecting this material world. The secular view of things, of course, sees no future restoration after death or history. And Eastern religions believe we lose our individuality and return to the great All-soul, so our material lives in this world are gone for ever. Even religions that believe in a heavenly paradise consider it a consolation for the losses and pain of this life and all the joys that might have been.

The biblical view of things is resurrection—not a future that is just a *consolation* for the life we never had but a *restoration* of the life you always wanted. This means that every horrible thing that ever happened will not only be undone and repaired but will in some way make the eventual glory and joy even greater.

A few years ago I had a horrible nightmare in which I dreamed that everyone in my family had died. When I awoke my relief was enormous – but there was much more than just relief. My delight in each member of my family was tremendously enriched. I looked at each one and realised how grateful I was for them, how deeply I loved them. Why? My joy had been greatly magnified by the nightmare. My delight on awakening took the terror up into itself, as it were, so that in the end my love for them was only greater for my having lost them and found them again. This same dynamic is at work when you lose some possession you take for granted. When you find it again (having thought it was gone for ever) you cherish and appreciate it in a far deeper way.

In Greek (specifically Stoic) philosophy there was a belief that history was an endless cycle. Every so often the universe would wind down and burn up in a great conflagration called a *palengenesia*, after which history, having been purified, started over. But in Matthew 19:28 Jesus spoke of his return to earth as *the* palingenesis. 'I tell you the truth, at the renewal of all things (Greek *palingenesis*), the Son of Man will sit on his glorious throne.' This was a radically new concept. Jesus insisted that his return will be with such power that the very material world and universe will be purged of all decay and brokenness. All will be healed and all might-have-beens will *be*.

Just after the climax of the trilogy *The Lord of the Rings*, Sam Gamgee discovers that his friend Gandalf was not dead (as he thought) but alive. He cries, 'I thought you were dead! But then I thought I was dead myself! *Is everything sad going to come untrue?*'[13] The answer of Christianity to that question is – yes. Everything sad is going to come untrue and it will somehow be *greater* for having once been broken and lost.

Embracing the Christian doctrines of the incarnation and cross brings profound consolation in the face of suffering. The doctrine of the resurrection can instil us with a powerful hope. It promises that we will get the life we most longed for, but it will be an infinitely more glorious world than if there had never been the need for bravery, endurance, sacrifice or salvation.[14]

Dostoevsky put it perfectly when he wrote:

> *I believe like a child that suffering will be healed and made up for, that all the humiliating absurdity of human contradictions will vanish like a pitiful mirage, like the despicable fabrication of the impotent and infinitely small Euclidean mind of man, that in the world's finale, at the moment of eternal harmony, something so precious will come to pass that it will suffice for all hearts, for the comforting of all resentments, for the atonement of all the crimes of humanity, of all the blood that they've shed; that it will make it not only possible to forgive but to justify all that has happened.*[15]

More succinctly, C. S. Lewis wrote:

> *They say of some temporal suffering, 'No future bliss can make up for it,' not knowing that Heaven, once attained, will work backwards and turn even that agony into a glory.*[16]

This is the ultimate defeat of evil and suffering. It will not only be ended but so radically vanquished that what has happened will only serve to make our future life and joy infinitely greater.

# THREE

## CHRISTIANITY IS A STRAITJACKET

*'Christians believe that they have the absolute truth that every-
one else has to believe – or else,' said Keith, a young artist living
in Brooklyn. 'That attitude endangers everyone's freedom.'*

*'Yes,' agreed Chloe, another young artist. 'A "one-Truth-fits all"
approach is just too confining. The Christians I know don't seem
to have the freedom to think for themselves. I believe each individual must determine truth for him- or herself.'*

IS a belief in absolute truth the enemy of freedom? Most people
I've met in New York City believe that it is. Christianity names
some beliefs 'heresy' and some practices 'immoral'. It bars from its
community those who transgress its doctrinal and moral boundaries. This seems to contemporary observers to endanger civic freedom, because it divides rather than unites our population. It also
appears to be culturally narrow, failing to recognise that various
cultures have different perspectives on reality. Finally, it seems to
enslave or at least infantilise its members, determining what they
must believe and practise in every particular. M. Scott Peck told of
counselling a woman named Charlene who said about Christianity:
'There's no room for *me* in that. That would be my death! . . . I
don't want to live for God. I will not. I want to live for . . . my own

sake.'[1] Charlene believed Christianity would stifle her creativity and growth. So did early-twentieth-century social activist Emma Goldman, who called Christianity 'the leveler of the human race, the breaker of man's will to dare and to do . . . an iron net, a straitjacket which does not let him expand or grow'.[2]

At the end of the movie *I, Robot* (2004), the robot named Sonny has fulfilled the objectives in his design program. But now he realises he no longer has a purpose. The movie concludes with a dialogue between Sonny and the other main character, Detective Spooner.

> Sonny: Now that I have fulfilled my purpose, I don't know what to do.
>
> Detective Spooner: I guess you'll have to find your way like the rest of us, Sonny . . . That's what it means to be free.

In this view, 'freedom' means that there is no overarching purpose for which we were created. If there were, we would be obligated to conform to it and to fulfil it, and that is limiting. True freedom is freedom to create your own meaning and purpose. The Supreme Court has enshrined this view in law when it opined 'the heart of liberty' is to 'define one's own concept of existence, of the meaning of the universe'.[3] Stephen Jay Gould concurs:

> *We are here because one odd group of fishes had a peculiar fin anatomy that could transform into legs for terrestrial creatures; because comets struck the earth and wiped out dinosaurs, thereby giving mammals a chance not otherwise available. . . . We may yearn for a 'higher' answer – but none exists. This explanation, though superficially troubling, if not terrifying, is ultimately liberating and exhilarating. We cannot read the meaning of life passively in the facts of nature. We must construct these answers for ourselves . . . [4]*

Christianity looks like an enemy of social cohesion, cultural adaptability and even authentic personhood. However, this objection is based on mistakes about the nature of truth, community, Christianity, and of liberty itself.

## Truth Is Unavoidable

The French philosopher Foucault writes: 'Truth is a thing of this world. It is produced only by multiple forms of constraint and that includes the regular effects of power.'[5] Inspired by Foucault, many say that all truth-claims are power plays. When you claim to have the truth, you are trying to get power and control over other people. Foucault was a disciple of Nietzsche, and to their credit they used this analysis on both the Left and the Right. If you claimed 'everyone should do justice to the poor' in front of Nietzsche, he would question whether you said that because you really loved justice and the poor or because you wanted to start a revolution that would give you control and power.

However, the objection that all truth is a power play falls prey to the same problem as the objection that all truth is culturally conditioned. If you try to explain away all assertions of truth as one or the other or something else you find yourself in an untenable position. C. S. Lewis writes in *The Abolition of Man*:

> But you cannot go on 'explaining away' for ever: you will find that you have explained explanation itself away. You cannot go on 'seeing through' things for ever. The whole point of seeing through something is to see something through it. It is good that the window should be transparent, because the street or garden beyond it is opaque. How if you saw through the garden too? . . . a wholly transparent world is an invisible world. To 'see through' all things is the same as not to see.[6]

If you say all truth-claims are power plays, then so is your statement. If you say (like Freud) that all truth-claims about religion and God are just psychological projections to deal with your guilt and insecurity, then so is your statement. To see through everything is not to see.

Foucault was pressing the truth of his analysis on others even as he denied the very category of truth. Some kind of truth-claim, then, seems unavoidable. The inconsistency of working against oppression when you refuse to admit there is such a thing as truth is the reason that postmodern 'theory' and 'deconstruction' is perhaps on the wane.[7] G. K. Chesterton made this very same point nearly a hundred years ago:

> *The new rebel is a sceptic, and will not trust anything . . . [but] therefore he can never be really a revolutionary. For all denunciation implies a moral doctrine of some kind. . . . Therefore the modern man in revolt has become practically useless for all purposes of revolt. By rebelling against everything he has lost his right to rebel against anything. . . . There is a thought that stops thought. That is the only thought that ought to be stopped.*[8]

## Community Can't Be Completely Inclusive

Christianity requires particular beliefs in order to be a member of its community. It is not open to all. This is socially divisive, critics argue. Human communities should instead be completely inclusive, open to all on the basis of our common humanity. Proponents of this view point out that many urban neighbourhoods contain residents of different races and religious beliefs who nonetheless live and work together as a community. All that is required for such community life is that each person respects the privacy and rights of others and works for equal access to education, jobs and political decision-making for all. Common moral beliefs are not necessary, it is said, in a 'liberal democracy'.

Unfortunately, the view just expressed is a vast oversimplification. Liberal democracy is based on an extensive list of assumptions – a preference of individual to community rights, a division between private and public morality, and the sanctity of personal choice. All of these beliefs are foreign to many other cultures.[9] A liberal democracy is based then (as is every community) on a shared set of very particular beliefs. Western society is based on shared commitments to reason, rights and justice, even though there is no universally recognised definition of any of these.[10] Every account of justice and reason is embedded in a set of some particular beliefs about the meaning of human life that is not shared with everyone.[11] The idea of a totally inclusive community is, therefore, an illusion.[12] Every human community holds in common some beliefs that necessarily create boundaries, including some people and excluding others from its circle.

Consider an illustration. Imagine that one of the board members of the local Gay, Lesbian and Transgender Community Centre announces, 'I've had a religious experience and now I believe homosexuality is a sin.' As the weeks go by, he persists in making that assertion. Imagine that a board member of the Alliance Against Same-Sex Marriage announces, 'I discovered that my son is gay and I think he has the right to marry his partner.' No matter how personally gracious and flexible the members of each group are, the day will come when each group will have to say, 'You must step off the board because you don't share a common commitment with us.' The first of these communities has the reputation for being inclusive and the second for being exclusive, but, in practice, both of them operate in almost the very same way. Each is based on common beliefs that act as boundaries, including some and excluding others. Neither community is being 'narrow' – they are just being communities.

Any community that did not hold its members accountable for specific beliefs and practices would have no corporate identity and would not really be a community at all.[13] We cannot consider a group exclusive simply because it has standards for its members. Is there then no way to judge whether a community is open and caring rather than narrow and oppressive? Yes, there is. Here is a far better set of tests: which community has beliefs that lead its members to treat people in other communities with love and respect – to serve them and meet their needs? Which community's beliefs lead it to demonise and attack those who violate their boundaries rather than treating them with kindness, humility and winsomeness? We should criticise Christians when they are condemning and ungracious to unbelievers.[14] But we should not criticise churches when they maintain standards for membership in accord with their beliefs. Every community must do the same.

## Christianity Isn't Culturally Rigid

Christianity is also reputed to be a cultural straitjacket. It allegedly forces people from diverse cultures into a single iron mould. It is seen as an enemy of pluralism and multiculturalism. In reality, Christianity has been more adaptive (and maybe less destructive) of diverse cultures than secularism and many other worldviews.

The pattern of Christian expansion differs from that of every other world religion. The centre and majority of Islam's population is still in the place of its origin – the Middle East. The original lands that have been the demographic centres of Hinduism, Buddhism and Confucianism have remained so. By contrast, Christianity was first dominated by Jews and centred in Jerusalem. Later it was dominated by Hellenists and centred in the Mediterranean.

Later the faith was received by the barbarians of Northern Europe and Christianity came to be dominated by western Europeans and then North Americans. Today most Christians in the world live in Africa, Latin America and Asia. Christianity soon will be centred in the southern and eastern hemispheres.

Two case studies are instructive. In 1900, Christians comprised 9 per cent of the African population and were outnumbered by Muslims four to one. Today, Christians comprise 44 per cent of the population,[15] and in the 1960s passed Muslims in number.[16] This explosive growth is now beginning in China.[17] Christianity is growing not only among the peasantry, but also among the social and cultural establishment, including the Communist party. At the current rate of growth, within thirty years Christians will constitute 30 per cent of the Chinese population of 1.5 billion.[18]

Why has Christianity grown so explosively in these places? African scholar Lamin Sanneh gives a most intriguing answer. Africans, he said, had a long tradition of belief in a supernatural world of good and evil spirits. When Africans began to read the Bible in their own languages many began to see in Christ the final solution to their own historic longings and aspirations as Africans.[19] Sanneh writes:

> *Christianity answered this historical challenge by a reorientation of the worldview. . . . People sensed in their hearts that Jesus did not mock their respect for the sacred nor their clamor for an invincible Savior, and so they beat their sacred drums for him until the stars skipped and danced in the skies. After that dance the stars weren't little anymore. Christianity helped Africans to become renewed Africans, not re-made Europeans.*[20]

Sanneh argues that secularism with its anti-supernaturalism and individualism is much more destructive of local cultures and

'African-ness' than Christianity is. In the Bible, Africans read of Jesus' power over supernatural and spiritual evil and of his triumph over it on the cross. When Africans become Christians, their African-ness is converted, completed and resolved, not replace with European-ness or something else.[21] Through Christianity, Africans get distance enough to critique their traditions yet still inhabit them.[22]

An interesting example of cultural adaptation is my own congregation, Redeemer Presbyterian Church of Manhattan. Its growth in this environment has surprised, even shocked observers. I am repeatedly asked, 'How are you reaching thousands of young adults in such a secular place?' The answer is that Christianity has done in New York City what it has done in all the other places that it has grown. It has adapted significantly and positively to the surrounding culture without compromising its main tenets.

Redeemer's basic doctrines – the deity of Christ, the infallibility of the Bible, the necessity of spiritual rebirth through faith in Christ's atoning death – are in unity with the orthodox, supernaturalist beliefs of the evangelical and Pentecostal churches of Africa, Asia, Latin America and the US South and Midwest. These beliefs often put us in conflict with views and practices of many people in the city. At the same time, we have been delighted to embrace many other aspects of urban, pluralistic culture. We emphasise the arts, value racial diversity, stress the importance of working for justice in the city for *all* its inhabitants, and communicate in the language and with the sensibility of our city-centre culture. Most of all we stress the grace of a Saviour who ate with people the establishment called 'sinners' and loved those who opposed him. All of these things are very important to Manhattan residents.

As a result, Redeemer attracts and reaches a very diverse, urban congregation. At one Redeemer Sunday service my wife, Kathy, was introduced to a man sitting in front of her, brought to church by John DeLorean. He was a speechwriter for a conservative Republican presidential candidate. Shortly thereafter she was tapped on the shoulder by a woman sitting behind her who wanted to introduce another guest. She had brought to church a man who was Madonna's chief songwriter at the time. Kathy was delighted they were both there, but she hoped they wouldn't meet each other before they had heard the sermon!

Some years ago a man from a southern US state visited Redeemer. He had heard that though we held to orthodox Christian doctrine, we had grown large in the midst of a sceptical, secular city. He expected to find that we were attracting people with avant-garde music, video monitors and clips, dramatic sketches, exceptionally hip settings and other kinds of eye-catching spectacle. To his surprise he found a simple and traditional service that, on the surface, seemed identical to those in his more conservative part of the world. Yet he could also see that the congregation contained many people who wouldn't have ever attended the churches he knew. After the service he met me and then said, 'This is a complete mystery to me. Where are the dancing bears? Where are the gimmicks? Why are these people here?'

I directed him to some 'downtown art-types' who had been coming to Redeemer for some time. They suggested that he look beneath the surface. One person said that the difference between Redeemer and other churches was profound, and lay in 'irony, charity and humility'. They said Redeemer lacked the pompous and highly sentimental language they found emotionally manipulative in other churches. Instead, Redeemer people addressed others with gentle, self-deprecating irony. Not only that, but beliefs were held here in charity and with humility, making Manhattanites feel included and welcomed, even if they disagreed with some of

Redeemer's beliefs. Most of all, they said, teaching and communication at Redeemer was intelligent and nuanced, showing sensitivity where they were sensitive.

All of these emphases meet with approval in Manhattan, but each one is grounded in historic Christian doctrine. For example, the emphasis on racial diversity comes right out of St Paul's letter to the Ephesians, chapter 2, in which Paul claims that the racial diversity of the church is an important witness to the truth of the Christian message. To take another example, Reinhold Niebuhr has pointed out that irony, amusement at seeing human beings try but fail to be Godlike, is a very Christian way of looking at things.[23] Because all these adaptive emphases have deep roots in historic Christian teaching, they are not simply marketing techniques.

Why has Christianity, more than any other major religion of the world, been able to infiltrate so many radically different cultures? There is, of course, a core of teachings (the Apostles' Creed, the Lord's Prayer, the Ten Commandments) to which all forms of Christianity are committed. Nevertheless, there is a great deal of freedom in how these absolutes are expressed and take form within a particular culture. For example, the Bible directs Christians to unite in acts of musical praise, but it doesn't prescribe the metre, rhythm, level of emotional expressiveness, or instrumentation – all this is left to be culturally expressed in a variety of ways. Historian Andrew Walls writes:

> Cultural diversity was built into the Christian faith . . . in Acts 15, which declared that the new gentile Christians didn't have to enter Jewish culture. . . . The converts had to work out . . . a Hellenistic way of being a Christian. [So] no one owns the Christian faith. There is no 'Christian culture' the way there is an 'Islamic culture' which you can recognize from Pakistan to Tunisia to Morocco. . . .[24]

Biblical texts such as Isaiah 60 and Revelation 21-22 depict a renewed, perfect, future world in which we retain our cultural differences (*'every tongue, tribe, people, nation'*). This means every human culture has (from God) distinct goods and strengths for the enrichment of the human race. As Walls indicates, while every culture has distortions and elements that will be critiqued and revised by the Christian message, each culture will also have good and unique elements to which Christianity connects and adapts.

Contrary to popular opinion, then, Christianity is not a Western religion that destroys local cultures. Rather, Christianity has taken more culturally diverse forms than other faiths.[25] It has deep layers of insight from the Hebrew, Greek and European cultures, and over the next hundred years will be further shaped by Africa, Latin America and Asia. Christianity may become the most truly 'catholic vision of the world',[26] having opened its leadership over the centuries to people from every tongue, tribe, people and nation.

## Freedom Isn't Simple

Christianity is supposedly a limit to personal growth and potential because it constrains our freedom to choose our own beliefs and practices. Immanuel Kant defined an enlightened human being as one who trusts in his or her own power of thinking, rather than in authority or tradition.[27] This resistance to authority in moral matters is now a deep current in our culture. Freedom to determine our own moral standards is considered a necessity for being fully human.

This oversimplifies, however. Freedom cannot be defined in strictly negative terms, as the absence of confinement and constraint. In fact, in many cases, confinement and constraint is actually a means to liberation.

If you have musical aptitude, you may give yourself to practise, practise, practise the piano for years. This is a restriction, a limit on your freedom. There are many other things you won't be able to do with the time you invest in practising. If you have the talent, however, the discipline and limitation will unleash your ability that would otherwise go untapped. What have you done? You've deliberately lost your freedom to engage in some things in order to release yourself to a richer kind of freedom to accomplish other things.

This does not mean that restriction, discipline and constraint are intrinsically, automatically liberating. For example, a five-foot-four, 9-stone young adult male should not set his heart on becoming a top American footballer. All the discipline and effort in the world will only frustrate and crush him (literally). He is banging his head against a physical reality – he simply does not have the potential. In our society many people have worked extremely hard to pursue careers that pay well rather than fit their talents and interests. Such careers are straitjackets that in the long run stifle and dehumanise us.

Disciplines and constraints, then, liberate us only when they fit with the reality of our nature and capacities. A fish, because it absorbs oxygen from water rather than air, is only free if it is restricted and limited to water. If we put it out on the grass, its freedom to move and even live is not enhanced, but destroyed. The fish dies if we do not honour the reality of its nature.

In many areas of life, freedom is not so much the absence of restrictions as finding the right ones, the liberating restrictions. Those that fit with the reality of our nature and the world produce greater power and scope for our abilities and a deeper joy and fulfilment. Experimentation, risk and making mistakes bring growth only if, over time, they show us our limits as well as our abilities. If we only grow intellectually, vocationally and physically through judicious constraints – why would it not also be true for spiritual and moral growth? Instead of insisting on freedom to create spiritual reality, shouldn't we be seeking to discover it and disciplining ourselves to live according to it?

The popular concept – that we should each determine our own morality – is based on the belief that the spiritual realm is nothing at all like the rest of the world. Does anyone really believe that? For many years after each of the morning and evening Sunday services I remained in the church for another hour to field questions. Hundreds of people stayed for the give-and-take discussions. One of the most frequent statements I heard was that 'Every person has to define right and wrong for him- or herself.' I always responded to the speakers by asking, 'Is there anyone in the world right now doing things you believe they should stop doing no matter what they personally believe about the correctness of their behaviour?' They would invariably say, 'Yes, of course.' Then I would ask, 'Doesn't that mean that you *do* believe there is some kind of moral reality that is "there" that is not defined by us, that must be abided by regardless of what a person feels or thinks?' Almost always, the response to that question was a silence, either a thoughtful or a grumpy one.

## Love, the Ultimate Freedom, Is More Constraining Than We Might Think

What then is the moral-spiritual reality we must acknowledge to thrive? What is the environment that liberates us if we confine ourselves to it, like water liberates the fish? Love. Love is the most liberating freedom-loss of all.

One of the principles of love – either love for a friend or romantic love – is that you have to lose independence to attain greater intimacy. If you want the 'freedoms' of love – the fulfilment, secu-rity, sense of worth that it brings – you must limit your freedom in many ways. You cannot enter a deep relationship and still make unilateral decisions or allow your friend or lover no say in how you live your life. To experience the joy and freedom of love, you must give up your personal autonomy. The French novelist Françoise Sa-gan expressed this well in an interview in *Le Monde*. She expressed that she was satisfied with the way she had lived her life and had no regrets:

> Interviewer: *Then you have had the freedom you wanted?*
> Sagan: *Yes . . . I was obviously less free when I was in love with someone. . . . But one's not in love all the time. Apart from that . . . I'm free.*[28]

Sagan is right. A love relationship limits your personal options. Again we are confronted with the complexity of the concept of 'freedom'. Human beings are most free and alive in relationships of love. We only become ourselves in love, and yet healthy love rela-tionships involve mutual, unselfish service, a mutual loss of indepen-dence. C. S. Lewis put it eloquently:

> *Love anything, and your heart will certainly be wrung and pos-sibly broken. If you want to make sure of keeping it intact, you must give your heart to no one, not even to an animal. Wrap it carefully round with hobbies and little luxuries; avoid all en-tanglements; lock it up safe in the casket or coffin of your selfish-ness. But in that casket – safe, dark, motionless, airless – it will change. It will not be broken; it will become unbreakable, impen-etrable, irredeemable. The alternative to tragedy, or at least to the risk of tragedy, is damnation.*[29]

Freedom, then, is not the absence of limitations and constraints but it is finding the right ones, those that fit our nature and liberate us.

For a love relationship to be healthy there must be a mutual loss of independence. It can't be just one way. Both sides must say to the other, 'I will adjust to you. I will change for you. I'll serve you even though it means a sacrifice for me.' If only one party does all the sacrificing and giving, and the other does all the ordering and taking, the relationship will be exploitative and will oppress and distort the lives of both people.

At first sight, then, a relationship with God seems inherently dehumanising. Surely it will have to be 'one way', God's way. God, the divine being, has all the power. I must adjust to God – there is no way that God could adjust to and serve me.

While this may be true in other forms of religion and belief in God, it is not true in Christianity. In the most radical way, God has adjusted to us – in his incarnation and atonement. In Jesus Christ he became a limited human being, vulnerable to suffering and death. On the cross, he submitted to our condition – as sinners – and died in our place to forgive us. In the most profound way, God has said to us, in Christ, 'I will adjust to you. I will change for you. I'll serve you though it means a sacrifice for me.' If he has done this for us, we can and should say the same to God and others. St Paul writes, 'the love of Christ *constrains* us' (2 Corinthians 5:14).

A friend of C. S. Lewis's was once asked, 'Is it easy to love God?' and he replied, 'It is easy to those who do it.'[30] That is not as paradoxical as it sounds. When you fall deeply in love, you want to please the beloved. You don't wait for the person to ask you to do something for her. You eagerly research and learn every little thing that brings her pleasure. Then you get it for her, even if it costs you money or great inconvenience. 'Your wish is my command,' you feel – and it doesn't feel oppressive at all. From the outside, bemused friends may think, 'She's leading him around by the nose,' but from the inside it feels like heaven.

For a Christian, it's the same with Jesus. The love of Christ constrains. Once you realise how Jesus changed for you and gave himself for you, you aren't afraid of giving up your freedom and therefore finding your freedom in him.

# FOUR

# THE CHURCH IS RESPONSIBLE
# FOR SO MUCH INJUSTICE

*'I have to doubt any religion that has so many fanatics and hypo-crites,' insisted Helen, a law student. 'There are so many people who are not religious at all who are more kind and even more moral than many of the Christians I know.'*

*'The church has a history of supporting injustice, of destroying culture,' responded Jessica, another law student. 'If Christianity is the true religion, how could this be?'*

MARK Lilla, a professor at the University of Chicago, wrote an account for *The New York Times Magazine* of his 'born-again' experience as a teenager. During college he 'de-converted' and abandoned his Christian faith. How did it happen? Moving from Detroit to Ann Arbor, Michigan, he entered a Christian community that had a national reputation for spiritual vitality, but it turned out to be a 'crushing disappointment'. The community was authoritarian and hierarchical, and the members were 'dogmatic . . . eager to bring me into line doctrinally'. Disillusioned by the combative and exploitative way he thought they used the Bible to control people's lives, 'the thought penetrated my mind – that the Bible might be wrong. . . . It was my first step out of the world of faith . . .'[1]

Many people who take an intellectual stand against Christianity do so against a background of personal disappointment with Christians and churches. We all bring to issues intellectual predispositions based on our experiences. If you have known many wise, loving, kind and insightful Christians over the years, and if you have seen churches that are devout in belief yet civic-minded and generous, you will find the intellectual case for Christianity much more plausible. If, on the other hand, the preponderance of your experience is with nominal Christians (who bear the name but don't practise it) or with self-righteous fanatics, then the arguments for Christianity will have to be extremely strong for you to concede that they have any cogency at all. Mark Lilla's determination that 'the Bible might be wrong' was not a pure act of philosophical reflection. He was resisting the way that a particular person, in the name of Christianity, was trying to exercise power over him.

So we have to address the behaviour of Christians – individual and corporate – that has undermined the plausibility of Christianity for so many people. Three issues stand out. First, there is the issue of Christians' glaring character flaws. If Christianity is the truth, why are so many non-Christians living better lives than the Christians? Second, there is the issue of war and violence. If Christianity is the truth, why has the institutional church supported war, injustice and violence over the years? Third, there is the issue of fanaticism. Even if Christian teaching has much to offer, why would we want to be together with so many smug, self-righteous, dangerous fanatics?

## Character Flaws

Anyone involved in the life of a church will soon discover the many flaws in the character of the average professing Christian. Church communities seem, if anything, to be characterised by more fighting and party spirit than do other voluntary organisations. Also, the moral failings of Christian leaders are well known. It may be true that the press takes too much pleasure in publicising them, but it doesn't create them. Church officials seem to be at least (if not more) corrupt than leaders in the world at large.

At the same time there are many formally irreligious people who live morally exemplary lives. If Christianity is all it claims to be, shouldn't Christians on the whole be much better people than everyone else?

This assumption is based on a mistaken belief concerning what Christianity actually teaches about itself. Christian theology has taught what is known as *common grace*. James 1:17 says, 'Every good and perfect gift comes down from above . . . from the father of lights.' This means that no matter who performs it, every act of goodness, wisdom, justice and beauty is empowered by God. God gives out good gifts of wisdom, talent, beauty and skill 'graciously' – that is, in a completely unmerited way. He casts them across *all* humanity, regardless of religious conviction, race, gender or any other attribute to enrich, brighten and preserve the world.

Christian theology also speaks of the seriously flawed character of real Christians. A central message of the Bible is that we can only have a relationship with God by sheer grace. Our moral efforts are too feeble and falsely motivated to ever merit salvation. Jesus, through his death and resurrection, has provided salvation for us, which we receive as a gift. All churches believe this in one form or another. Growth in character and changes in behaviour occur in a gradual process after a person becomes a Christian. The mistaken belief that a person must 'clean up' his or her own life in order to merit God's presence is not Christianity. This means, though, that the church will be filled with immature and broken people who still have a long way to go emotionally, morally and spiritually. As the saying has it: 'The church is a hospital for sinners, not a museum for saints.'

Good character is largely attributable to a loving, safe and stable family and social environment – conditions for which we were not responsible. Many have had instead an unstable family background, poor role models and a history of tragedy and disappointment. As a result, they are burdened with deep insecurities, hypersensitivity, and a lack of self-confidence. They may struggle with uncontrolled anger, shyness, addictions and other difficulties as a result.

Now imagine that someone with a very broken past becomes a Christian and her character improves significantly over what it was. Nevertheless, she still may be less secure and self-disciplined than someone who is so well adjusted that she feels no particular need for religious affiliation at all. Suppose you meet both of these women the same week. Unless you know the starting points and life journeys of each woman, you could easily conclude that Christianity isn't worth much, and that Christians are inconsistent with their own high standards. It is often the case that people whose lives have been harder and who are 'lower on the character scale' are more likely to recognise their need for God and turn to Christianity. So we should expect that many Christians' lives would not compare well to those of the non-religious[2] (just as the health of people in the hospital is comparatively worse than people visiting museums).

## Religion and Violence

Doesn't orthodox religion lead inevitably to violence? Christopher Hitchens, the author of *God Is Not Great: How Religion Poisons Everything* argues that it does. In his chapter 'Religion Kills', he gives personal accounts of religion-fuelled violence in Belfast,

Beirut, Bombay, Belgrade, Bethlehem and Baghdad. His argument is that religion takes racial and cultural differences and aggravates them. 'Religion is not unlike racism,' he writes. 'One version of it inspires and provokes the other. Religion has been an enormous multiplier of tribal suspicion and hatred. . . .'[3]

Hitchens' point is fair. Religion 'transcendentalises' ordinary cultural differences so that parties feel they are in a cosmic battle between good and evil. This is why Hitchens argues that 'religion poisons everything'. So it would seem. Christian nations institutionalised imperialism, violence and oppression through the Inquisition and the African slave trade. The totalitarian and militaristic Japanese empire of the mid-twentieth century grew out of a culture deeply influenced by Buddhism and Shintoism. Islam is the soil for much of today's terrorism, while Israeli forces have often been ruthless too. Hindu nationalists, in the name of their religion, carry out bloody strikes on both Christian churches and Muslim mosques. All of this evidence seems to indicate that religion aggravates human differences until they boil over into war, violence and the oppression of minorities.[4]

There are problems with this view, however. The Communist Russian, Chinese and Cambodian regimes of the twentieth century rejected all organised religion and belief in God. A forerunner of all these was the French Revolution, which rejected traditional religion for human reason. These societies were all rational and secular, yet each produced massive violence against its own people without the influence of religion. Why? Alister McGrath points out that when the idea of God is gone, a society will 'transcendentalise' something else, some other concept, in order to appear morally and spiritually superior. The Marxists made the State into such an absolute, while the Nazis did it to race and blood. Even the ideals of liberty and equality can be used in this way in order to do violence to opponents. In 1793, when Madame Roland went to the guillotine on trumped-up charges, she bowed to the statue personifying liberty in the Place de la Révolution and said, *'Liberty, what crimes are committed in your name.'*[5]

Violence done in the name of Christianity is a terrible reality and must be both addressed and redressed. There is no excusing it. In the twentieth century, however, violence has been inspired as much by secularism as by moral absolutism. Societies that have rid themselves of all religion have been just as oppressive as those steeped in it. We can only conclude that there is some violent impulse so deeply rooted in the human heart that it expresses itself regardless of what the beliefs of a particular society might be – whether socialist or capitalist, whether religious or irreligious, whether individualistic or hierarchical. Ultimately, then, the fact of violence and warfare in a society is no necessary refutation of the prevailing beliefs of that society.

## Fanaticism

Perhaps the biggest deterrent to Christianity for the average person today is not so much violence and warfare but the shadow of fanaticism. Many non-believers have friends or relatives who have become 'born again' and seem to have gone off the deep end. They soon begin to express loudly their disapproval of various groups and sectors of our society – especially movies and television, the Democratic party, homosexuals, evolutionists, activist judges, members of other religions, and the values taught in state schools. When arguing for the truth of their faith they often appear intolerant and self-righteous. This is what many people would call fanaticism.

Many people try to understand Christians along a spectrum from 'nominalism' at one end to 'fanaticism' at the other. A nominal

Christian is someone who is Christian in name only, who does not practise it and perhaps barely believes it. A fanatic is someone who is thought to over-believe and over-practise Christianity. In this schematic, the best kind of Christian would be someone in the middle, someone who doesn't go all the way with it, who believes it but is not too devoted to it. The problem with this approach is that it assumes that the Christian faith is basically a form of moral improvement. Intense Christians would therefore be intense moralists or, as they were called in Jesus' time, Pharisees. Pharisaic people assume they are right with God because of their moral behaviour and right doctrine. This leads naturally to feelings of superiority towards those who do not share their religiosity, and from there to various forms of abuse, exclusion and oppression. This is the essence of what we think of as fanaticism.

What if, however, the essence of Christianity is salvation by grace, salvation not because of what we do but because of what Christ has done for us? Belief that you are accepted by God by sheer grace is profoundly humbling. The people who are fanatics, then, are so not because they are too committed to the gospel but because they're not committed to it enough.

Think of people you consider fanatical. They're overbearing, self-righteous, opinionated, insensitive and harsh. Why? It's not because they are too Christian but because they are not Christian enough. They are fanatically zealous and courageous, but they are not fanatically humble, sensitive, loving, empathetic, forgiving or understanding – as Christ was. Because they think of Christianity as a self-improvement programme they emulate the Jesus of the whips in the temple, but not the Jesus who said, 'Let him who is without sin cast the first stone' (John 8:7). What strikes us as overly fanatical is actually a failure to be fully committed to Christ and his gospel.

## The Biblical Critique of Religion

Extremism and fanaticism, which lead to injustice and oppression, are a constant danger within any body of religious believers. For Christians, however, the antidote is not to tone down and moderate their faith, but rather to grasp a fuller and truer faith in Christ. The biblical prophets understood this well. In fact, the scholar Merold Westphal documents how Marx's analysis of religion as an instrument of oppression was anticipated by the Hebrew prophets Isaiah, Jeremiah, Amos, and even by the message of the New Testament Gospels. Marx, according to Westphal, was unoriginal in his critique of religion – the Bible beat him to it![6]

Jesus conducts a major critique of religion. His famous Sermon on the Mount (Matthew chapters 5, 6 and 7) does not criticise irreligious people, but rather religious ones. In his famous discourse the people he criticises pray, give to the poor, and seek to live according to the Bible, but they do so in order to get acclaim and power for themselves. They believe they will get leverage over others and even over God because of their spiritual performance ('They think they will be heard for their many words' – Matthew 6:7). This makes them judgemental and condemning, quick to give criticism, and unwilling to take it. They are fanatics.

In his teaching, Jesus continually says to the respectable and upright, 'The tax collectors and the prostitutes enter the kingdom before you' (Matthew 21:31). He continuously condemns in white-hot language their legalism, self-righteousness, bigotry and love of wealth and power ('You clean the outside of the cup and dish, but inside you are full of greed and wickedness. . . . You neglect justice and the love of God . . . You load people down with burdens they can hardly carry, and you yourselves will not lift one finger to help them. . . . [You] devour widows' houses and for a show make long prayers' – Luke 11:39-46; 20:47). We should not be surprised to discover it was the Bible-believing religious establishment who put Jesus to death. As Swiss theologian Karl Barth put it, it was the church, not the world, who crucified Christ.[7]

Jesus followed the lead of the Hebrew prophets such as Isaiah, who said to the people of his day:

> Day after day they seek me out; they seem eager to know my ways, as if they were a nation that does what is right and has not forsaken the commands of its God. They seem eager for God to come near them. 'Why have we fasted,' they say, 'and you have not seen it? Why have we humbled ourselves, and you have not noticed?' Yet on the day of your fasting, you do as you please and exploit all your workers. . . . Is not this the kind of fasting I have chosen: to loose the chains of injustice . . . to set the oppressed free and break every yoke? Is it not to share your food with the hungry and to provide the poor wanderer with shelter—when you see the naked, to clothe him . . . ? (Isaiah 58:2-7)

What were the prophets and Jesus criticising? They were not against prayer and fasting and obedience to biblical directions for life. The tendency of religious people, however, is to use spiritual and ethical observance as a lever to gain power over others and over God, appeasing him through ritual and good works. This leads to both an emphasis on external religious forms as well as greed, materialism and oppression in social arrangements. Those who believe they have pleased God by the quality of their devotion and moral goodness naturally feel that they and their group deserve deference and power over others. The God of Jesus and the prophets, however, saves completely by grace. He cannot be manipulated by religious and moral performance – he can only be reached through repentance, through the *giving up* of power. If we are saved by sheer grace we can only become grateful, willing servants of God and of everyone around us. Jesus charged his disciples: 'Whoever wants to be great among you must be your servant, and whoever wants to be first must be servant of all' (Mark 10:43-45).

In Jesus' and the prophets' critique, self-righteous religion is always marked by insensitivity to issues of social justice, while true faith is marked by profound concern for the poor and marginalised. The Swiss theologian John Calvin, in his commentaries on the Hebrew prophets, says that God so identifies with the poor that their cries express divine pain. The Bible teaches us that our treatment of them equals our treatment of God.[8]

While the church has inexcusably been party to the oppression of people at times, it is important to realise that the Bible gives us tools for analysis and unflinching critique of religiously supported injustice *from within the faith*. Historian C. John Sommerville claims that even strong secular critics of Christianity are really using resources from within it to denounce it.[9] Many criticise the church for being power-hungry and self-regarding, but there are many cultures in which the drive for power and respect is considered a good. Where, then, did we get this list of virtues by which we can discern the church's sins, asks Sommerville? We actually got it from within the Christian faith.

To illustrate this point to his students, Sommerville invites them to do a thought experiment. He points out that the pre-Christian northern European tribes, like the Anglo-Saxons, had societies based on the concept of honour. They were shame-based cultures in which earning and insisting upon respect from others was paramount. The Christian monks who were trying to convert them had a set of values based on charity, on wanting the best for others. To see the difference he asks his students to imagine seeing a little old lady coming down the street at night carrying a big purse. Why not just knock her over and take the purse and its money? The answer of an honour-shame culture is that you do *not* take her purse, because if you pick on the weak you would be a despicable person. No one would respect you and you would not respect yourself. That ethic, of course, is self-regarding. You are focused on how the action will affect your honour and reputation. There is, however, another train of thought to take. You may imagine how much it would hurt to be mugged, and how the loss of money might harm people who depend on her. So you don't take the money because you want the best for her and for her dependents. This is an other-regarding ethic; you are thinking completely about her.

Over the years Sommerville found that the overwhelming majority of his students reasoned according to the second, other-regarding ethic. As a historian, he then showed them how Christian their moral orientation was. Christianity changed those honour-based cultures in which pride was valued rather than humility, dominance rather than service, courage rather than peaceableness, glory rather than modesty, loyalty to one's own tribe rather than equal respect for all.[10]

The typical criticisms by secular people about the oppressiveness and injustices of the Christian church actually come from Christianity's own resources for critique of itself. The shortcomings of the church can be understood historically as the imperfect adoption and practice of the principles of the Christian gospel. Sommerville says that when the Anglo-Saxons first heard the Christian gospel message they were incredulous. They couldn't see how any society could survive that did not fear and respect strength. When they did convert, they were far from consistent. They tended to merge the Christian other-regarding ethic with their older ways. They supported the Crusades as a way of protecting God's honour and theirs. They let monks, women and serfs cultivate charitable virtues, but these virtues weren't considered appropriate for men of honour and action. No wonder there is so much to condemn in church history. But to give up Christian standards would be to leave us with no basis for the criticism.[11]

What is the answer, then, to the very fair and devastating criticisms of the record of the Christian church? The answer is *not* to abandon the Christian faith, because that would leave us with neither the standards nor the resources to make correction. Instead we should move to a fuller and deeper grasp of what Christianity is. The Bible itself has taught us to expect the abuses of religion and it has also told us what to do about them. Because of this, Christian history gives us many remarkable examples of self-correction. Let's look at perhaps the two leading examples of this.

## Justice in Jesus' Name

A deep stain on Christian history is the African slave trade. Since Christianity was dominant in the nations that bought and sold slaves during that time, the churches must bear responsibility along with their societies for what happened. Even though slavery in some form was virtually universal in every human culture over the centuries, it was Christians who first came to the conclusion that it was wrong. The social historian Rodney Stark writes:

> *Although it has been fashionable to deny it, anti-slavery doctrines began to appear in Christian theology soon after the decline of Rome and were accompanied by the eventual disappearance of slavery in all but the fringes of Christian Europe. When Europeans subsequently instituted slavery in the New World, they did so over strenuous papal opposition, a fact that was conveniently 'lost' from history until recently. Finally, the abolition of New World slavery was initiated and achieved by Christian activists.*[12]

Christians began to work for abolition not because of some general understanding of human rights, but because they saw it as violating the will of God. Older forms of indentured servanthood and the bond-service of biblical times had often been harsh, but Christian abolitionists concluded that race-based, life-long chattel slavery, established through kidnapping, could not be squared with biblical teaching either in the Old Testament or the New.[13] Christian activists such as William Wilberforce in Great Britain, John Woolman in America, and many, many others devoted their entire lives, in the name of Christ, to ending slavery. The slave trade was so tremendously lucrative that there was enormous incentive within the church to justify it. Many church leaders defended the institution. The battle for self-correction was titanic.[14]

When the abolitionists finally had British society poised to abolish slavery in their empire, planters in the colonies foretold that emancipation would cost investors enormous sums and the prices of commodities would skyrocket catastrophically. This did not deter the abolitionists in the House of Commons. They agreed to compensate the planters for all freed slaves, an astounding sum up to half of the British government's annual budget. The Act of Emancipation was passed in 1833, and the costs were so high to the British people that one historian called the British abolition of slavery 'voluntary econocide'.

Rodney Stark notes how historians have been desperately trying to figure out why the abolitionists were willing to sacrifice so much to end slavery. He quotes the historian Howard Temperley, who says that the history of abolition is puzzling because most historians believe all political behaviour is self-interested. Yet despite the fact that hundreds of scholars over the last fifty years have looked for ways to explain it, Temperley says, 'no one has succeeded in showing that those who campaigned for the end of the slave trade . . . stood to gain in any tangible way . . . or that these measures were other than economically costly to the country'. Slavery was abolished because it was wrong, and Christians were the leaders in saying so.[15] Christianity's self-correcting apparatus, its critique of religiously supported acts of injustice, had asserted itself.

Another classic case of this is the Civil Rights movement in the United States in the mid-twentieth century. In an important history of the movement, David L. Chappell demonstrates that it was not a political but primarily a religious and spiritual movement. White Northern liberals who were the allies of the African-American civil rights leaders were not proponents of civil disobedience or of a direct attack on segregation. Because of their secular belief in the goodness of human nature, they thought that education and enlightenment would bring about inevitable social and racial progress. Chappell argues that black leaders were much more rooted in the biblical understanding of the sinfulness of the human heart and in the denunciations of injustice that they read in the Hebrew prophets. Chappell also shows how it was the vibrant faith of rank-and-file African-Americans that empowered them to insist on justice despite the violent opposition to their demands. Thus Chappell says there is no way to understand what happened until you see the Civil Rights movement as a religious revival.[16]

When Martin Luther King, Jr confronted racism in the white church in the South, he did not call on Southern churches to become more secular. Read his sermons and 'Letter from Birmingham Jail' and see how he argued. He invoked God's moral law and the Scripture. He called white Christians to be *more true* to their own beliefs and to realise what the Bible really teaches. He did not say 'Truth is relative and everyone is free to determine what is right or wrong for them.' If everything is relative, there would have been no incentive for white people in the South to give up their power. Rather, Dr King invoked the prophet Amos, who said, 'Let justice roll down like waters, and righteousness as a mighty stream'

(Amos 5:24). The greatest champion of justice in our era knew the antidote to racism was not less Christianity, but a deeper and truer Christianity.

Wilberforce and King were not by any means the only leaders who have turned the tide against injustice in the name of Christ. After apartheid was abolished in South Africa, everyone expected a bloodbath in which former victims would take violent vengeance on their persecutors and former oppressors would defend themselves with force. Instead, Christian leaders like Desmond Tutu set up the remarkable South African Commission for Truth and Reconciliation in the mid-1990s. Its name expressed its principle and mission. It invited victims to come forward to tell their stories publicly. It also invited former perpetrators of oppression and violence to come forward, tell the truth, and ask for amnesty. No side was exempt from appearing before the commission. The commission heard reports of human rights violations and considered amnesty applications from all sides, from the former apartheid state as well as from the African National Congress. Though not without its flaws and critics, the commission helped bring about the transition of majority rule with far less bloodshed than anyone could have expected.

In the late twentieth century the Catholic Church in eastern Europe refused to die under Communism. Through 'patience, candles and crosses' it began the chain of events that brought down all those totalitarian regimes. The Polish priest Jerzy Popieluszko, through his preaching and activism, led the movement for a free trade union in Communist Poland in the early 1980s. When he was murdered by the secret police, 250,000 people came to his funeral, including Lech Walesa, whose Solidarity movement would help bring down the Communist government. Many of those who went to his funeral marched past the secret police headquarters with a banner that read 'We Forgive'.[17] The Christian underpinnings of the resistance movement were unmistakable.

There is a long list of martyrs who stood up for the oppressed in Jesus' name, such as Archbishop Oscar Romero of El Salvador. Romero was made archbishop for his conservative, orthodox, doctrinal views. In his new post he saw irrefutable evidence of chronic and violent human rights abuses by the government. He began to speak out fearlessly against it, and as a result he was shot to death in 1980 while saying Mass.

The famous Lutheran martyr Dietrich Bonhoeffer was pastoring two German-speaking churches in London when Hitler came to power. He refused to stay at a safe distance and returned to his country to head an illegal seminary for the Confessing Church, the Christian congregations that refused to sign an oath of allegiance to the Nazis. Bonhoeffer wrote the classic *The Cost of Discipleship*, in which he critiqued the religion and church of his day. In echoes of Jesus and the prophets, Bonhoeffer revealed the spiritual deadness and self-satisfied complacency that made it possible for so many to co-operate with Hitler and turn a blind eye to those being systematically marginalised and destroyed by the Nazis. Bonhoeffer was eventually arrested and hanged.

In his last letters from prison, Bonhoeffer reveals how his Christian faith gave him the resources to give up everything for the sake of others. Marx argued that if you believe in a life after this one you won't be concerned about making this world a better place. You can also argue the opposite. If this world is all there is, and if the goods of this world are the only love, comfort and wealth I will ever have, why should I sacrifice them for others? Bonhoeffer, however, had a joy and hope in God that made it possible for him to do what he did:

*It is not a religious act that makes the Christian, but participation in the sufferings of God in the secular life. That is metanoia [repentance]: not in the first place thinking about one's own needs, problems, sins and fears, but allowing oneself to be caught*

66

*up into the way of Jesus Christ. . . . Pain is a holy angel. . . . Through him men have become greater than through all the joys of the world. . . . The pain of longing, which often can be felt physically, must be there, and we shall not and need not talk it away. But it needs to be overcome every time, and thus there is an even holier angel than the one of pain, that is the one of joy in God.*[18]

Why mention all of these examples? They are evidence that Dr King was right. When people have done injustice in the name of Christ they are not being true to the spirit of the one who himself died as a victim of injustice and who called for the forgiveness of his enemies. When people give their lives to liberate others as Jesus did, they are realising the true Christianity that Martin Luther King, Jr, Dietrich Bonhoeffer and other Christian voices have called for.

# FIVE

## How Can a Loving God Send People to Hell?

*'I doubt the existence of a judgemental God who requires blood to pacify his wrath,' said a frowning Hartmut, a graduate student from Germany. 'Someone had to die before the Christian God would pardon us. But why can't he just forgive? And then there's all those places in the Old Testament where God commands that people be slaughtered.'*

*'All that is troubling, I agree,' responded Josie, who worked for an art gallery in Soho. 'But I have even more of a problem with the doctrine of hell. The only God that is believable to me is a God of love. The Bible's God is no more than a primitive deity who must be appeased with pain and suffering.'*

IN 2005, Rick Warren, mega-church pastor and author of the bestselling book *The Purpose Driven Life*, spoke to leading journalists at a forum sponsored by the Pew Foundation. Some of those present were troubled by the civil implications of one particular Christian belief, namely that God consigns some people to eternal punishment. One speaker said to Warren:

*Maybe you can hold in your mind the contradiction, which is that Wendy [a non-Christian reporter present] is a full American citizen deserving of every protection that the most senior member of your church deserves. But when she dies, she's going to go to hell because she is not saved. The question is, do you think your followers – or the people who come to church, the people who read your books, the people you are talking to all over the world—are sophisticated enough to hold this contradiction in their minds? . . .* [1]

Warren responded that his church saw no contradiction between these things, but many of the journalists were unconvinced. They suggested that any Christian who thinks that there are people bound for hell must perceive such people as unequal in dignity and worth. In this, they reflected the deep misgivings of many today about the Christian concept of a God who judges people and sends them to hell. That belief, they contend, leads to exclusion, abuse, division and even violence.

In our culture, divine judgement is one of Christianity's most offensive doctrines. As a minister and preacher I often find myself speaking on biblical texts that teach the wrath of God, the final judgement, and the doctrine of hell. For many years I always held a question-and-answer session immediately after each service. There I was regularly grilled by New Yorkers about these teachings. I found their deep distress over this aspect of historic Christian faith perfectly understandable. Although this objection to hell and judgement may seem to be more of a feeling of revulsion than a doubt, we still can find a number of very specific beliefs hidden inside it. Let's look at each one in turn.

## A God of Judgement Simply Can't Exist

Robert Bellah's influential work *Habits of the Heart* speaks of the 'expressive individualism' that dominates American culture. In his book Bellah notes that 80 per cent of Americans agree with the statement 'an individual should arrive at his or her own religious beliefs independent of any church or synagogue'.[2] He concludes that the most fundamental belief in American culture is that moral truth is relative to individual consciousness. Our culture, therefore, has no problem with a God of love who supports us no matter how we live. It does, however, object strongly to the idea of a God who punishes people for their sincerely held beliefs, even if they are mistaken. This objection, however, has a cultural history to it.

In C. S. Lewis's classic *The Abolition of Man*, he outlines what he considers to be a major difference between the ancient and the modern views of reality. Lewis attacks our smug belief that ancient people believed in magic and later modern science came along and supplanted it. As an expert in the medieval age and how it gave way to modernity, Lewis knew that there had been very little magic in the Middle Ages, that the high noon of magic was in the sixteenth and seventeenth centuries, at the very time that modern science was developing. The same cause, he contended, gave rise to them both.

*The serious magical endeavour and the serious scientific endeavour are twins: one was sickly and died, the other was strong and throve. But they are twins. They were born of the same impulse.*[3]

Lewis describes that impulse – a new approach to moral and spiritual reality.

*There is something which unites magic and applied science while separating both from the 'wisdom' of earlier ages. For the wise men of old the cardinal problem had been how to conform the soul to reality, and the solution had been knowledge, self-discipline and virtue. For magic and applied science alike the problem is how to subdue reality to the wishes of men: the solution is a tech-*

*nique; and both, in the practice of this technique, are ready to do*
*things hitherto regarded as disgusting and impious. . . .*[4]

In ancient times it was understood that there was a transcendent
moral order outside the self, built in to the fabric of the universe. If
you violated that metaphysical order there were consequences just
as severe as if you violated physical reality by placing your hand in a
fire. The path of wisdom was to learn to live in conformity with this
unyielding reality. That wisdom rested largely in developing quali-
ties of character, such as humility, compassion, courage, discretion
and loyalty.

Modernity reversed this. Ultimate reality was seen not so much
as a supernatural order but as the natural world, and that was mal-
leable. Instead of trying to shape our desires to fit reality, we now
seek to control and shape reality to fit our desires. The ancients
looked at an anxious person and prescribed spiritual character
change. Modernity talks instead about stress-management techniques.

Lewis knew that readers might think he was against the scientific method as such, but he protested that he was not. He wanted
us to realise, however, that the modernity was born in 'dreams of
power'. Writing during the Second World War, Lewis was standing
in the midst of some of the bitterest fruit of the modern spirit.
Lewis's friend J. R. R. Tolkien wrote *The Lord of the Rings* about
the consequences of seeking power and control rather than wisdom
and glad enjoyment of the 'givenness' of God's creation.[5]

The spirit of modernity, then, gave us the responsibility to determine right or wrong. Our new confidence that we can control
the physical environment has spilled over so we now think we can
reshape the metaphysical realm as well. It seems to our minds unfair, therefore, that we should determine that it is all right to have
sex outside of marriage and later discover that there is a God who is

going to punish us for that. We believe so deeply in our personal rights in this realm that the very idea of a divine Judgement Day seems impossible. However, as Lewis shows us, this belief is tied to a quest for control and power that has had terrible consequences in recent world history. Not all the human race today has accepted modernity's view of things. Why should we act as if it is inescapable?

In one of my after-service discussions a woman told me that the very idea of a judging God was offensive. I said, 'Why aren't you offended by the idea of a forgiving God?' She looked puzzled. I continued, 'I respectfully urge you to consider your cultural location when you find the Christian teaching about hell offensive.' I went on to point out that secular Westerners get upset by the Christian doctrines of hell, but they find biblical teaching about turning the other cheek and forgiving enemies appealing. I then asked her to consider how someone from a very different culture sees Christianity. In traditional societies the teaching about 'turning the other cheek' makes absolutely no sense. It offends people's deepest instincts about what is right. For them the doctrine of a God of judgement, however, is no problem at all. That society is repulsed by aspects of Christianity that Western people enjoy, and are attracted by the aspects that secular Westerners can't stand.

Why, I concluded, should Western cultural sensibilities be the final court in which to judge whether Christianity is valid? I asked the woman gently whether she thought her culture superior to non-Western ones. She immediately answered 'no'. 'Well then,' I asked, 'why should your culture's objections to Christianity trump theirs?'

For the sake of argument, let's imagine that Christianity is not the product of any one culture but is actually the transcultural truth of God. If that were the case we would expect that it would contradict and offend every human culture at some point, because human cultures are ever-changing and imperfect. If Christianity were the truth it would have to be offending and correcting your thinking at some place. Maybe this is the place, the Christian doctrine of divine judgement.

## A God of Judgement Can't Be a God of Love

In Christianity God is both a God of love and of justice. Many people struggle with this. They believe that a loving God can't be a judging God. Like most other Christian ministers in our society, I have been asked literally thousands of times, 'How can a God of love be also a God filled with wrath and anger? If he is loving and perfect, he should forgive and accept everyone. He shouldn't get angry.'

I always start my response by pointing out that all loving people are sometimes filled with wrath, not just despite of but because of their love. If you love a person and you see someone ruining them – even they themselves – you get angry. As Becky Pippert puts it in her book *Hope Has Its Reasons*:

> *Think how we feel when we see someone we love ravaged by unwise actions or relationships. Do we respond with benign tolerance as we might toward strangers? Far from it. . . . Anger isn't the opposite of love. Hate is, and the final form of hate is indifference. . . . God's wrath is not a cranky explosion, but his settled opposition to the cancer . . . which is eating out the insides of the human race he loves with his whole being.*[6]

The Bible says that God's wrath flows from his love and delight in his creation. He is angry at evil and injustice because it is destroying its peace and integrity.

The Lord is righteous in all his ways and loving toward
all he has made . . .

The Lord watches over those who love him, but all the
wicked he will destroy.
(Psalms 145:17-20)

It is at this point that many people complain that those who believe
in a God of judgement will not approach enemies with a desire to
reconcile with them. If you believe in a God who smites evildoers,
you may think it perfectly justified to do some of the smiting yourself. Yale theologian Miroslav Volf, a Croatian who has seen the violence in the Balkans, does not see the doctrine of God's judgement
that way. He writes:

> *If God were* not angry *at injustice and deception and did* not
> *make a final end to violence – that God would not be worthy of*
> *worship. . . . The only means of prohibiting all recourse to violence*
> *by* ourselves *is to insist that violence is legitimate only when it*
> *comes from God. . . . My thesis that the practice of non-violence*
> *requires a belief in divine vengeance will be unpopular with*
> *many . . . in the West. . . . [But] it takes the quiet of a suburban*
> *home for the birth of the thesis that human non-violence [results*
> *from the belief in] God's refusal to judge. In a sun-scorched land,*
> *soaked in the blood of the innocent, it will invariably*
> *die . . . [with] other pleasant captivities of the liberal mind.*[7]

In this fascinating passage Volf reasons that it is the *lack* of belief in
a God of vengeance that 'secretly nourishes violence'.[8] The human
impulse to make perpetrators of violence pay for their crimes is
almost an overwhelming one. It cannot possibly be overcome
with platitudes like 'Now don't you see that violence won't solve

anything?' If you have seen your home burned down and your relatives killed and raped, such talk is laughable – and it shows no real concern for justice. Yet victims of violence are drawn to go far beyond justice into the vengeance that says, 'You put out one of my eyes, so I will put out both of yours.' They are pulled inexorably into an endless cycle of vengeance, of strikes and counterstrikes nurtured and justified by the memory of terrible wrongs.

Can our passion for justice be honoured in a way that does not nurture our desire for blood vengeance? Volf says the best resource for this is belief in the concept of God's divine justice. If I don't believe that there is a God who will eventually put all things right, I *will* take up the sword and will be sucked into the endless vortex of retaliation. Only if I am sure that there's a God who will right all wrongs and settle all accounts perfectly do I have the power to refrain.

Czeslaw Milosz, the Nobel Prize-winning Polish poet, wrote the remarkable essay 'The Discreet Charms of Nihilism'. In it he remembers how Marx had called religion 'the opiate of the people' because the promise of an afterlife (Marx said) led the poor and the working class to put up with unjust social conditions. But, Milosz continued:

> *And now we are witnessing a transformation. A true opium of the people is a belief in nothingness after death – the huge solace of thinking that our betrayals, greed, cowardice, murders are not going to be judged . . . [but] all religions recognize that our deeds are imperishable.*[9]

Many people complain that belief in a God of judgement will lead to a more brutal society. Milosz had personally seen, in both Nazism and Communism, that a loss of belief in a God of judgement can lead to brutality. If we are free to shape life and morals any way we choose without ultimate accountability, it can lead to violence. Volf and Milosz argue that the doctrine of God's final judgement is a necessary undergirding for human practices of love and peace-making.

## A Loving God Would Not Allow Hell

'Ah,' you may say, 'fighting evil and injustice in the world is one thing, but sending people to hell is another. The Bible speaks of eternal punishment. How does that fit in with the love of God? I cannot reconcile even the *idea* of hell with a loving God.' How do we address this understandable recoiling?

Modern people inevitably think that hell works like this: God gives us time, but if we haven't made the right choices by the end of our lives, he casts our souls into hell for all eternity. As the poor souls fall through space, they cry out for mercy, but God says, 'Too late! You had your chance! Now you will suffer!' This caricature misunderstands the very nature of evil. The biblical picture is that sin separates us from the presence of God, which is the source of all joy and indeed of all love, wisdom or good things of any sort. Since we were originally created for God's immediate presence, only before his face will we thrive, flourish and achieve our highest potential. If we were to lose his presence totally, that would be hell – the loss of our capability for giving or receiving love or joy.

A common image of hell in the Bible is that of fire.[10] Fire disintegrates. Even in this life we can see the kind of soul disintegration that self-centredness creates. We know how selfishness and self-absorption leads to piercing bitterness, nauseating envy, paralyzing anxiety, paranoid thoughts and the mental denials and distortions that accompany them. Now ask the question: 'What if when we die we don't end, but spiritually our life extends on into eternity?'

Hell, then, is the trajectory of a soul, living a self-absorbed, self-centred life, going on and on forever.

Jesus' parable of Lazarus and the Rich Man in Luke 16 supports the view of hell we are presenting here. Lazarus is a poor man who begs at the gate of a cruel rich man. They both die and Lazarus goes to heaven while the rich man goes to hell. There he looks up and sees Lazarus in heaven 'in Abraham's bosom':

> So he called to him, 'Father Abraham, have pity on me and send Lazarus to dip the tip of his finger in water and cool my tongue, because I am in agony in this fire.' But Abraham replied, 'Son, remember that in your lifetime you received your good things, while Lazarus received bad things, but now he is comforted here and you are in agony. And besides all this, between us and you a great chasm has been fixed, so that those who want to go from here to you cannot, nor can anyone cross over from there to us.' He answered, 'Then I beg you, father, send Lazarus to my father's house, for I have five brothers. Let him warn them, so that they will not also come to this place of torment.' Abraham replied, 'They have Moses and the Prophets; let them listen to them.' 'No, father Abraham,' he said, 'but if someone from the dead goes to them, they will repent.' He said to him, 'If they do not listen to Moses and the Prophets, they will not be convinced even if someone rises from the dead.' (Luke 16:24-31)

What is astonishing is that though their statuses have now been reversed, the rich man seems to be blind to what has happened. He still expects Lazarus to be his servant and treats him as his water boy. He does not ask to get out of hell, yet strongly implies that

God never gave him and his family enough information about the afterlife. Commentators have noted the astonishing amount of denial, blame-shifting and spiritual blindness in this soul in hell. They have also noted that the rich man, unlike Lazarus, is never given a personal name. He is only called a 'Rich Man,' strongly hinting that since he had built his identity on his wealth rather than on God, once he lost his wealth he lost any sense of a self.

In short, hell is simply one's freely chosen identity apart from God on a trajectory into infinity. We see this process 'writ small' in addictions to drugs, alcohol, gambling and pornography. First, there is disintegration, because as time goes on you need more and more of the addictive substance to get an equal kick, which leads to less and less satisfaction. Second, there is the isolation, as increasingly you blame others and circumstances in order to justify your behaviour. 'No one understands! Everyone is against me!' is muttered in greater and greater self-pity and self-absorption. When we build our lives on anything but God, that thing – though a good thing – becomes an enslaving addiction, something we *have* to have to be happy. Personal disintegration happens on a broader scale. In eternity, this disintegration goes on forever. There is increasing isolation, denial, delusion and self-absorption. When you lose all humility you are out of touch with reality. No one ever asks to leave hell. The very idea of heaven seems to them a sham.

In his fantasy *The Great Divorce*, C. S. Lewis describes a busload of people from hell who come to the outskirts of heaven. There they are urged to leave behind the sins that have trapped them in hell – but they refuse. Lewis's descriptions of these people are striking because we recognise in them the self-delusion and self-absorption that are 'writ small' in our own addictions.[11]

> *Hell begins with a grumbling mood, always complaining, always blaming others . . . but you are still distinct from it. You may*

*even criticise it in yourself and wish you could stop it. But there may come a day when you can no longer. Then there will be no you left to criticise the mood or even to enjoy it, but just the grumble itself, going on forever like a machine. It is not a question of God 'sending us' to hell. In each of us there is something growing, which will BE Hell unless it is nipped in the bud.*[12]

The people in hell are miserable, but Lewis shows us why. We see raging like unchecked flames their pride, their paranoia, their self-pity, their certainty that everyone else is wrong, that everyone else is an idiot! All their humility is gone, and thus so is their sanity. They are utterly, finally locked in a prison of their own self-centredness, and their pride progressively expands into a bigger and bigger mushroom cloud. They continue to go to pieces for ever, blaming everyone but themselves. Hell is that, writ large.

That is why it is a travesty to picture God casting people into a pit who are crying 'I'm sorry! Let me out!' The people on the bus from hell in Lewis's parable would rather have their 'freedom', as they define it, than salvation. Their delusion is that, if they glorified God, they would somehow lose power and freedom, but in a supreme and tragic irony, their choice has ruined their own potential for greatness. Hell is, as Lewis says, 'the greatest monument to human freedom'. As Romans 1:24 says, God 'gave them up to . . . their desires'. All God does in the end with people is give them what they most want, including freedom from himself. What could be more fair than that? Lewis writes:

*There are only two kinds of people – those who say to God, 'Thy will be done' to God or those to whom God in the end says, 'Thy will be done.' All that are in Hell choose it. Without that self-choice it wouldn't be Hell. No soul that seriously and constantly desires joy will ever miss it.*[13]

## Hell and the Equality of People

Let's return to the doubtful journalists at the Pew Forum with Rick Warren. They were concerned that any Christian who believes that some people are bound for hell must necessarily perceive such people to be unequal, less deserving of civil rights. This concern misunderstands what the Bible teaches about the nature of salvation and damnation.

As C. S. Lewis points out, the journey to hell is a process, which can begin with something as apparently innocuous as a grumbling mood. No one can look out at a congregation on a Sunday morning, a crowd at Yankee Stadium, or the audience at the Metropolitan Opera, and be sure of who is ultimately going to arrive in heaven or hell. Today's outspoken believer may be tomorrow's apostate, and today's outspoken unbeliever may be tomorrow's convert. We must not make settled, final decisions about anyone's spiritual state or fate.

After speaking about the Christian faith to a gathering in a Manhattan town house, I was approached by two women who had heard my presentation. They both told me that believing in eternal judgement made me a very narrow person. I asked them, 'You think I'm wrong about these religious questions, and I think you are wrong. Why doesn't that make you as narrow as me?' One woman retorted, 'That's different. You think we are eternally lost! We don't think you are. That makes you more narrow than us.' I didn't agree, and here is what I proposed to them.

Both the Christian and the secular person believe that self-centredness and cruelty have very harmful consequences. Because Christians believe souls don't die, they also believe that moral and spiritual errors affect the soul for ever. Liberal, secular people also believe that there are terrible moral and spiritual errors, like exploitation and oppression. But since they don't believe in an afterlife, they don't think the consequences of wrongdoing go on into eternity. Because Christians think wrongdoing has infinitely more long-term consequences than secular people do, does that mean they are somehow narrower?

Imagine two people arguing over the nature of a cookie. Jack thinks the cookie is poison, and Jill thinks it is not. Jack thinks Jill's mistaken view of the cookie will send her to the hospital or worse. Jill thinks Jack's mistaken view of the cookie will keep him from having a fine dessert. Is Jack more narrow-minded than Jill just because he thinks the consequences of her mistake are more dire? I don't believe anyone would think so. Christians, therefore, aren't more narrow because they think wrong thinking and behaviour have eternal effects.

## 'I Believe in a God of Love'

During my college years and my early twenties I, like so many others, questioned the Christian faith I was raised in. There were subjective reasons for my doubts. Christianity just didn't seem real to me experientially. I had not developed a prayer life and had never experienced God personally. There were also intellectual problems I was having with Christianity, all of which I am addressing elsewhere in this book. There was one, however, I will talk about here.

I was troubled by those Christians who stressed hellfire and damnation. Like so many of my generation I believed that, if there was a core to all religions, it was a loving God. I wanted to believe in a God of love who accepted people regardless of their beliefs and practices. I began to take courses in the other major religions of the world – Buddhism, Hinduism, Islam, Confucianism and Judaism. I have profited to this day from those studies. However, my explorations in other faiths proved me wrong on this particular point about the centrality of a loving God.

I found no other religious text outside of the Bible that said God created the world out of love and delight. Most ancient pagan religions believed the world was created through struggles and violent battles between opposing gods and supernatural forces. I turned to look more closely at Buddhism, the religion I liked best at the time. However, despite its great emphasis on selflessness and detached service to others, Buddhism did not believe in a personal God at all, and love is the action of a person.

Later on, after I became a minister, I was a speaker and panellist for several years in a monthly discussion programme in Philadelphia between a Christian church and a mosque. Each month a speaker from the church and a speaker from the mosque would give a biblical and Qu'ranic perspective on a topic. When we covered the topic of God's love, it was striking how different our conceptions were. I was told repeatedly by Muslim speakers that God was indeed loving in the sense of being merciful and kind to us. But when Christians spoke of the Lord as our spouse, of knowing God intimately and personally, and of having powerful effusions of his love poured into our hearts by the Holy Spirit, our Muslim friends baulked. They told us that it was disrespectful, in their view, to speak of anyone knowing God personally.

Today many of the sceptics I talk to say, as I once did, they can't believe in the God of the Bible, who punishes and judges people, because they 'believe in a God of Love'. I now ask, what makes them think God is Love? Can they look at life in the world today and say, 'This proves that the God of the world is a God of love'? Can they look at history and say, 'This all shows that the God of history is a God of love'? Can they look at the religious texts of the world and conclude that God is a God of love? By no means is that the dominant, ruling attribute of God as understood in any of the major faiths. I must conclude that the source of the idea that God is Love is the Bible itself. And the Bible tells us that the God of love is also a God of judgement who will put all things in the world to rights in the end.

The belief in a God of pure love – who accepts everyone and judges no one – is a powerful act of faith. Not only is there no evidence for it in the natural order, but there is almost no historical, religious textual support for it outside of Christianity. The more one looks at it, the less justified it appears.

# SIX

## SCIENCE HAS DISPROVED CHRISTIANITY

*'My scientific training makes it difficult if not impossible to accept the teachings of Christianity,' said Thomas, a young Asian medical resident. 'As a believer in evolution, I can't accept the Bible's prescientific accounts of the origin of life.'*

*'And the Bible is filled with accounts of miracles,' added Michelle, a medical student. 'They simply could not have happened.'*

THE bestselling books by Richard Dawkins, Daniel C. Dennett, and Sam Harris assume that science in general, and evolutionary science in particular, has made belief in God unnecessary and obsolete. Dawkins said very famously that 'although atheism might have been logically tenable before Darwin, Darwin made it possible to be an intellectually fulfilled atheist'.[1] In *The God Delusion* he goes much further. He argues that you cannot be an intelligent scientific thinker and still hold religious beliefs. It is one or the other. To support his thesis he points out that a study in 1998 showed that only about 7 per cent of American scientists in the National Academy of Sciences believe in a personal God.[2] This is proof that the more intelligent, rational and scientifically minded you are, the less you will be able to believe in God.

84

Is Dawkins right? Has science essentially disproved Christian beliefs? Must we choose between thinking scientifically and belief in God?

## Aren't Miracles Scientifically Impossible?

The first reason that many people think science has disproved traditional religion is that most of the major faiths believe in miracles, the intervention of God into the natural order. The miraculous is particularly important for Christian belief. Christians annually celebrate the miracle of the incarnation, the birth of Jesus, each Christmas, and the miracle of the bodily resurrection of Jesus from the dead each Easter. The New Testament is filled with accounts of miracles that Jesus performed during the course of his ministry. Scientific mistrust of the Bible began with the Enlightenment belief that miracles cannot be reconciled to a modern, rational view of the world. Armed with this presupposition, scholars turned to the Bible and said, 'The biblical accounts can't be reliable because they contain descriptions of miracles.' The premise behind such a claim is 'Science has proven that there is no such thing as miracles.'[3] But embedded in such a statement is a leap of faith.

It is one thing to say that science is only equipped to test for natural causes and cannot speak to any others. It is quite another to insist that science proves that no other causes could possibly exist. John Macquarrie writes: 'Science proceeds on the assumption that whatever events occur in the world can be accounted for in terms of other events . . . just as immanent and this-worldly. [So] . . . Miracle is irreconcilable with our modern understanding of both science and history.'[4]

Macquarrie is quite right to assert that, when studying a

phenomenon, the scientist must always assume there is a natural cause. That is because natural causes are the only kind its methodology can address. It is another thing to insist that science has proven there can't *be* any other kind. There would be no experimental model for testing the statement: 'No supernatural cause for any natural phenomenon is possible.' It is therefore a philosophical presupposition and not a scientific finding. Macquarrie's argument is ultimately circular. He says that science, by its nature, can't discern or test for supernatural causes, and therefore, those causes can't exist.

The philosopher Alvin Plantinga responds:

*Macquarrie perhaps means to suggest that the very practice of science requires that one reject the idea (e.g.) of God raising someone from the dead.... [This] argument ... is like the drunk who insisted on looking for his lost car keys only under the streetlight on the grounds that the light was better there. In fact, it would go the drunk one better: it would insist that because the keys would be hard to find in the dark, they* must *be under the light.*[5]

The other hidden premise in the statement 'miracles cannot happen' is 'there can't be a God who does miracles'. If there is a Creator God, there is nothing illogical at all about the possibility of miracles. After all, if he created everything out of nothing, it would hardly be a problem for him to rearrange parts of it as and when he wishes. To be sure that miracles cannot occur you would have to be sure beyond a doubt that God didn't exist, and that is an article of faith. The existence of God can be neither demonstrably proven nor disproven.

## Isn't Science in Conflict with Christianity?

It is common to believe today that there is a war going on between science and religion. One of the reasons for this perception is that the media needs to report news events as stories with protagonists and antagonists. It gives wide publicity to battles between secular and religious people over the teaching of evolution in schools, stem-cell research, in vitro fertilisation, and many other areas of medicine and science. These battles give credibility to the claims of Dawkins, Harris and others that it is either-or – you can be either scientific and rational or religious.

Over the years at Redeemer I've talked to many people trained in science and biology who were very wary of orthodox Christian belief. One young medical student said to me, 'The Bible denies evolution, which most educated people accept. It bothers me terribly that so many Christians, because of their belief in the Bible, can take such an unscientific mind-set.' His concern is quite understandable. Here's how I responded to him.

Evolutionary science assumes that more complex life-forms evolved from less complex forms through a process of natural selection. Many Christians believe that God brought about life this way. For example, the Catholic Church, the largest church in the world, has made official pronouncements supporting evolution as being compatible with Christian belief.[6] However, Christians may believe in evolution as a process without believing in 'philosophical naturalism' – the view that everything has a natural cause and that organic life is solely the product of random forces guided by no one. When evolution is turned into an All-encompassing Theory explaining absolutely everything we believe, feel and do as the product of natural selection, then we are not in the arena of science, but of philosophy. Evolution as an All-encompassing Theory has insurmountable difficulties as a worldview. We will look at these difficulties in Chapter 9.

Dawkins argues that if you believe in evolution as a biological mechanism you must also believe in philosophical naturalism. But why? The same year that Dawkins's *The God Delusion* was published, Francis Collins published *The Language of God*. Collins is an eminent research scientist and head of the Human Genome Project. He believes in evolutionary science and critiques the Intelligent Design movement that denies the transmutation of species. However, Collins believes that the fine-tuning, beauty and order of nature nonetheless point to a divine Creator, and describes his conversion from atheism to Christianity. Here then is what Dawkins says can't exist, someone with a firm belief in evolution as biological mechanism, but who completely rejects philosophical naturalism. Collins, of course, is not alone.[7]

Contrary to Dawkins's simplistic schema, there are many different models proposed about how God relates to the development of the life-forms we see today. Ian Barbour lays out four different ways that science and religion may be related to each other: conflict, dialogue, integration and independence. At the one end of the spectrum, in 'conflict', are both the proponents of 'creation science' and, ironically, thinkers like Dawkins. Each side has bought in to the warfare model of the relationship of science to faith. Many creationists' view of Genesis 1 makes any kind of evolutionary process impossible, while the philosophical naturalism of Dawkins makes religious belief totally invalid. At the other end of the spectrum, there are those who believe faith is mainly a private, subjective thing and therefore does not speak to the empirical realm at all. In this view science and religion have nothing to say to each other at all. Barbour himself thinks this view gives away too much, and prefers the spectrum of more moderate and complicated approaches in which science and religious faith recognise their respective spheres of authority.[8]

It is the conflict model, however, that gets the most publicity. Fortunately, this view is losing credibility with a growing number of scholars. The history of the secularisation of American institutions is treated in an important and influential book edited by Christian Smith.[9] In it Smith argues that the conflict model of the relationship of science to religion was a deliberate exaggeration used by both scientists and educational leaders at the end of the nineteenth century to undermine the church's control of their institutions and increase their own cultural power.[10] The absolute warfare model of science and reason was the product not so much of intellectual necessity but rather of a particular cultural strategy. Many scientists see no incompatibility between faith in God and their work.

Two famous studies that support this contention were done in 1916 and 1997. The American psychologist James Leuba conducted the first survey of scientists, asking them if they believed in a God who actively communicates with humanity, at least through prayer. Forty per cent said they did, 40 per cent said they did not, and 20 per cent were not sure. In 1997, Edward Larson and Larry Witham repeated this survey asking the very same questions of scientists. They reported in the scientific journal *Nature* that they had found that the numbers had not changed significantly in eighty years.[11]

What, then, of Dawkins' claim that nearly all prominent scientists disbelieve in God? In *The God Delusion* he cites Larson and Witham's follow-up correspondence in *Nature* a year later. There they noted that when they asked the same questions about belief in God to members of the National Academy of Sciences only 7 per cent said 'yes'.[12] Dawkins cites this statistic as evidence that intelligent scientific thinking almost always leads to the conclusion that

God does not exist. There are, however, major problems with the way Dawkins, and even Larson and Witham, interpret the data from these studies.

First, keep in mind the original question posed to the scientists in both surveys. Scientists are asked if they believe in a God who personally communicates with humanity. To hold that a transcendent God created the universe is not enough to be listed as a 'believer'. Any NAS scientist who believes in a God who does not communicate directly with humanity is automatically put into the category of disbeliever. The surveys were only designed to 'see' scientists with conservative, traditional belief. Those with a more general belief in God are screened out by the way the question is formulated. Second, Dawkins reads the data as establishing a causal relationship between the scientific mind and atheism. His assumption is that NAS scientists disbelieve because they are scientifically minded. However, the study does not and cannot prove what the cause of NAS scientists' disbelief in God really is. Alister McGrath, a theologian with an Oxford doctorate in biophysics, writes that most of the many unbelieving scientists he knows are atheists on other grounds than their science. Many complex factors lead a person to belief or disbelief in God. Some are personal experiences, some are intellectual, and some are social. Sociologists of knowledge like Peter Berger have shown that our peer group and primary relationships shape our beliefs much more than we want to admit. Scientists, like non-scientists, are very affected by the beliefs and attitudes of the people from whom they want respect. In McGrath's experience, most of his atheist colleagues brought their assumptions about God to their science rather than basing them on their science.[13]

Also, Dawkins gives readers the impression that all atheistic scientists would agree with him that no rational, scientific mind could believe in God. But that is simply not the case. Stephen Jay Gould, the late Harvard scientist and evolutionist who was himself an atheist, knew all about these studies, but could not conclude with Dawkins that science necessarily clashed with Christian faith. He wrote:

> *Either half my colleagues are enormously stupid, or else the science of Darwinism is fully compatible with conventional religious beliefs – and equally compatible with atheism.*[14]

When Gould spoke of 'half his colleagues', he was probably not thinking strictly of survey data. He simply knew that a great number of his most respected scientific colleagues had traditional religious beliefs about God. One of the reasons Gould does not agree with Dawkins is that he was much more willing to concede that science might not be able to account for everything about human existence to every thinker's satisfaction.

Another scholar who makes this point is the philosopher Thomas Nagel, who critiqued Dawkins' approach in a review of *The God Delusion* in the journal *The New Republic*. Nagel, too, is an atheist, but thinks Dawkins is wrong to insist that, if we are going to be scientific at all, we must embrace 'physicalist naturalism . . . that the ultimate explanation of everything must lie in particle physics, string theory, or whatever purely extensional laws govern the elements of which the material world is composed'. He asks, for example, whether we really believe that our moral intuitions, such as that genocide is morally wrong, are not real but only the result of neurochemistry hardwired into us. Can physical science do full justice to reality as human beings experience it? Nagel doubts that. He writes:

> *The reductionist project usually tries to reclaim some of the originally excluded aspects of the world, by analyzing them in*

91

*physical – that is, behavioral or neurophysiological – terms; but it denies reality to what cannot be so reduced. I believe the project is doomed – that conscious experience, thought, value, and so forth are not illusions, even though they cannot be identified with physical facts.*[15]

This is why even many atheists believe Dawkins is wrong, that science cannot explain everything, and why scientific thought can be compatible with religious belief.

Even though the concept of warfare between science and religion still has much popular credence, we should disabuse ourselves of the notion that we have to choose between the two, or that if you want to be a Christian you will have to be in conflict with science. A majority of scientists consider themselves deeply or moderately religious – and those numbers have increased in recent decades.[16] There is no necessary disjunction between science and devout faith.

## Doesn't Evolution Disprove the Bible?

What about the more specific issue of how evolutionary science fits with the biblical account of creation in Genesis 1 and 2? Surely there we have a head-on collision. No, that's not the case.

Different Christian thinkers use all of Barbour's models of relating science to faith – conflict, dialogue, integration and independence. Some Christians in the highly publicised Creation Science movement take the conflict model and insist that Genesis 1 teaches that God created all life-forms in a period of six twenty-four-hour days just several thousand years ago. At the other end of the spectrum are Christians who take the independence model and simply say that God was the primary cause in beginning the world and after that natural causes took over. Other thinkers occupy the central positions. Some hold that God created life and then guided natural selection to develop all complex life-forms from simpler ones. In this view, God acts as a top-down cause without violating the process of evolution. Others, believing there are gaps in the fossil record and claiming that species seem to 'appear' rather than develop from simpler forms, believe that God performed large-scale creative acts at different points over longer periods of time.

The relationship of science to the Bible hinges not only on how we read the scientific record but how we interpret certain key biblical passages, such as Genesis 1. Christians who accept the Bible's authority agree that the primary goal of biblical interpretation is to discover the biblical author's original meaning as he sought to be understood by his audience. This has always meant interpreting a text according to its literary genre. For example, when Christians read the Psalms they read it as poetry. When they read Luke, which claims to be an eyewitness account (see Luke 1:1-4), they take it as history. Any reader can see that the historical narrative should be read as history and that the poetic imagery is to be read as metaphorical.

The difficulty comes in the few places in the Bible where the genre is not easily identifiable, and we aren't completely sure how the author expects it to be read. Genesis 1 is a passage whose interpretation is up for debate among Christians, even those with a 'high' view of inspired Scripture.[17] I personally take the view that Genesis 1 and 2 relate to each other the way Judges 4 and 5 and Exodus 14 and 15 do. In each couplet one chapter describes a historical event and the other is a song or poem about the theological meaning of the event. When reading Judges 4 it is obvious that it is a sober recounting of what happened in the battle, but when we read Judges 5, Deborah's Song about the battle, the language is poetic and metaphorical. When Deborah sings that the stars in the heavens came down to fight for the Israelites, we understand that she means that metaphorically. I think Genesis 1 has the earmarks of poetry and is therefore a 'song' about the wonder and meaning of God's creation. Genesis 2 is an account of how it happened. There will always be debates about how to interpret some passages – including Genesis 1. But it is false logic to argue that if one part of Scripture can't be taken literally then none of it can be. That isn't true of any human communication.

What can we conclude? Since Christian believers occupy different positions on both the meaning of Genesis 1 and on the nature of evolution, those who are considering Christianity as a whole should not allow themselves to be distracted by this intramural debate. The sceptical enquirer does not need to accept any one of these positions in order to embrace the Christian faith. Rather, he or she should concentrate on and weigh the central claims of Christianity. Only after drawing conclusions about the person of Christ, the resurrection, and the central tenets of the Christian message should one think through the various options with regard to creation and evolution.

Representatives of these different views often imply that their approach is the One True Christian Position on Evolution.[18] Indeed, I'm sure that many reading this will be irritated that I don't take time here to adjudicate between the competing views. For the record I think God guided some kind of process of natural selection, and yet I reject the concept of evolution as All-encompassing Theory. One commentator on Genesis captures this balance well:

*If 'evolution' is . . . elevated to the status of a world-view of the way things are, then there is direct conflict with biblical faith. But if 'evolution' remains at the level of scientific biological hypothesis, it would seem that there is little reason for conflict between the implications of Christian belief in the Creator and the*

*scientific explorations of the way which – at the level of biology –*
*God has gone about his creating processes.*[19]

# Healing the World

I don't want to be too hard on people who struggle with the idea of
God's intervention in the natural order. Miracles are hard to believe
in, and they should be. In Matthew 28 we are told that the apostles
met the risen Jesus on a mountainside in Galilee. 'When they saw
him, they worshipped him; but some doubted' (verse 17). That is a
remarkable admission. Here is the author of an early Christian
document telling us that some of the founders of Christianity
couldn't believe the miracle of the resurrection, even when they
were looking straight at him with their eyes and touching him with
their hands. There is no other reason for this to be in the account
unless it really happened.

The passage shows us several things. It is a warning not to think
that only we modern, scientific people have to struggle with the
idea of the miraculous, while ancient, more primitive people did
not. The apostles responded like any group of modern people –
some believed their eyes and some didn't. It is also an encouragement to patience. All the apostles ended up as great leaders in the
church, but some had a lot more trouble believing than others.

The most instructive thing about this text is, however, what it
says about the purpose of biblical miracles. They lead not simply to
cognitive belief, but to *worship*, to awe and wonder. Jesus' miracles
in particular were never magic tricks, designed only to impress and
coerce. You never see him say something like: 'See that tree over
there? Watch me make it burst into flames!' Instead, he used miraculous power to heal the sick, feed the hungry and raise the dead.
Why? We modern people think of miracles as the suspension of the
natural order, but Jesus meant them to be the restoration of the

natural order. The Bible tells us that God did not originally make the world to have disease, hunger and death in it. Jesus has come to redeem the world where it is wrong and heal where it is broken. His miracles are not just proofs that he has power but also wonderful foretastes of what he is going to do with that power. Jesus' miracles are not just a challenge to our minds, but a promise to our hearts, that the world we all want is coming.

# SEVEN

# You Can't Take the
# Bible Literally

*'I see much of the Bible's teaching as historically inaccurate,'*
*said Charles, an investment banker. 'We can't be sure the Bible's*
*account of events is what really happened.'*

*'I'm sure you're right, Charles,' answered Jaclyn, a woman*
*working in finance. 'But my biggest problem with the Bible is*
*that it is culturally obsolete. Much of the Bible's social teaching*
*(for example, about women) is socially regressive. So it is impos-*
*sible to accept the Bible as the complete authority Christians*
*think it is.'*

WHEN I was in college in the late 1960s I took some courses
on the Bible as literature and was confronted with the prevailing wisdom of the time. My professors taught that the New
Testament Gospels originated as the oral traditions of various
church communities around the Mediterranean. These stories
about Jesus were shaped by those communities to address the questions and needs peculiar to each church. Leaders made certain that
the Jesus in these stories supported the policies and beliefs of their
communities. The oral traditions were then passed down over the
years, evolving through the addition of various legendary materials.
Finally, long after the actual events, the Gospels assumed written

form. By then it was almost impossible to know to what degree, if any, they represented the actual historical events.

Who then was the original Jesus? The scholars I read proposed that the real, 'historical Jesus' was a charismatic teacher of justice and wisdom who provoked opposition and was executed. After his death, they said, different parties and viewpoints emerged among his followers about who he was. Some claimed he was divine and risen from the dead, others that he was just a human teacher who lived on spiritually in the hearts of his disciples. After a power struggle, the 'divine Jesus' party won and created texts that promoted its views. They allegedly suppressed and destroyed all the alternative texts showing us a different sort of Jesus. Recently, some of these suppressed, alternate views of Jesus have come to light – like the 'Gnostic' gospels of Thomas and Judas. This shows, it is said, that early Christianity was very diverse in its doctrinal beliefs.

If this view of the New Testament's origins and development is true, it would radically change our understanding of the content and meaning of Christianity itself. It would mean that no one could really know what Jesus said and did, and that the Bible could not be the authoritative norm over our life and beliefs. It would mean that most of the classic Christian teachings – Jesus's deity, atonement and resurrection – are mistaken and based on legends.

As a student I was initially shaken by this. How could all of these prominent scholars be wrong? Then, however, as I did my own firsthand research, I was surprised at how little evidence there actually was for these historical reconstructions. To my encouragement the evidence for this older, sceptical view of the Bible has been crumbling steadily for the past thirty years, even as it has been promoted by the popular media through books and movies such as *The Da Vinci Code*.

Anne Rice was one person who was startled to discover how weak the case for a merely human 'historical Jesus' really is. Rice became famous as the author of *Interview with the Vampire* and other works that could be called 'horror-erotica'. Raised a Catholic, she lost her faith at a secular college, married an atheist, and became wealthy writing novels about Lestat, who is both a vampire and a rock star. It shocked the literary and media world when Rice announced that she had returned to Christianity.

Why did she do it? In the afterword to her new novel, *Christ the Lord: Out of Egypt*, she explained that she had begun doing extensive research about the historical Jesus by reading the work of Jesus scholars at the most respected academic institutions. Their main thesis was that the biblical documents we have aren't historically reliable. She was amazed at how weak their arguments were.

> *Some books were no more than assumptions piled on assumptions. . . . Conclusions were reached on the basis of little or no data at all. . . . The whole case for the nondivine Jesus who stumbled into Jerusalem and somehow got crucified . . . that whole picture which had floated around the liberal circles I frequented as an atheist for thirty years – that case was not made. Not only was it not made, I discovered in this field some of the worst and most biased scholarship I'd ever read.*[1]

The Christian faith requires belief in the Bible.[2] This is a big stumbling block for many. I meet many New Yorkers for the first time after they have been invited to one of Redeemer's services. The centrepiece of each service is a sermon based on a text of the Bible. The average visitor is surprised or even shocked to find us listening to the Bible so carefully. Most would say that they know there are many great stories and sayings in the Bible, but today 'you can't take it *literally*'. What they mean is that the Bible is not entirely trustworthy because some parts – maybe many or most parts – are scientifically impossible, historically unreliable and culturally regressive. We looked at the first of these issues, of science and the Bible, in the previous chapter. Now we will look at the other two.

## 'We Can't Trust the Bible *Historically*'

It is widely believed that the Bible is a historically unreliable collection of legends. A highly publicised forum of scholars, 'the Jesus Seminar', has stated that no more than 20 per cent of Jesus' sayings and actions in the Bible can be historically validated.[3] How do we respond to this? It is beyond the range of this book to examine the historic accuracy of each part of the Bible. Instead, we will ask whether we can trust the Gospels, the New Testament accounts of Jesus' life, to be historically reliable.[4] By this I mean the 'canonical' Gospels – Matthew, Mark, Luke and John – that the church recognised very early on as authentic and authoritative.

It is often asserted that the New Testament Gospels were written so many years after the events happened that the writers' accounts of Jesus' life can't be trusted – that they are highly embellished if not wholly imagined. Many believe that the canonical Gospels were only four out of scores of other texts and that they were written to support the church hierarchy's power while the rest (including the so-called 'Gnostic Gospels') were suppressed. This belief has been given new plausibility in the popular imagination by the bestselling book *The Da Vinci Code*. In this novel, the original Jesus is depicted as a great but clearly human teacher who many years after his death was made into a resurrected God by church leaders who did so to gain status in the Roman Empire.[5] However, there are several good reasons why the Gospel accounts should be considered historically reliable rather than legends.[6]

## The timing is far too early for the Gospels to be legends.

The canonical Gospels were written at the very most forty to sixty years after Jesus' death.[7] Paul's letters, written just fifteen to twenty-five years after the death of Jesus, provide an outline of all the events of Jesus' life found in the Gospels – his miracles, claims, crucifixion and resurrection. This means that the biblical accounts of Jesus' life were circulating within the lifetimes of hundreds who had been present at the events of his ministry. The Gospel author Luke claims that he got his account of Jesus' life from eyewitnesses who were still alive (Luke 1:1-4).

In his landmark book *Jesus and the Eyewitnesses*, Richard Bauckham marshals much historical evidence to demonstrate that at the time the Gospels were written there were still numerous well-known living eyewitnesses to Jesus' teaching and life events. They had committed them to memory and they remained active in the public life of the churches throughout their lifetimes, serving as ongoing sources and guarantors of the truth of those accounts. Bauckham uses evidence within the Gospels themselves to show that the Gospel writers named their eyewitness sources within the text to assure readers of their accounts' authenticity.

Mark, for example, says that the man who helped Jesus carry his cross to Calvary 'was the father of Alexander and Rufus' (Mark 15:21). There is no reason for the author to include such names unless the readers know or could have access to them. Mark is saying, 'Alexander and Rufus vouch for the truth of what I am telling you, if you want to ask them.' Paul also appeals to readers to check with living eyewitnesses if they want to establish the truth of what he is saying about the events of Jesus' life (1 Corinthians 15:1-6).[8] Paul refers to a body of five hundred eyewitnesses who saw the risen Christ at once. You can't write that in a document designed for public reading unless there really were surviving witnesses whose testimony agreed and who could confirm what the author said. All this decisively refutes the idea that the Gospels were anonymous, collective, evolving oral traditions. Instead they were oral histories taken down from the mouths of the living eyewitnesses who preserved the words and deeds of Jesus in great detail.

It is not only Christ's supporters who were still alive. Also still alive were many bystanders, officials and opponents who had actually heard him teach, seen his actions and watched him die. They would have been especially ready to challenge any accounts that were fabricated. For a highly altered, fictionalised account of an event to take hold in the public imagination it is necessary that the eyewitnesses (and their children and grandchildren) all be long dead. They must be off the scene so they cannot contradict or debunk the embellishments and falsehoods of the story. The Gospels were written far too soon for this to occur.

It would have been impossible, then, for this new faith to spread as it did had Jesus never said or done the things mentioned in the Gospel accounts. Paul could confidently assert to government officials that the events of Jesus' life were public knowledge: 'These things were not done in a corner,' he said to King Agrippa (Acts 26:26). The people of Jerusalem had *been* there – they had been in the crowds that heard and watched Jesus. The New Testament documents could not say Jesus was crucified when thousands of people were still alive who knew whether he was or not. If there had not been appearances after his death, if there had not been an empty tomb, if he had not made these claims, and these public documents claimed they happened, Christianity would never have got off the ground. The hearers would have simply laughed at the accounts.

The four canonical Gospels were written much earlier than the so-called Gnostic Gospels. The Gospel of Thomas, the best known of the Gnostic documents, is a translation from the Syriac, and scholars have shown that the Syriac traditions in Thomas can be dated to 175 A.D. at the earliest, more than a hundred years after the time that the canonical Gospels were in widespread use.[9] Adam Gopnik in *The New Yorker* wrote that the Gnostic Gospels were so late that they '. . . no more challenge the basis of the Church's faith than the discovery of a document from the nineteenth century written in Ohio and defending King George would be a challenge to the basis of American democracy'.[10] The Gospels of Matthew, Mark, Luke and John, however, were recognised as authoritative eyewitness accounts almost immediately, and so we have Irenaeus of Lyons in 160 A.D. declaring that there were four, and only four, Gospels. The widespread idea, promoted by *The Da Vinci Code*, that the Emperor Constantine determined the New Testament canon, casting aside the earlier and supposedly more authentic Gnostic Gospels, simply is not true.[11]

As for *The Da Vinci Code*, people know the book and the movie plot is fictitious, but many find plausible the historical background that the author, Dan Brown, claims is true. The bestseller depicts Constantine in 325 A.D. as decreeing Jesus' divinity and suppressing all the evidence that he was just a human teacher. Even in a document like Paul's letter to the Philippians, however, which all historians date at no more than twenty years after the death of Christ, we see that Christians were worshipping Jesus as God (Philippians 2). Belief in the deity of Christ was part of the dynamic from the beginning in the growth of the early Christian church. One historian comments:

*[Dan Brown says] that the Emperor Constantine imposed a whole new interpretation on Christianity at the Council of Nicea in 325. That is, he decreed the belief in Jesus' divinity and suppressed all evidence of his humanity. This would mean Christianity won the religious competition in the Roman Empire by*

*an exercise of power rather than by any attraction it exerted. In*
*actual historical fact, the Church had won that competition*
*long before that time, before it had any power, when it was still*
*under sporadic persecution. If a historian were cynical, you*
*would say Constantine chose Christianity because it had already*
*won and he wanted to back a winner.*[12]

### The content is far too counterproductive for the Gospels to be legends.

The working theory of many people today is that the Gospels were
written by the leaders of the early church to promote their policies,
consolidate their power and build their movement. That theory
does not fit at all with what we actually find in the Gospels.

If this popular view is correct, we would expect to see many
places in the Gospels where Jesus takes sides in debates that were
going on in the early church. That is how (it is reasoned) the Gospels were shaped by Christian leaders to support their party. However, we do not find this. We know, for example, that one of the
great controversies in the earliest church was that some believed
Gentile Christians should be required to be circumcised. In light of
that great conflict, it is remarkable that nowhere in the Gospel accounts does Jesus say anything about circumcision. The most likely
reason that Jesus is silent about circumcision is that the early church
did *not* feel free to fabricate things and put words in Jesus' mouth
that he didn't utter.

Why would the leaders of the early Christian movement have
made up the story of the crucifixion if it didn't happen? Any listener
of the Gospel in either Greek or Jewish culture would have automatically suspected that anyone who had been crucified was a criminal, whatever the speaker said to the contrary. Why would any
Christian make up the account of Jesus asking God in the garden of

Gethsemane if he could get out of his mission? Or why ever make up the part on the cross when Jesus cries out that God had abandoned him? These things would have only offended or deeply confused first-century prospective converts. They would have concluded that Jesus was weak and failing his God. Why invent women as the first witnesses of the resurrection in a society where women were assigned such low status that their testimony was not admissible evidence in court?[13] It would have made far more sense (if you were inventing the tale) to have male pillars of the community present as witnesses when Jesus came out of the tomb. The only plausible reason that all of these incidents would be included in these accounts is that they actually happened.

Also, why constantly depict the apostles – the eventual leaders of the early Church – as petty and jealous, almost impossibly slow-witted, and in the end as cowards who either actively or passively failed their master? Richard Bauckham makes similar arguments about the depiction of Peter's denial of Jesus, even to the point of his calling down a curse on his master (Mark 14:71). Why would anyone in the early church want to play up the terrible failures of their most prominent leader? No one would have made such a story up, and even though it is true, Bauckham reasons that no one but Peter himself would have dared to recount it unless Peter himself was the source and had authorised its preservation and propagation.[14]

Again, a comparison with the 'Gnostic Gospels' is illuminating. The Gospel of Thomas and similar documents express a philosophy called 'Gnosticism', in which the material world is a dark, evil place from which our spirits need to be rescued by secret illumination, or 'gnosis'. This fits in very well with the worldview of the Greeks and Romans but is utterly different than that of the first-century Jewish world of which Jesus was part.[15] Contrary, then, to *The Da Vinci Code* and similar accounts, it is not the canonical Gospels that 'suck up' to the 'powers that be' in the ancient world, but it is the Gnostic texts that do it. It was the canonical Gospels, with their positive view of material creation and their emphasis on the poor and the oppressed that offended the dominant views of the Graeco-Roman world. The canonical Gospels not only give us a far more historically credible picture of what the original Jesus was really like, but they boldly challenge the worldview of their Greek and Roman readers.

**The literary form of the Gospels is too detailed to be legend.**

C. S. Lewis was a world-class literary critic. When reading the Gospels, he noted:

> *I have been reading poems, romances, vision literature, legends and myths all my life. I know what they are like. I know none of them are like this. Of this [gospel] text there are only two possible views. Either this is reportage . . . or else, some unknown [ancient] writer . . . without known predecessors or successors, suddenly anticipated the whole technique of modern novelistic, realistic narrative . . .* [16]

Lewis meant that ancient fiction was nothing like modern fiction. Modern fiction is realistic. It contains details and dialogue and reads like an eyewitness account. This genre of fiction, however, only developed within the last three hundred years. In ancient times, romances, epics or legends were high and remote – details were spare and only included if they promoted character development or drove the plot. That is why if you are reading *Beowulf* or *The Iliad* you don't see characters noticing the rain or falling asleep with a sigh. In modern novels, details are added to create the aura of realism, but that was never the case in ancient fiction.

The Gospel accounts are not fiction. In Mark 4, we are told that Jesus was asleep on a cushion in the stern of a boat. In John 21 we are told that Peter was a hundred yards out in the water when he saw Jesus on the beach. He then jumped out of the boat and together they caught 153 fish. In John 8, as Jesus listened to the men who caught a woman in adultery, we are told he doodled with his finger in the dust. We are never told what he was writing or why he did it. None of these details are relevant to the plot or character development at all. If you or I were making up an exciting story about Jesus, we would include such remarks just to fill out the story's air of realism. But that kind of fictional writing was unknown in the first century. The only explanation for why an ancient writer would mention the cushion, the 153 fish, and the doodling in the dust is because the details had been retained in the eyewitnesses' memory.

Richard Bauckham has compiled a great deal of research by psychologists on the marks of recollective memory. He looks at the marks of eyewitness accounts of events and how they differ from speculative or fictional accounts, or of composite historical reconstructions. Recollective memory is selective – it fixes on unique and consequential events, it retains irrelevant detail (as Lewis observes), it takes the limited vantage point of a participant rather than that of an omniscient narrator, and it shows signs of frequent rehearsal.[17] Bauckham then shows these same marks in the Gospel narratives. Vivid and important events can stay with you for decades if frequently rehearsed and/or retold. Factor in the fact that disciples in the ancient world were expected to memorise masters' teachings, and that many of Jesus' statements are presented in a form that was actually designed for memorisation, and you have every reason to trust the accounts.

Bauckham also looks to anthropology for evidence that the Gospel writers did not feel free to embellish or fabricate words or events in the life of Jesus. Critical scholars from earlier in the twentieth century assumed the early Christians would have used a relatively fluid process for transmitting popular folktales and that they would have felt free to change the tales from the past in order to correspond to their present realities and situation. Bauckham, however, cites Jan Vansina's study of oral traditions in primitive African cultures, in which fictional legends and historical accounts are clearly distinguished from each other and much greater care is taken to preserve historical accounts accurately. This finding undermines a hundred years of critical Gospel scholarship.

> *Gospels scholars, from the form critics onward, [believed] that early Christians in the transmission of Jesus traditions would not have made any distinction between the past time of the history of Jesus and their own present because oral societies do not make such distinctions. This is untrue.*[18]

As I write today, there seems to be a flood of what David Van Biema of *Time* magazine calls 'biblical revisionism' following in the footsteps of Dan Brown and *The Da Vinci Code*. He refers to the recent claim that Jesus' tomb has been found, and that he married Mary Magdalene and had children. Other scholars have published books claiming similar new insights from the Gnostic Gospels. More seem sure to come. Van Biema quotes *Publishers Weekly* senior religion editor Lynn Garrett, who speaks of what she calls 'the *Da Vinci Code* effect': 'Speculative histories were out there before Dan Brown wrote,' says Garrett. 'But they didn't make the bestseller lists and their authors didn't go on *The Daily Show*.'[19]

All these revisionist histories completely ignore the growing body of careful scholarship that shows there were a very large number of eyewitnesses to Jesus' life who lived on for years. As British scholar Vincent Taylor famously remarked, if the sceptics about the

Bible are right, 'the disciples must have been translated into heaven immediately after the resurrection'.[20] That is the only way that legendary elements could have come into the story of Jesus by the time the Gospels were written, but that did not happen. So, ironically, as the popular media is promoting accounts of Jesus' life based on the highly sceptical biblical scholarship that arose a century ago, the actual foundations of that scholarship are eroding fast.[21]

### 'We can't trust the Bible *culturally*.'

When I first came to New York City almost twenty years ago, the main problem people had with the Bible was in the areas just discussed – science and history. Today things have shifted somewhat. I find more people now especially upset by what they call the outmoded and regressive teaching of the Bible. It seems to support slavery and the subjugation of women. These positions appear so outrageous to contemporary people that they have trouble accepting any other parts of the Bible's message.

In the early days of Redeemer I spent a lot of time with people who were reading the Bible for the first time. As a result I was constantly responding to people who were choking on some particularly indigestible verse. I remember one black-clad young artist who came up to me after a service. He had just discovered the verse 'slaves obey your masters' (Ephesians 6:5ff.) and was almost apoplectic. Here's how I advised him and other people on how to deal with a Scripture text that appeared objectionable or offensive to them.

Many people simply run viscerally from any consideration of the Bible once they find such a biblical passage. I counsel them instead to slow down and try out several different perspectives on the issues that trouble them. That way they can continue to read, learn and profit from the Bible even as they continue to wrestle with some of its concepts.

One possibility I urge them to consider is that the passage that bothers them might not teach what it appears to them to be teaching. Many of the texts people find offensive can be cleared up with a decent commentary that puts the issue into historical context. Take the text 'slaves obey your masters'. The average reader today immediately and understandably thinks of the African slave trade of the eighteenth and nineteenth centuries, or of the human trafficking and sexual slavery practised in many places today. We then interpret the texts to teach that such slavery is permissible, even desirable.

This is a classic case of ignoring the cultural and historical distance between us and the writer and readers of the original text. In the first-century Roman Empire, when the New Testament was written, there was not a great difference between slaves and the average free person. Slaves were not distinguishable from others by race, speech or clothing. They looked and lived like most everyone else, and were not segregated from the rest of society in any way. From a financial standpoint, slaves made the same wages as free labourers, and therefore were not usually poor. Also, slaves could accrue enough personal capital to buy themselves out. Most important of all, very few slaves were slaves for life. Most could reasonably hope to be manumitted within ten or fifteen years, or by their late thirties at the latest.[22]

By contrast, New World slavery was much more systematically and homogeneously brutal. It was 'chattel' slavery, in which the slave's whole person was the property of the master – he or she could be raped or maimed or killed at the will of the owner. In the older bond-service or indentured servanthood, only slaves' productivity – their time and skills – were owned by the master, and only temporarily. African slavery, however, was race-based, and its default mode was slavery for life. Also, the African slave trade was begun and re-sourced through kidnapping. The Bible unconditionally condemns kidnapping and trafficking in slaves (1 Timothy 1:9-11; cf. Deuter-onomy 24:7). Therefore, while the early Christians did not go on a campaign to abolish first-century slavery completely, later Christians did so when faced with New World-style slavery, which could not be squared in any way with biblical teaching.[23]

Some texts may not teach what they at first appear to teach. Some people, however, have studied particular biblical texts care-fully and come to understand what they teach, and yet they *still* find them outrageous and regressive. What should they do then?

I urge people to consider that their problem with some texts might be based on an unexamined belief in the superiority of their historical moment over all others. We must not universalise our time any more than we should universalise our culture. Think of the implication of the very term 'regressive'. To reject the Bible as regressive is to assume that you have now arrived at the ultimate historic moment, from which all that is regressive and progressive can be discerned. That belief is surely as narrow and exclusive as the views in the Bible you regard as offensive.

Consider the views of contemporary British people and how they differ from the views of their ancestors, the Anglo-Saxons, a thousand years ago. Imagine that both are reading the Bible and they come to the Gospel of Mark, chapter 14. First they read that Jesus claims to be the Son of Man, who will come with angels at the end of time to judge the whole world according to his righteousness (verse 62). Later they read about Peter, the leading apostle, who de-nies his master three times and at the end even curses him to save his skin (verse 71). Yet later Peter is forgiven and restored to leadership (Mark 16:7; John 21:15ff.). The first story will make contemporary British people shudder. It sounds so judgemental and exclusive. However, they will love the story about how even Peter can be restored and forgiven. The first story will not bother the Anglo-Saxons at all. They know all about Domesday, and they are glad to get more information about it! However, they will be shocked at the second story. Disloyalty and betrayal at Peter's level must never be forgiven, in their view. He doesn't deserve to live, let alone become the foremost disciple. They will be so appalled by this that they will want to throw the Bible down and read no more of it.

Of course, we think of the Anglo-Saxons as primitive, but someday others will think of us and our culture's dominant views as primitive. How can we use our time's standard of 'progressive' as the plumbline by which we decide which parts of the Bible are valid and which are not? Many of the beliefs of our grandparents and great-grandparents now seem silly and even embarrassing to us. That process is not going to stop now. Our grandchildren will find many of our views outmoded as well. Wouldn't it be tragic if we threw the Bible away over a belief that will soon look pretty weak or wrong? To stay away from Christianity because part of the Bible's teaching is offensive to you assumes that if there is a God he wouldn't have any views that upset you. Does that belief make sense?

I have one more bit of advice to people struggling with some of the Bible's teaching. We should make sure we distinguish between the major themes and message of the Bible and its less primary teachings. The Bible talks about the person and work of Christ and also about how widows should be regarded in the church. The first of these subjects is much more foundational. Without it the secondary teachings don't make sense. We should therefore consider the Bible's teachings in their proper order.

Let's take a hot issue today as a good example. If you say, 'I can't accept what the Bible says about gender roles,' you must keep in mind that Christians themselves differ over what some texts mean, as they do about many, many other things. However, they all confess in the words of the Apostles' Creed that Jesus rose from the dead on the third day. Don't worry about gender roles until you figure out what you think about the central teachings of the faith.

You may appeal, 'But I can't accept the Bible if what it says about gender is outmoded.' I would respond to that with this question – are you saying that because you don't like what the Bible says about sex that Jesus couldn't have been raised from the dead? I'm sure you wouldn't insist on such a non sequitur. If Jesus is the Son of God, then we have to take his teaching seriously, including his confidence in the authority of the whole Bible. If he is not who he says he is, why should we care what the Bible says about anything else?

Think of it like this. If you dive into the shallow end of the biblical pool, where there are many controversies over interpretation, you may get scraped up. But if you dive into the centre of the biblical pool, where there is consensus – about the deity of Christ, his death and resurrection – you will be safe. It is therefore important to consider the Bible's core claims about who Jesus is and whether he rose from the dead before you reject it for its less central and more controversial teachings.

## A Trustworthy Bible or a Stepford God?

If we let our unexamined beliefs undermine our confidence in the Bible, the cost may be greater than we think.

If you don't trust the Bible enough to let it challenge and correct your thinking, how could you ever have a *personal* relationship with God? In any truly personal relationship, the other person has to be able to contradict you. For example, if a wife is not allowed to contradict her husband, they won't have an intimate relationship. Remember the (two!) movies *The Stepford Wives*? The husbands of Stepford, Connecticut, decide to have their wives turned into robots who never cross the wills of their husbands. A Stepford wife was wonderfully compliant and beautiful, but no one would describe such a marriage as intimate or personal.

Now, what happens if you eliminate anything from the Bible that offends your sensibility and crosses your will? If you pick and choose what you want to believe and reject the rest, how will you ever have a God who can contradict you? You won't! You'll have a Stepford God! A God, essentially, of your own making, and not a God with whom you can have a relationship and genuine interaction. Only if your God can say things that outrage you and make you struggle (as in a real friendship or marriage!) will you know that you have got hold of a real God and not a figment of your imagination. So an authoritative Bible is not the enemy of a personal relationship with God. It is the precondition for it.

# Intermission

*Come, let us argue it out.*
—Isaiah 1:18

INTERMISSION means literally to be between journeys or missions. That is where we are now. Underlying all doubts about Christianity are alternate beliefs, unprovable assumptions about the nature of things. So far I've examined the beliefs beneath the seven biggest objections or doubts people in our culture have about the Christian faith. I respect much of the reasoning behind them, but in the end I don't believe any of them make the truth of Christianity impossible or even improbable. We have another journey to take, however. It is one thing to argue that there are no sufficient reasons for disbelieving Christianity. It is another to argue that there are sufficient reasons *for* believing it. That is what I will try to do in the last part of this volume.

'Wait,' someone should ask. 'You are going to give us sufficient grounds for believing Christianity? How do you define Christianity? And how do you define "sufficient"?' Let's take these questions in order.

115

## Which Christianity?

From the outside the various Christian churches and traditions can look extremely different, almost like distinct religions. This is partially because the public worship services look so different. It is also because, as I said in Chapter 3, Christianity is the faith that is most spread across the cultures and regions of the world. Therefore it has assumed an enormous number of different cultural forms. Another reason that Christians look so different from one another is the great theological rifts that have occurred over the centuries. The first great division was between the eastern Greek and western Roman church in the eleventh century. Today these are known as the Eastern Orthodox and Roman Catholic Churches. The second great schism was within the Western church, between Roman Catholicism and Protestantism.

All Christians who take truth and doctrine seriously will agree that these differences between churches are highly significant. They make a major difference in how one's faith is held and practised. Nevertheless, all Orthodox, Catholic and Protestant Christians assent together to the great creeds of the first thousand years of church history, such as the Apostle's, Nicene, Chalcedonian and Athanasian creeds. In these creeds the fundamental Christian view of reality is laid out. There is the classical expression of the Christian understanding of God as three-in-one. Belief in the Trinity creates a profoundly different view of the world from that of polytheists, non-Trinitarian monotheists and atheists, as I will show in Chapter 13. There is also a strong statement of the full deity and humanity of Jesus Christ in these creeds. Christians, therefore, do not look upon Jesus as one more teacher or prophet, but as Saviour of the world. These teachings make Christians far more like than unlike one another.

What is Christianity? For our purposes, I'll define Christianity as the body of believers who assent to these great ecumenical creeds.

They believe that the triune God created the world, that humanity has fallen into sin and evil, that God has returned to rescue us in Jesus Christ, that in his death and resurrection Jesus accomplished our salvation for us so we can be received by grace, that he established the church, his people, as the vehicle through which he continues his mission of rescue, reconciliation and salvation, and that at the end of time Jesus will return to renew the heavens and the earth, removing all evil, injustice, sin and death from the world.

All Christians believe all this – but no Christians believe just this. As soon as you ask 'How does the church act as vehicle for Jesus's work in the world?' and 'How does Jesus's death accomplish our salvation?' and 'How are we received by grace?' Catholic, Orthodox and Protestant Christians will give you different answers. Despite the claims of many to be such, there are no truly 'generic' non-denominational Christians. Everyone has to answer these 'how' questions in order to live a Christian life, and those answers immediately put you into one tradition and denomination or another.

It is important for readers to understand this. I am making a case in this book for the truth of Christianity in general – not for one particular strand of it. Some sharp-eyed Presbyterian readers will notice that I am staying quiet about some of my particular theological beliefs in the interest of doing everything I can to represent all Christians. Yet when I come to describe the Christian gospel of sin and grace, I will necessarily be doing it as a Protestant Christian, and I won't be sounding notes that a Catholic author would sound.

## Which Rationality?

I want to show that there are sufficient reasons for believing Christianity. Prominent disbelievers in Christianity today – Richard Dawkins, Daniel Dennett, Sam Harris and Christopher Hitchens – insist that sufficient reasons do not exist for the existence of God.

Dawkins, for example, says that the claim of God's existence is a scientific hypothesis that should be open to rational demonstration.[1] He and his co-sceptics want a logical or empirical argument for God that is airtight and therefore convinces almost everyone. They won't believe in God until they get it.

Is there anything wrong with that? I think so. These authors are evaluating Christian arguments by what some have called 'strong rationalism'.[2] Its proponents laid down what was called the 'verification principle', namely, that no one should believe a proposition unless it can be proved rationally by logic or empirically by sense experience.[3] What is meant by the word 'proved'? Proof, in this view, is an argument so strong that no person whose logical faculties are operating properly would have any reason for disbelieving it. Atheists and agnostics ask for this kind of 'proof' for God, but are not alone in holding to strong rationalism. Many Christians claim that their arguments for faith are so strong that all who reject them are simply closing their minds to the truth out of fear or stubbornness.[4]

Despite all the books calling Christians to provide proofs for their beliefs, you won't see philosophers doing so, not even the most atheistic. The great majority think that strong rationalism is nearly impossible to defend.[5] To begin with, it can't live up to its own standards. How could you empirically prove that no one should believe something without empirical proof? You can't, and that reveals it to be, ultimately, a belief.[6] Strong rationalism also assumes that it is possible to achieve 'the view from nowhere', a position of almost complete objectivity, but virtually all philosophers today agree that is impossible. We come to every individual evaluation with all sorts of experiences and background beliefs that strongly influence our thinking and the way our reason works. It is not fair, then, to demand an argument that all rational people would have to bow to.

The philosopher Thomas Nagel is an atheist, but in his book *The Last Word* he admits that he can't come to the question of God in anything like a detached way. He confesses that he has 'fear of religion', and he doubts that anyone can address this issue without very powerful motives for seeing the arguments go one way or the other.

> *I am talking of . . . the fear of religion itself. I speak from experience, being strongly subject to this fear myself: I want atheism to be true. . . . It isn't just that I don't believe in God and, naturally, hope that I'm right in my belief. It's that I hope there is no God! I don't want there to be a God: I don't want the universe to be like that. . . . I am curious whether there is anyone who is genuinely indifferent as to whether there is a God – anyone who, whatever his actual belief about the matter, doesn't particularly* want *either one of the answers to be correct.*[7]

Imagine a judge who comes to a case in which one of the parties is a company in which she has a heavy financial investment. Because she has a deep desire to see the case go in a particular way, she will recuse herself from sitting in judgement on the case. Nagel is saying that when it comes to God, we are all like the judge. Depending on our experiences with religion, on our other beliefs and commitments, and on how we are living our lives – we all are deeply interested in seeing the case for God go one way or the other. The trouble is, we can't recuse ourselves. Because he rejects strong rationalism, Nagel has, despite his scepticism, wonderful respect towards belief and religion. He differs markedly from the tone and stance of writers like Dawkins and Harris.

The philosophical indefensibility of 'strong rationalism' is the reason that the books by Dawkins and Dennett have been getting such surprisingly rough treatment in scholarly journals. As just one example, the Marxist scholar Terry Eagleton wrote a scathing review of Richard Dawkins' *The God Delusion* in the *London Review of Books*. Eagleton attacks both of Dawkins' naive ideas, namely that faith has no rational component, and that reason isn't based to a great degree on faith.

> *Dawkins considers that all faith is blind faith, and that Christian and Muslim children are brought up to believe unquestioningly. Not even the dim-witted clerics who knocked me about at grammar school thought that. For mainstream Christianity, reason, argument and honest doubt have always played an integral role in belief. . . . Reason, to be sure, doesn't go all the way down for believers, but it doesn't for most sensitive, civilized non-religious types either. Even Richard Dawkins lives more by faith than by reason. We hold many beliefs that have no unimpeachably rational justification, but are nonetheless reasonable to entertain. . . .* [8]

If we reject strong rationalism, are we then stuck in relativism – without any way to judge one set of beliefs from another? Not at all. In Chapters 2 and 3 I argued that complete relativism is impossible to maintain.[9] The approach I will take in the rest of this volume is called 'critical rationality'.[10] It assumes that there are some arguments that many or even most rational people will find convincing, even though there is no argument that will be persuasive to everyone regardless of viewpoint. It assumes that some systems of belief are more reasonable than others, but that all arguments are rationally avoidable in the end. That is, you can always find reason to escape it that is not sheer bias or stubbornness. Nevertheless, this doesn't mean that we can't evaluate beliefs, only that we should not expect conclusive proof, and to demand it is unfair. Not even scientists proceed that way.

Scientists are very reluctant to ever say that a theory is 'proved'. Even Richard Dawkins admits that Darwin's theory cannot be finally proven, that 'new facts may come to light which will force our successors . . . to abandon Darwinism or modify it beyond recognition'.[11] But that doesn't mean that science cannot test theories and find some far more empirically verifiable than others. A theory is considered empirically verified if it organises the evidence and explains phenomena better than any conceivable alternative theory. That is, if, through testing, it leads us to expect with accuracy many and varied events better than any other rival account of the same data, then it is accepted, though not (in the strong rationalist sense) 'proved'.

In *Is There a God?* Oxford philosopher Richard Swinburne argues powerfully that belief in God can be tested and justified (but not proven) in the same way.[12] The view that there is a God, he says, leads us to expect the things we observe – that there is a universe at all, that scientific laws operate within it, that it contains human beings with consciousness and with an indelible moral sense. The theory that there is no God, he argues, does not lead us to expect any of these things. Therefore, belief in God offers a better empirical fit, it explains and accounts for what we see better than the alternative account of things. No view of God can be proven, but that does not mean that we cannot sift and weigh the grounds for various religious beliefs and find that some or even one is the most reasonable.

## God the Playwright

I don't want anyone to think that I am adopting 'critical rationality' as some sort of second best, however. If the God of the Bible really does exist, 'critical rationality' would be exactly the way we ought to approach the question of his being and existence.

When a Russian cosmonaut returned from space and reported that he had not found God, C. S. Lewis responded that this was like Hamlet going into the attic of his castle looking for Shakespeare. If there is a God, he wouldn't be another object in the universe that could be put in a lab and analysed with empirical methods. He would relate to us the way a playwright relates to the characters in his play. We (characters) might be able to know quite a lot about the playwright, but only to the degree the author chooses to put information about himself in the play. Therefore, in no case could we 'prove' God's existence as if he were an object wholly within our universe like oxygen and hydrogen or an island in the Pacific.

Lewis gives us another metaphor for knowing the truth about God when he writes that he believes in God 'as I believe the sun has risen, not only because I see it, but because by it I see everything else'.[13] Imagine trying to look directly at the sun in order to learn about it. You can't do it. It will burn out your retinas, ruining your capacity to take it in. A far better way to learn about the existence, power and quality of the sun is to look at the world it shows you, to recognise how it sustains everything you see and enables you to see it.

Here, then, we have a way forward. We should not try to 'look into the sun', as it were, demanding irrefutable proofs for God. Instead we should 'look at what the sun shows us'. Which account of the world has the most 'explanatory power' to make sense of what we see in the world and in ourselves? We have a sense that the world is not the way it ought to be. We have a sense that we are very flawed and yet very great. We have a longing for love and beauty that nothing in this world can fulfil. We have a deep need to know meaning and purpose. Which worldview best accounts for these things?

Christians do not claim that their faith gives them omniscience or absolute knowledge of reality. Only God has that. But they believe that the Christian account of things – creation, fall, redemption and restoration – makes the most sense of the world. I ask you to put on Christianity like a pair of spectacles and look at the world with it. See what power it has to explain what we know and see.

If the God of the Bible exists, he is not a man in the attic, but the Playwright. That means we won't be able to find him like we would find a passive object with the powers of empirical investigation. Rather, we must find the clues to his reality that he has written into the universe, including into us. That is why, if God exists, we would expect to find that he appeals to our rational faculties. If we were made 'in his image' as rational, personal beings, there should be some resonance between his mind and ours. It also means that reason alone won't be enough. The Playwright can only be known through personal revelation. That is why we have to take a look at what the Bible says about God and the human condition.

In the Christian view, however, the ultimate evidence for the existence of God is Jesus Christ himself. If there is a God, we characters in his play have to hope that he put some information about himself in the play. But Christians believe he did more than give us information. He wrote *himself* into the play as the main character in history, when Jesus was born in a manger and rose from the dead. He is the one with whom we have to do.

## PART 2

# THE REASONS FOR FAITH

# EIGHT

## THE CLUES OF GOD

*If one puts aside the existence of God and the survival after life as too doubtful . . . one has to make up one's mind as to the use of life. If death ends all, if I have neither to hope for good nor to fear evil, I must ask myself what I am here for, and how in these circumstances I must conduct myself. Now the answer is plain, but so unpalatable that most will not face it. There is no meaning for life, and [thus] life has no meaning.*

—Somerset Maugham, *The Summing Up*

*It was true, I had always realised it – I hadn't any 'right' to exist at all. I had appeared by chance, I existed like a stone, a plant, a microbe. I could feel nothing to myself but an inconsequential buzzing. I was thinking . . . that here we are eating and drinking, to preserve our precious existence, and that there's nothing, nothing, absolutely no reason for existing.*

—Jean-Paul Sartre, *Nausea*

HOW can we believe in Christianity if we don't even know whether God exists? Though there cannot be irrefutable proof for the existence of God, many people have found strong clues for his reality – divine fingerprints – in many places.

I once met regularly with a brilliant young scientist who was haunted by a general sense that God existed. Much of what I am writing in this chapter and the next I discovered during my conversations with him. He looked at one argument for God after another, and though many of them had a great deal of merit, he found that ultimately every one of them was rationally avoidable at some point. This troubled him greatly. 'I can't believe unless I find at least *one* absolutely airtight proof for God,' he said to me. I pointed out to him that he was assuming 'strong rationalism' and he got some relief when together we realised that he had no airtight proof for *that*. Then we began to go back and review the lines of reasoning that he had been calling 'proofs' and began to look at them instead as clues. When we went about it with that perspective he began to see that, cumulatively, the clues of God had a lot of force to them.

The philosopher Alvin Plantinga believes that there are no proofs of God that will convince all rational persons. However, he believes that there are at least two to three dozen very good arguments for the existence of God.[1] Most readers who take the time to think through Plantinga's list will find some items compelling and others not. However, the accumulated weight of the ones you find appealing can be very formidable. I will trace out just a handful of them.

## The Mysterious Bang

Those of a more rational mind-set have always been fascinated by the question, 'Why is there something rather than nothing?' This question has become even more interesting to people in the wake of the Big Bang theory. There's evidence that the universe is expanding explosively and outwardly from a single point. Stephen Hawking wrote: 'Almost everyone now believes that the universe, and time itself, had a beginning at the Big Bang.'[2] Scientist Francis Collins puts this clue in layman's language in his book *The Language of God*:

> *We have this very solid conclusion that the universe had an origin, the Big Bang. Fifteen billion years ago, the universe began with an unimaginably bright flash of energy from an infinitesimally small point. That implies that before that, there was nothing. I can't imagine how nature, in this case the universe, could have created itself. And the very fact that the universe had a beginning implies that someone was able to begin it. And it seems to me that had to be outside of nature.*[3]

Everything we know in this world is 'contingent', has a cause outside of itself. Therefore the universe, which is just a huge pile of such contingent entities, would itself have to be dependent on some cause outside of itself. Something had to make the Big Bang happen – but what? What could that be but something outside of nature, a supernatural, non-contingent being that exists from itself.

Sam Harris, in his review of Francis Collins' book, makes the classic objection to this line of reasoning. 'In any case,' he writes, 'even if we accepted that our universe simply had to be created by an intelligent being, this would not suggest that this being is the God of the Bible.'[4] That is perfectly right. If we are looking at this as an argument proving the existence of a personal God, it doesn't get us all the way there. However, if we are looking for a clue – a clue that there is something besides the natural world – it is very provocative for many people.

## The Cosmic Welcome Mat

For organic life to exist, the fundamental regularities and constants of physics – the speed of light, the gravitational constant, the strength of the weak and strong nuclear forces – must all have values that together fall into an extremely narrow range. The probability of this perfect calibration happening by chance is so tiny as to be statistically negligible.[5] Again, Collins puts it well:

> *When you look from the perspective of a scientist at the universe, it looks as if it knew we were coming. There are 15 constants – the gravitational constant, various constants about the strong and weak nuclear force, etc. – that have precise values. If any one of those constants was off by even one part in a million, or in some cases, by one part in a million million, the universe could not have actually come to the point where we see it. Matter would not have been able to coalesce, there would have been no galaxy, stars, planets or people.*[6]

Some have said that it is as if there were a large number of dials that all had to be tuned to within extremely narrow limits – and they were. It seems extremely unlikely that this would happen by chance. Stephen Hawking concludes: 'The odds against a universe like ours emerging out of something like the Big Bang are enormous. I think there are clearly religious implications.' Elsewhere he says, 'It would be very difficult to explain why the universe would have begun in just this way except as the act of a God who intended to create beings like us.'[7]

This has been called the 'Fine-Tuning Argument' or the 'Anthropic Principle', namely that the universe was prepared for human beings. As an argument it must be a pretty powerful one, because there are a lot of fierce rebuttals being published about it. The most common rejoinder, which Richard Dawkins makes in his book *The God Delusion*, is that there may be trillions of universes. Given the enormous number of universes existing over enormous amounts of time and space, it is inevitable that some of them are fine-tuned to sustain our kind of life. The one we are in is one, so here we are.[8]

Again, as a 'proof', the Fine-Tuning Argument is rationally avoidable. Though there's not a shred of proof that there are many universes, there's also no way to prove that there aren't.

However, as a clue, this line of thinking has force. Alvin Plantinga gives this illustration. He imagines a man dealing himself twenty straight hands of four aces in the same game of poker. As his companions reach for their six-shooters the poker player says, 'I know it looks suspicious! But what if there is an infinite succession of universes, so that for any possible distribution of poker hands, there is one universe in which this possibility is realised? We just happen to find ourselves in one where I always deal myself four aces without cheating!'[9] This argument will have no effect on the other poker players. It is technically possible that the man just happened to deal himself twenty straight hands of four aces. Though you could not prove he had cheated, it would be unreasonable to conclude that he hadn't.

The philosopher John Leslie poses a similar illustration. He imagines a man who is sentenced to be executed by a firing squad consisting of fifty expert marksmen.[10] They all fire from six feet away and not one bullet hits him. Since it is possible that even expert marksmen could miss from close range it is technically possible that all fifty just happened to miss at the same moment. Though you could not prove they had conspired to miss, it would be unreasonable to draw the conclusion that they hadn't.

It is technically possible that we just happened to be in the one universe in which organic life occurred. Though you could not prove that the fine-tuning of the universe was due to some sort of design, it would be unreasonable to draw the conclusion that it wasn't. Although organic life could have just happened without a Creator, does it make sense to live as if that infinitely remote chance is true?

## The Regularity of Nature

There is something about nature that is much more striking and inexplicable than its design. All scientific, inductive reasoning is based on the assumption of the regularity (the 'laws') of nature, that water will boil tomorrow under the identical conditions of to-day. The method of induction requires generalising from observed cases to all cases of the same kind. Without inductive reasoning we couldn't learn from experience, we couldn't use language, we couldn't rely on our memories.

Most people find that normal and untroubling. But not philosophers! David Hume and Bertrand Russell, as good secular men, were troubled by the fact that we haven't got the slightest idea of why nature-regularity is happening now, and moreover we haven't the slightest rational justification for assuming it will continue to-morrow. If someone were to say, 'Well the future has always been like the past in the past,' Hume and Russell reply that you are assuming the very thing you are trying to establish. To put it another way, science cannot prove the continued regularity of nature, it can only take it on faith.

There have been many scholars in the last decades who have argued that modern science arose in its most sustained form out of Christian civilisation because of its belief in an all-powerful, personal God who created and sustains an orderly universe.[11] As a proof for the existence of God, the regularity of nature is escapable. You can always say, 'We don't know why things are as they are.' As a clue for God, however, it is helpful.

## The Clue of Beauty

Arthur C. Danto, the art critic at *The Nation*, once described a work of art that gave him a sense of 'obscure but inescapable meaning'.[12] In other words, while great art does not 'hit you over the head' with a simple message, it always gives you a sense that life is not a 'tale told by an idiot, full of sound and fury, signifying nothing'. It fills you with hope and gives you the strength to carry on, though you cannot define what it is that moves you.

Leonard Bernstein once rhapsodised about the effect of Beethoven on him:

*Beethoven . . . turned out pieces of breath-taking rightness. Rightness – that's the word! When you get the feeling that whatever note succeeds the last is the only possible note that can rightly happen at that instant, in that context, then chances are you're listening to Beethoven. Melodies, fugues, rhythms – leave them to the Tchaikovskys and Hindemiths and Ravels. Our boy has the real goods, the stuff from Heaven, the power to make you feel at the finish: Something is right in the world. There is something that checks throughout, that follows its own law consistently: something we can trust, that will never let us down.*[13]

If there is no God, and everything in this world is the product of (as Bertrand Russell famously put it) 'an accidental collocation of atoms', then there is no actual purpose for which we were made – we are accidents. If we are the product of accidental natural forces, then what we call 'beauty' is nothing but a neurological hardwired response to particular data. You only find certain scenery to be beautiful because you had ancestors who knew you would find food there and they survived because of that neurological feature and now we have it too. In the same way, though music feels significant, that significance is an illusion. Love too must be seen in this light. If we are the result of blind natural forces, then what we call 'love' is simply a biochemical response, inherited from ancestors who survived because this trait helped them survive.

Bernstein and Danto are testifying to the fact that even though we as secular people believe that beauty and love are just biochemical responses, in the presence of great art and beauty we inescapably feel that there *is* real meaning in life, there *is* truth and justice that will never let us down, and love means everything. Notice that Bernstein, though by no means an orthodox religious person, can't refrain from even using the term 'Heaven' when talking about Beethoven. We may, therefore, be secular materialists who believe truth and justice, good and evil, are complete illusions. But in the presence of art or even great natural beauty, our hearts tell us another story.

Another prominent artist who is apparently telling us the same thing is John Updike. In his short story 'Pigeon Feathers' a young teenager says to this mother, 'Don't you see, if when we die there's nothing, all your sun and fields and what not are all, ah, *horror*? It's just an ocean of horror.' Later, in the presence of the beauty of pigeon feathers, of their texture and colour, he is overwhelmed by a certainty that there is a God behind the world who will allow him to live for eternity.[14] Updike seems to be saying that regardless of the beliefs of our mind about the random meaninglessness of life, before the face of beauty we know better.

'So what?' someone might object. 'Just because we feel something is true doesn't make it so!' Are we, however, only talking about feelings here? What is evoked in these experiences is, more accurately, appetite or desire. Goethe refers to this as *selige sehnsucht* – blessed longing. We not only feel the reality but also the absence of what we long for.

St Augustine in his *Confessions* reasoned that these unfulfillable desires are clues to the reality of God. How so? Indeed (as it was just objected) just because we *feel* the desire for a steak dinner doesn't mean we will get it. However, while hunger doesn't prove that the particular meal desired will be procured, doesn't the appetite for food in us mean that food exists? Isn't it true that innate desires correspond to real objects that can satisfy them, such as sexual desire (corresponding to sex), physical appetite (corresponding to food), tiredness (corresponding to sleep), and relational desires (corresponding to friendship)?

Doesn't the unfulfillable longing evoked by beauty qualify as an innate desire? We have a longing for joy, love and beauty that no amount or quality of food, sex, friendship or success can satisfy. We want something that nothing in this world can fulfil. Isn't that at least a clue that this 'something' that we want exists?[15] This unfulfillable longing, then, qualifies as a deep, innate human desire, and that makes it a major clue that God is there.[16]

## The Clue-Killer

In our culture there is a very influential school of thought that claims to have the answers to all of these so-called clues. This is the school of evolutionary biology that claims everything about us can be explained as a function of natural selection. A book that seeks to explain all clues about God in this way is *Breaking the Spell: Religion as a Natural Phenomenon* by Daniel Dennett. Dennett claims that if we have religious feelings it is only because those traits once helped certain people survive their environment in greater numbers and therefore passed that genetic code on to us. He sums up his view when he writes:

> *Everything we value – from sugar and sex and money to music and love and religion – we value for reasons. Lying behind, and*

*distinct from, our reasons are evolutionary reasons, free-floating
rationales that have been endorsed by natural selection.*[17]

In *The New York Times Magazine*, Robin Marantz Henig surveyed
what evolutionists think about religion in an article, 'Why Do We
Believe? How Evolutionary Science Explains Faith in God'.[18] We
know that 'the idea of an infallible God is comfortable and familiar,
something children readily accept'.[19] Why? Some evolutionists
such as David Sloan Wilson think belief in God made people hap-
pier and more unselfish, which meant their families and tribes
survived and they got better mates. Others such as Scott Atran and
Richard Dawkins posit that belief in God is an accidental by-product
of other traits that did give adaptive advantage. Our ancestors who
survived were most prone to detect agents in the brush even when
they weren't there, and were most likely to impose narratives, causal
reasoning, on everything that happened around them. However, these
same traits make us more likely to believe in God – to see agents and
narratives and intelligences where they don't actually exist.[20]

Despite fierce debates within the field, evolutionary theorists all
agree that our capacity to believe in God is hardwired into our
physiology because it was directly or indirectly associated with
traits that helped our ancestors adapt to their environment. That's
why arguments for God appeal to so many of us. That's all there is
to it. The clues are clues to nothing.

However, there are many who believe not only that the clue-
killer argument has a fatal contradiction in it, but that it actually
points to another clue for God.

In the last part of Dawkins' *The God Delusion* he admits that
since we are the product of natural selection, we can't completely
trust our own senses. After all, evolution is interested only in pre-
serving adaptive behaviour, not true belief.[21] In the *New York
Times Magazine* article, another scientist says, 'In some circum-

stances a symbolic belief that departs from factual reality fares better.'[22] In other words, paranoid false beliefs are often more effective at helping you survive than accurate ones.

I don't believe Dawkins or other evolutionary theorists realise the full implications of this crucial insight. Evolution can only be trusted to give us cognitive faculties that help us live on, *not* to provide ones that give us an accurate and true picture of the world around us.[23] Patricia Churchland puts it like this:

> *The principle chore of [brains] is to get the body parts where they should be in order that the organism may survive. Improvements in sensorimotor control confer an evolutionary advantage: a fancier style of representing [the world] is advantageous so long as it . . . enhances the organism's chances for survival. Truth, whatever that is, takes the hindmost.*[24]

Thomas Nagel, the prominent philosopher and atheist, agrees in the last chapter of his book *The Last Word*. He writes that to be sure my mind is telling me what is really, truly out there in the world, I must 'follow the rules of logic because they are correct – not merely because I am biologically programmed to do so'. However, according to evolutionary biology laws of reason would have to make sense to us only because they help us survive, not because they necessarily tell us truth. So, Nagel asks:

> *[Can we have any] continued confidence in reason as a source of knowledge about the nonapparent character of the world? In itself, I believe an evolutionary story [of the human race] tells against such confidence.*[25]

Evolutionists say that if God makes sense to us, it is not because he is really there, it's only because that belief helped us survive and so we are hardwired for it. However, if we can't trust our belief-forming faculties to tell us the truth about God, why should we trust them to tell us the truth about anything, including evolutionary science? If our cognitive faculties only tell us what we need to survive, not what is true, why trust them about anything at all?

It seems that evolutionary theorists have to do one of two things. They could backtrack and admit that we can trust what our minds tell us about things, including God. If we find arguments or clues to God's existence that seem compelling to us, well, maybe he's really there. Or else they could go forward and admit that we can't trust our minds about anything. What is not fair is to do what so many evolutionary scientists are doing now. They are applying the scalpel of their scepticism to what our minds tell us about God but not to what our minds are telling us about evolutionary science itself.

This is a huge Achilles' heel in the whole enterprise of evolutionary biology and theory. Alvin Plantinga points out that Charles Darwin himself saw this major vulnerability. To a friend, Darwin wrote that:

*the horrid doubt always arises whether the convictions of man's mind, which has been developed from the mind of the lower animals, are of any value or at all trustworthy.*[26]

Plantinga then proceeds to argue that it is ultimately irrational to accept evolutionary 'naturalism', the theory that everything in us is caused only by natural selection. If it were true, we couldn't trust the methods by which we arrived at it or any scientific theory at all.[27]

*People like Dawkins hold that there is a conflict between science and religion . . . the truth of the matter, however, is that the conflict is between science and naturalism, not between science and belief in God. . . . It's as likely, given unguided evolution, that we live in a sort of dream world as that we actually know something about ourselves and our world.*[28]

Despite popular books like those of Dennett, Dawkins and Harris, which try to use the evolutionary clue-killer on religion, more and more thinkers are seeing through it, and not just orthodox believers, but those like Thomas Nagel. Leon Wieseltier, the literary editor of *The New Republic*, points out the flaw in the clue-killer argument in his review of Dennett's book *Breaking the Spell*.

*[Dennett] portrays reason in service to natural selection, and as a product of natural selection. But if reason is a product of natural selection, then how much confidence can we have in a rational argument for natural selection? The power of reason is owed to the independence of reason, and to nothing else. . . . Evolutionary biology cannot invoke the power of reason even as it destroys it.*[29]

It comes down to this: if, as the evolutionary scientists say, what our brains tells us about morality, love and beauty is not real – if it is merely a set of chemical reactions designed to pass on our genetic code – then so is what *their* brains tell them about the world. Then why should they trust them?

## The Clue-Killer Is Really a Clue

I think that ultimately the supposed clue-killer ends up showing us one more clue for God to put beside the others.

The first clue is the very existence of the world, the Big Bang. The secular person rightly responds, 'But that doesn't prove God exists. Maybe the Big Bang just caused itself.' The second clue is the fine-tuning of the universe, the one-in-a-trillion-trillion chance that our universe supports organic and human life. Again the secular person can very fairly respond: 'But that doesn't prove God. It could be through sheer random circumstance that this universe is the one that was formed.' Another clue is the regularity of nature. All scientific, inductive reasoning is based on the assumption of this, though we haven't the slightest rational justification for assuming it will continue. When believers have responded that this is a clue to God's existence, non-believers retort, rightly, 'We don't know why nature is regular, it just is. That doesn't prove God.'

Another clue is the clue of beauty and meaning. If we are the product of the meaningless, accidental forces of nature, believers ask, how do you account for the sense we have that beauty matters, that love and life are significant? The secular person responds: 'This doesn't prove God. We can explain all such "senses" and convictions through evolutionary biology. Our religious, aesthetic and moral intuitions are there only because they helped our ancestors survive.' However, as many thinkers point out, if this argument proves anything at all it proves too much. If we can't trust our belief-forming faculties in one area, we should not trust them in any area. If there is no God, we should not trust our cognitive faculties at all.

Oh, but we do, and that's the final clue. If we believe God exists, then our view of the universe gives us a basis for believing that cognitive faculties work, since God could make us able to form true beliefs and knowledge. If we believe in God, then the Big Bang is not mysterious, nor the fine-tuning of the universe, nor the regularities of nature. All the things that we see make perfect sense. Also, if God exists our intuitions about the meaningfulness of beauty and love are to be expected.

If you don't believe in God, not only are all these things profoundly inexplicable, but your view – that there is no God – would lead you *not* to expect them. Though you have little reason to believe your rational faculties work, you go on using them. You have no basis for believing that nature will go on regularly, but you continue to use inductive reasoning and language. You have no good reason to trust your senses that love and beauty matter, but you keep on doing it. C. S. Lewis puts this vividly:

> *You can't, except in the lowest animal sense, be in love with a girl if you know (and keep on remembering) that all the beauties both of her person and of her character are a momentary and accidental pattern produced by the collision of atoms, and that your own response to them is only a sort of psychic phosphorescence arising from the behaviour of your genes. You can't go on getting very serious pleasure from music if you know and remember that its air of significance is a pure illusion, that you like it only because your nervous system is irrationally conditioned to like it.*[30]

Of course none of the clues we have been looking for actually proves God. Every one of them is rationally avoidable. However, their cumulative effect is, I think, provocative and potent. Though the secular view of the world is rationally possible, it doesn't make as much sense of all these things as the view that God exists. That's why we call them clues. The theory that there is a God who made the world accounts for the evidence we see better than the theory that there is no God. Those who argue against the existence of God go right on using induction, language and their cognitive faculties, all of which make far more sense in a universe in which a God has created and supports them all by his power.

## Beyond the Clues

I can imagine someone saying at this point, 'So, it's all inconclusive! All you are saying is that, on the whole, God probably exists, but nobody can make an airtight case. That means no one can know if there's a God or not.'

I don't agree.

In the next chapter I want to do something very personal. I don't want to argue why God may exist. I want to demonstrate that you already know that God does exist. I'd like to convince the reader that, whatever you may profess intellectually, belief in God is an unavoidable, 'basic' belief that we cannot prove but can't not know. We *know* God is there. That is why even when we believe with all our minds that life is meaningless, we simply can't live that way. We know better.

# NINE

# THE KNOWLEDGE OF GOD

CHARLIE:    *Of course there's a God! We all basically know there is.*

CYNTHIA:    *I know no such thing.*

CHARLIE:    *Of course you do! When you think to yourself – and most of our waking life is taken up thinking to ourself – you must have that feeling that your thoughts aren't entirely wasted, that in some sense they are being heard. I think it's this sensation of silently being listened to with total comprehension that represents our innate belief in a supreme being, an all-comprehending intelligence. What it shows is that some kind of belief is innate in all of us. At some point most of us lose that, after which it can only be regained by a conscious act of faith.*

CYNTHIA:    *And you've experienced that?*

CHARLIE:    *No, I haven't. I hope to someday.*

               —*Metropolitan* (1990, USA, Whit Stillman)

CONSERVATIVE writers and speakers are constantly complaining that the young people of our culture are relativistic and amoral. As a pastor in Manhattan I have been neck-deep in sophisticated twentysomethings for almost two decades, and I have not found this to be the case. The secular, young adults I have known have a very finely honed sense of right and wrong. There are many things happening in the world that evoke their moral outrage. There is a problem with their moral outlook, however.

## Free-Floating Morality

In many cases I have to put on my philosophy-professor hat in order to be a good pastor to people. A young couple once came to me for some spiritual direction. They 'didn't believe in much of anything' they said. How could they begin to figure out if there even was a God? I asked them to tell me about something they felt was really, really wrong. The woman immediately spoke out against practices that marginalised women. I said I agreed with her fully since I was a Christian who believed God made all human beings, but I was curious why she thought it was wrong. She responded, 'Women are human beings and human beings have rights. It is wrong to trample on someone's rights.' I asked her how she knew that.

Puzzled, she said, 'Everyone knows it is wrong to violate the rights of someone.' I said, 'Most people in the world don't "know" that. They don't have a Western view of human rights. Imagine if someone said to you "everyone knows that women are inferior". You'd say, "That's not an argument, it's just an assertion." And you'd be right. So let's start again. If there is no God as you believe and everyone has just evolved from animals, why would it be wrong to trample on someone's rights?' Her husband responded: 'Yes, it is true we are just bigger-brained animals, but I'd say animals have rights too. You shouldn't trample on their rights, either.' I asked whether he held animals guilty for violating the rights of other animals if the stronger ones ate the weaker ones. 'No, I couldn't do that.' So he only held human beings guilty if they trampled on the weak? 'Yes.' Why this double standard, I asked. Why did the couple insist that human beings had to be different from animals, so that they were *not* allowed to act as was natural to the rest of the animal world. Why did the couple keep insisting that humans had this great, unique individual dignity and worth? Why did they believe in human rights? 'I don't know', the woman said, 'I guess they are just there, that's all.'

The conversation was much more congenial than this very compressed account conveys. The young couple laughed at the weakness of some of their responses, which showed me that they were open to exploration and that encouraged me to be more pointed than I would ordinarily have been. However, this conversation reveals how our culture differs from all the others that have gone before. People still have strong moral convictions, but unlike people in other times and places, they don't have any visible basis for *why* they find some things to be evil and other things good. It's almost like their moral intuitions are free-floating in mid-air – far off the ground.

Polish poet Czeslaw Milosz spoke of this:

*What has been surprising in the post-Cold War period are those beautiful and deeply moving words pronounced with veneration in places like Prague and Warsaw, words which pertain to the old repertory of the rights of man and the dignity of the person. I wonder at this phenomenon because maybe underneath there is an abyss. After all, those ideas had their foundation in religion, and I am not over-optimistic about the survival of religion in a scientific-technological civilization. Notions that seemed buried forever have suddenly been resurrected. But how long can they stay afloat if the bottom is taken out?*[1]

I don't believe Milosz is right. I think that people will definitely go on holding to their beliefs in human dignity even when conscious belief in God is gone. Why is this the case? I have a radical thesis. I think people in our culture know unavoidably that there is a God, but they are repressing what they know.

## The Concept of Moral Obligation

It is common to hear people say, 'No one should impose their moral views on others, because everyone has the right to find truth inside him or herself.' This belief leaves the speaker open to a series of very uncomfortable questions. Aren't there people in the world who are doing things you believe are *wrong* – things that they should stop doing no matter what they personally believe about the correctness of their behaviour? If you do (and everyone does!), doesn't that mean you *do* believe that there is some kind of moral standard that people should abide by regardless of their individual convictions? This raises a question. Why is it impossible (in practice) for anyone to be a consistent moral relativist even when they claim that they are? The answer is that we all have a pervasive, powerful and unavoidable belief not only in moral values but also in moral *obligation*. Sociologist Christian Smith puts it like this:

> *'Moral' . . . is an orientation toward understandings about what is right and wrong, just and unjust, that are not established by our own actual desires or preferences but instead are believed to exist apart from them, providing standards by which our desires and preferences can themselves be judged.*[2]

All human beings have moral feelings. We call it a conscience. When considering doing something that we feel would be wrong, we tend to refrain. Our moral sense does not stop there, however. We also believe that there are standards 'that exist apart from us' by

146

which we evaluate moral feelings. Moral obligation is a belief that some things ought not to be done regardless of how a person feels about them within herself, regardless of what the rest of her community and culture says, and regardless of whether it is in her self-interest or not. The young couple had no doubts that people in other cultures should honour women's rights, for example.

Though we have been taught that all moral values are relative to individuals and cultures, we can't live like that. In actual practice we inevitably treat *some* principles as absolute standards by which we judge the behaviour of those who don't share our values. What gives us the right to do that, if all moral beliefs are relative? Nothing gives us the right. Yet we can't stop it. People who laugh at the claim that there is a transcendent moral order do not think that racial genocide is just impractical or self-defeating, but that it is *wrong*. The Nazis who exterminated Jews may have claimed that they didn't feel it was immoral at all. We don't care. We don't care if they sincerely felt they were doing a service to humanity. They ought not to have done it.

We do not only have moral feelings, but we also have an ineradicable belief that moral standards exist, outside of us, by which our internal moral feelings are evaluated. Why? Why do we think those moral standards exist?

## The Evolutionary Theory of Moral Obligation

A common answer today comes from what I called in the last chapter the 'clue-killer', sociobiology or evolutionary psychology. This view holds that altruistic people, those who act unselfishly and co-operatively, survived in greater numbers than those who were selfish and cruel. Therefore altruistic genes were passed down to us and now the great majority of us feel that unselfish behaviour is 'right'.

There are, however, many flaws in this theory, and it has been given some devastating critiques.[3] An individual's self-sacrificing, altruistic behaviour towards his or her blood kin might result in a greater survival rate for the individual's family or extended clan, and therefore result in a greater number of descendants with that person's genetic material. For evolutionary purposes, however, the opposite response – hostility to all people outside one's group – should be just as widely considered moral and right behaviour. Yet today we believe that sacrificing time, money, emotion and even life – especially for someone 'not of our kind' or tribe – is *right*. If we see a total stranger fall in the river we jump in after him, or feel guilty for not doing so. In fact, most people will feel the obligation to do so even if the person in the water is an enemy. How could that trait have come down by a process of natural selection? Such people would have been less likely to survive and pass on their genes. On the basis of strict evolutionary naturalism (the belief that everything about us is here because of a process of natural selection) that kind of altruism should have died out of the human race long ago. Instead, it is stronger than ever.

Other arguments to demonstrate the reproductive benefits of altruism have also run into trouble. Some contend that altruistic behaviour brings many indirect reciprocal benefits to the practitioner from others, but this can't account for our motivation to practise such acts when no one knows about them. Others have contended that sacrificial behaviour benefits an entire group or society, enabling the entire society to pass on its genetic code. However, there is consensus that natural selection does not work on whole populations.[4]

Evolution, therefore, cannot account for the origin of our moral feelings, let alone for the fact that we all believe there are external moral standards by which moral feelings are evaluated.[5]

## The Problem of Moral Obligation

This sense of moral obligation creates a problem for those with a secular understanding of the world. Carolyn Fluehr-Lobban is an anthropologist whose professional field is dominated by what she calls 'cultural relativism' – a view that all moral beliefs are culturally created (that is, we believe them because we are part of a community that gives them plausibility) and that there is no basis for objectively judging one culture's morality to be better than another. Yet she was appalled by practices in societies she was studying that oppressed women. She decided that she should promote women's interests in the societies wherever she worked as an anthropologist.

This immediately created a conundrum for her. She knew that her belief in women's equality was rooted in a socially located (Northern European, eighteenth-century) individualistic mode of thought. What right did she have to promote her views over those of the non-Western societies where she worked? Her response:

*Anthropologists continue to express strong support for cultural relativism. One of the most contentious issues arises from the fundamental question: What authority do we Westerners have to impose our own concept of universal rights on the rest of humanity. . . . [But] the cultural relativists' argument is often used by repressive governments to deflect international criticism of their abuse of their citizens. . . . I believe that we should not let the concept of relativism stop us from using national and international forums to examine ways to protect the lives and dignity of people in every culture. . . . When there is a choice between defending human rights and defending cultural relativism, anthropologists should choose to protect and promote human rights. We cannot just be bystanders.*[6]

The author poses a difficult question: 'If all cultures are relative, then so is the idea of universal human rights, so how can I decide to impose my values on this culture?' But she doesn't answer her own question. She has just said that her charge of oppression is based on a Western concept of individual freedom, but she has no answer for this conundrum. She simply declares that women are being oppressed and she feels she has to stop it. We have to bring our Western values to these other nations. Our values are better than theirs. Period.

## The Difficult Issue of Human Rights

Fluehr-Lobban is struggling with a major crisis in the field of human rights. Jürgen Habermas has written that, despite their European origins, 'human rights' in Asia, Africa and South America now 'constitute the only language in which the opponents and victims of murderous regimes and civil wars can raise their voices against violence, repression, and persecution'.[7] This reveals the enormous importance of the morality of human rights, which Michael J. Perry defines as the twofold conviction that every human being has inherent dignity and that it is obligatory that we order our lives in accordance with this fact. It is wrong to violate the equal dignity of other human beings.[8] But why should we believe that? On what does this dignity depend?

In his essay 'Where Do Rights Come From?'[9] Harvard law professor Alan Dershowitz lays out the possibilities. Some say human rights come from God. If we were all created in God's image, then every human being would be sacred and inviolable. Dershowitz rejects this as an answer, since so many millions of people are agnostic. Others say human rights come from nature, or what has been called 'natural law'. They argue that nature and human nature, if it is

150

examined, will reveal that some kinds of behaviour are 'fitting' with the way things are, and are right. However, Dershowitz points out that nature thrives on violence and predation, on the survival of the fittest. There is no way to derive the concept of the dignity of every individual from the way things really work in nature.

Another theory claims that human rights are created by us, the people who write the laws. Many argue that it is in the interests of societies to create human rights because honouring individual dignity means that in the long run everyone in the community is better off. However, what if a majority decides it is *not* in their interest to grant human rights? If rights are nothing but a majority creation then there is nothing to appeal to when they are legislated out of existence. Dershowitz, quoting Ronald Dworkin, argues that this third view of human rights is inadequate:

> *It is no answer to say that if individuals have these rights then the community is better off in the long run ... because when we say someone has a* right *to speak his mind freely, we mean he is entitled to do so even if this would not be in the general interest.*

If human rights are created by majorities, of what use are they? Their value lies in that they can be used to insist that majorities honour the dignity of minorities and individuals despite their conception of their 'greater good'. Rights cannot be created – they must be *discovered*, or they are of no value. As Dworkin concludes, if we want to defend individual rights, we must try to discover *something beyond utility* that argues for these rights.[10]

What could that 'something' be? Neither Dworkin nor Dershowitz can really give an answer. Dworkin ends up appealing to a form of majority rule anyway. In *Life's Dominion: An Argument*

*About Abortion, Euthanasia, and Individual Freedom* (1995), he
writes:

> *The life of a single human organism commands respect and
> protection . . . because of our wonder at the . . . processes that
> produce new lives from old ones. . . . The nerve of the sacred lies
> in the value we attach to a process or enterprise or project rather
> than to its results considered independently from how they were
> produced. . . .* [11]

Law professor Michael J. Perry responds:

> *The nonreligious source of normativity, for Dworkin, is the
> great value 'we' attach to every human being understood as a
> creative masterpiece; it is 'our' wonder at the processes that
> produce new lives from old ones. . . . But to whom is Dworkin
> referring with his 'we' and 'our'? Did the Nazis value the Jews
> intrinsically? The conspicuous problem with Dworkin's . . .
> secular argument [for rights] is that Dworkin assumes a con-
> sensus among human agents that does not exist and never has
> existed.*[12]

Perry's new book, *Toward a Theory of Human Rights*, is very significant. Perry concludes that though it is clear 'there is a religious
ground for the morality of human rights . . . It is far from clear that
there is a non-religious ground,[13] a *secular* ground, for human
rights.'[14] Perry lays out Nietzsche's well-known insistence that, if
God is dead, any and all morality of love and human rights is base-
less. If there is no God, argue Nietzsche, Sartre and others, there
can be no good reason to be kind, to be loving or to work for peace.
Perry quotes Philippa Foot who says that secular thinkers accepted
the idea that there is no God and no given meaning to human life,

but have not 'really joined battle with Nietzsche about morality. By and large we have just gone on taking moral judgements for granted as if nothing had happened.'[15] Why do we keep on doing this?

## The Grand 'Sez Who?'

The reason is laid out in a classic essay by late Yale law professor Arthur Leff. Most people feel that human rights are not created by us but are found by us, that they are there and must be honoured by majorities, whether they like them or not. But, Leff says:

> *When would it be impermissible to make the formal intellectual equivalent of what is known in barrooms and schoolyards as 'the grand Sez Who'? In the absence of God . . . each . . . ethical and legal system . . . will be differentiated by the answer it chooses to give to one key question: who among us . . . ought to be able to declare 'law' that ought to be obeyed? Stated that baldly, the question is so intellectually unsettling that one would expect to find a noticeable number of legal and ethical thinkers trying not to come to grips with it. . . . Either God exists or He does not, but if He does not, nothing and no one else can take His place. . . .* [16]

If there is no God, then there is no way to say any one action is 'moral' and another 'immoral' but only 'I like this'. If that is the case, who gets the right to put their subjective, arbitrary moral feelings into law? You may say 'the majority has the right to make the law', but do you mean that then the majority has the right to vote to exterminate a minority? If you say, 'No, that is wrong,' then you are back to square one. 'Who sez' that the majority has a moral obligation not to kill the minority? Why should your moral convictions be obligatory for those in opposition? Why should your view prevail over the will of the majority? The fact is, says Leff, if there is no God, then all moral statements are arbitrary, all moral valuations are subjective and internal, and there can be no external moral standard by which a person's feelings and values are judged. Yet Leff ends this intellectual essay in a most shocking way:

> *As things are now, everything is up for grabs. Nevertheless: napalming babies is bad. Starving the poor is wicked. Buying and selling each other is depraved. . . . There is such a thing as evil. All together now: Sez Who? God help us.*

Nietzsche, of course, understood this. 'The masses blink and say: "We are all equal – Man is but man, before God we are all equal." Before God! But now this God has died.'[17] Raimond Gaita, an atheist thinker, reluctantly writes:

> *Only someone who is religious can speak seriously of the sacred. . . . We may say that all human beings are inestimably precious, that they are ends in themselves, that they are owed unconditional respect, that they possess inalienable rights, and, of course, that they possess inalienable dignity. In my judgment these are ways of trying to say what we feel a need to say when we are estranged from the conceptual resources [i.e. God] we need to say it. . . . Not one of [these statements about human beings] has the power of the religious way of speaking . . . that we are sacred because God loves us, his children.*[18]

Leff is not simply concluding that there is no basis for human rights without God. He is also pointing out (as are Dershowitz and Dworkin, in their own way) that despite the fact that we can't justify or ground human rights in a world without God, we still know they exist. Leff is not just speaking generically, but personally. Without

God he can't justify moral obligation, and yet he can't *not know* it exists.

## The Argument for God from the Violence of Nature

Why would we know this? To sharpen our focus on the significance of this indelible knowledge of moral obligation, consider the observations of writer Annie Dillard. Dillard lived for a year by a creek in the mountains of Virginia expecting to be inspired and refreshed by closeness to 'nature'. Instead, she came to realise that nature was completely ruled by one central principle – violence by the strong against the weak.

> *There is not a person in the world that behaves as badly as praying mantises. But wait, you say, there is no right or wrong in nature; right and wrong is a human concept! Precisely! We are moral creatures in an amoral world. . . . Or consider the alternative . . . it is only human feeling that is freakishly amiss. . . . All right then – it is our emotions that are amiss. We are freaks, the world is fine, and let us all go have lobotomies to restore us to a natural state. We can leave . . . lobotomized, go back to the creek, and live on its banks as untroubled as any muskrat or reed. You first.*[19]

Annie Dillard saw that all of nature is based on violence. Yet we inescapably believe it is wrong for stronger human individuals or groups to kill weaker ones. If violence is totally natural why would it be wrong for strong humans to trample weak ones? There is no basis for moral obligation unless we argue that nature is in some part unnatural. We can't know that nature is broken in some way unless there is some *super*natural standard of normalcy apart from nature by which we can judge right and wrong. That means there would have to be heaven or God or some kind of divine order outside of nature in order to make that judgement.

There is only one way out of this conundrum. We can pick up the biblical account of things and see if it explains our moral sense any better than a secular view. If the world was made by a God of peace, justice and love, then that is why we know that violence, oppression and hate are wrong. If the world is fallen, broken and needs to be redeemed, that explains the violence and disorder we see.

If you believe human rights are a reality, then it makes much more sense that God exists than that he does not. If you insist on a secular view of the world and yet you continue to pronounce some things right and some things wrong, then I hope you see the deep disharmony between the world your intellect has devised and the real world (and God) that your heart knows exists. This leads us to a crucial question. If a premise ('There is no God') leads to a conclusion you know isn't true ('Napalming babies is culturally relative') then *why not change the premise?*

## The Endless, Pointless Litigation of Existence

I have not tried to prove the existence of God to you. My goal has been to show you that you already know God is there. To some degree I have been treating the non-existence of God as an intellectual problem, but it is much more than that. It not only makes all moral choices meaningless, but it makes all life meaningless too. The playwright Arthur Miller reveals this vividly through the character Quentin in *After the Fall*. Quentin says:

*For many years I looked at life like a case at law. It was a series of proofs. When you're young you prove how brave you are, or smart; then, what a good lover; then, a good father; finally, how wise, or powerful or [whatever.] But underlying it all, I see now, there was a presumption. That one moved . . . on an upward path toward some elevation, where . . . God knows what . . . I would be justified, or even condemned. A verdict anyway. I think now that my disaster really began when I looked up one day . . . and the bench was empty. No judge in sight. And all that remained was the endless argument with oneself, this pointless litigation of existence before an empty bench. . . . Which, of course, is another way of saying – despair.*[20]

What is he saying? We all live as if it is better to seek peace instead of war, to tell the truth instead of lying, to care and nurture rather than to destroy. We believe that these choices are not pointless, that it matters which way we choose to live. Yet if the Cosmic Bench is truly empty, then 'who sez' that one choice is better than the others? We can argue about it, but it's just pointless arguing, endless litigation. If the Bench is truly empty, then the whole span of human civilisation, even if it lasts a few million years, will be just an infinitesimally brief spark in relation to the oceans of dead time that preceded it and will follow it. There will be no one around to remember any of it. Whether we are loving or cruel in the end would make no difference at all.[21]

Once we realise this situation there are two options. One is that we can simply refuse to think out the implications of all this. We can hold on to our intellectual belief in an empty Bench and yet live as if our choices are meaningful and as if there is a difference between love and cruelty. Why would we do that? A cynic might say that this is a way of 'having one's cake and eating it, too'. That is, you get the benefit of having a God without the cost of following him. But there is no integrity in that.

The other option is to recognise that you *do* know there is a

God. You could accept the fact that you live as if beauty and love have meaning, as if there is meaning in life, as if human beings have inherent dignity – all because you know God exists. It is dishonest to live as if he is there and yet fail to acknowledge the one who has given you all these gifts.

# TEN

## THE PROBLEM OF SIN

*Can we doubt that presently our race will more than realise our boldest imaginations, that it will achieve unity and peace, and that our children will live in a world made more splendid and lovely than any palace or garden that we know, going on from strength to strength in an ever-widening circle of achievement? What man has done, the little triumphs of his present state . . . form but the prelude to the things that man has yet to do.*

—H. G. Wells, *A Short History of the World* (1937)

*The cold-blooded massacres of the defenceless, the return of deliberate and organised torture, mental torment, and fear to a world from which such things had seemed well nigh banished – has come near to breaking my spirit altogether . . . 'Homo Sapiens', as he has been pleased to call himself, is played out.*

—H. G. Wells, *Mind at the End of Its Tether* (1946)

IT is hard to avoid the conclusion that there is something fundamentally wrong with the world. According to Christianity our biggest problem is sin. Yet the concept of 'sin' is offensive or ludicrous to many. This is often because we don't understand what Christians mean by the term.

## Sin and Human Hope

Many have the impression that the Christian doctrine of sin is bleak and pessimistic about human nature. Nothing could be further from the truth. When I was brand new in the ministry a young man came to see me whose wife had just left him. He was feeling angry at what she had done, guilty over his own flaws that had led her to do it, and despondent before the whole situation. I said that what he needed more than anything was hope. He quickly agreed and asked how he could get some. As gently as possible I said that the good news was – he was a sinner. Because he was a sinner he wasn't simply the helpless victim of psychological drives or social systems. Years later I came across a passage in a sermon by Barbara Brown Taylor, who said more eloquently what I tried to say that day.

> *Neither the language of medicine nor of law is adequate substitute for the language of [sin.] Contrary to the medical model, we are not entirely at the mercy of our maladies. The choice is to enter into the process of repentance. Contrary to the legal model, the essence of sin is not [primarily] the violation of laws but a wrecked relationship with God, one another, and the whole created order. 'All sins are attempts to fill voids,' wrote Simone Weil. Because we cannot stand the God-shaped hole inside of us, we try stuffing it full of all sorts of things, but only God may fill [it].*[1]

Andrew Delbanco is a humanities professor at Columbia University. Some years ago he was doing research on Alcoholics Anonymous and was attending AA meetings around the country. One Saturday morning in a New York City church basement he was listening to a 'crisply dressed young man' who was talking about his problems. In his narrative he was absolutely faultless. All his mistakes were due to the injustice and betrayals of others. He spoke of how he was going to avenge himself on all who had wronged him. 'His every gesture gave the impression of grievously wounded pride,' Delbanco wrote. It was clear that the young man was trapped in his need to justify himself, and that things could only get worse and worse in his life until he recognised this. While he was speaking, a black man in his forties, in dreadlocks and dark shades, leaned over to Delbanco and said, 'I used to feel that way too, before I achieved low self-esteem.' Delbanco wrote later in his book, *The Real American Dream: A Meditation on Hope*:

> *This was more than a good line. For me it was the moment I understood in a new way the religion I had claimed to know something about. As the speaker bombarded us with phrases like 'got to take control of my life,' and 'I've got to really believe in myself' – the man beside me took refuge in the old Calvinist doctrine that pride is the enemy of hope. What he meant by his joke about self-esteem was that he learned no one can save himself by dint of his own efforts. He thought the speaker was still lost – lost in himself, but without knowing it.*[2]

By 'low self-esteem' the man in the dreadlocks did not mean the young man should come to hate himself. He meant that the well-dressed young man was 'lost in himself' until he could admit he was a very flawed human being, a sinner. He would never be liberated to see his own flaws in their true light, to forgive those who had wronged him, or to humbly seek and receive forgiveness from others. The Christian doctrine of sin, properly understood, can be a great resource for human hope, but what is that doctrine?

161

## The Meaning of Sin

The famous Danish philosopher Søren Kierkegaard wrote a fascinating little book called *The Sickness Unto Death* in 1849. In it he defined 'sin' in a way that is rooted in the Bible but also is accessible to contemporary people. 'Sin is: in despair not wanting to be oneself before God. . . . Faith is: that the self in being itself and wanting to be itself is grounded transparently in God.'[3] Sin is the despairing refusal to find your deepest identity in your relationship and service to God. Sin is seeking to become oneself, to get an identity, apart from him.

What does this mean? Everyone gets their identity, their sense of being distinct and valuable, from somewhere or something. Kierkegaard asserts that human beings were made not only to believe in God in some general way, but to love him supremely, centre their lives on him above anything else, and build their very identities on him. Anything other than this is sin.

Most people think of sin primarily as 'breaking divine rules', but Kierkegaard knows that the very first of the Ten Commandments is to 'have no other gods before me'. So, according to the Bible, the primary way to define sin is not just the doing of bad things, but the making of good things into *ultimate* things. It is seeking to establish a sense of self by making something else more central to your significance, purpose and happiness than your relationship to God.

In the movie *Rocky*, the title character's girlfriend asks him why it is so important for him to 'go the distance' in the boxing match. 'Then I'll know I'm not a bum,' he replies. In the movie *Chariots of Fire* one of the main characters explains why he works so hard at running the hundred-yard dash for the Olympics. He says that when each race begins, 'I have ten lonely seconds to justify my existence.' Both of these men looked to athletic achievement as the defining force that gave meaning to their lives.

Ernest Becker won the Pulitzer Prize for his book *The Denial of Death*. He begins it by noting that a child's need for self-worth 'is *the* condition for his life', so much so that every person is desperately seeking what Becker calls 'cosmic significance'. He immediately warns the reader not to take this term lightly.[4] Our need for worth is so powerful that whatever we base our identity and value on we essentially 'deify'. We will look to it with all the passion and intensity of worship and devotion, even if we think of ourselves as highly irreligious. He uses romantic love as an illustration:

> *The self-glorification that [modern man] needed in his innermost nature he now looked for in the love partner. The love partner becomes the divine ideal within which to fulfill one's life. Spiritual and moral needs now become focused on one individual.*[5]

Becker is not saying that everyone looks to romance and love for a sense of self. Many look not to romance but rather to work and career for cosmic significance:

> *[Sometimes] his work has to carry the burden of justifying him. What does 'justifying' mean? . . . He lives the fantasy of the control of life and death, of destiny.*[6]

But all this only sets the stage for continual disappointment:

> *No human relationship can bear [this] burden of godhood. . . . If your partner is your 'All' then any shortcoming in him becomes a major threat to you. . . . What is it that we want when we elevate the love partner to this position? We want to be rid of . . . our feeling of nothingness . . . to know our existence has not been in*

*vain. We want redemption – nothing less. Needless to say, humans cannot give this.*[7]

This is exactly Kierkegaard's point. Every person must find *some* way to 'justify their existence', and to stave off the universal fear that they're 'a bum'. In more traditional cultures, the sense of worth and identity comes from fulfilling duties to family and giving service to society. In our contemporary individualistic culture, we tend to look to our achievements, our social status, our talents or our love relationships. There is an infinite variety of identity-bases. Some get their sense of 'self' from gaining and wielding power, others from human approval, others from self-discipline and control. But everyone is building their identity on something.[8]

## The Personal Consequences of Sin

Defining sin this way, we can see several ways that sin destroys us personally. Identity apart from God is inherently unstable. Without God, our sense of worth may seem solid on the surface, but it never is – it can desert you in a moment. For example, if I build my identity on being a good parent, I have no true 'self' – I am just a parent, nothing more. If something goes wrong with my children or my parenting, there is no 'me' left. Theologian Thomas Oden writes:

*Suppose my god is sex or my physical health or the Democratic Party. If I experience any of these under genuine threat, then I feel myself shaken to the depths. Guilt becomes neurotically intensified to the degree that I have idolized finite values. . . . Suppose I value my ability to teach and communicate clearly. . . . If*

*clear communication has become an absolute value for me, a*
*center of value that makes all my other values valuable . . . then*
*if I [fail in teaching well] I am stricken with neurotic guilt. Bit-*
*terness becomes neurotically intensified when someone or some-*
*thing stands between me and something that is my ultimate*
*value.*[9]

If anything threatens your identity you will not just be anxious but
paralysed with fear. If you lose your identity through the failings of
someone else you will not just be resentful, but locked into bitterness. If you lose it through your own failings, you will hate or despise yourself as a failure as long as you live. Only if your identity is
built on God and his love, says Kierkegaard, can you have a self that
can venture anything, face anything.

There is no way to avoid this insecurity outside of God. Even if
you say, 'I will not build *my* happiness or significance on anyone or
thing,' you will actually be building your identity on your personal
freedom and independence. If anything threatens *that*, you will
again be without a self.

An identity not based on God also leads inevitably to deep forms
of addiction. When we turn good things into ultimate things, we
are, as it were, spiritually addicted. If we take our meaning in life
from our family, our work, as cause, or some achievement other
than God, they enslave us. We have to have them. St Augustine said
that 'our loves are not rightly ordered'. He famously said to God,
'Our hearts are restless until they find their rest in Thee!' If we try
to find our ultimate rest in anything else, our hearts become dislo-
cated, 'out of joint'. The good things that enslave us are good
things that deserve to be loved. But when our heart loves become
inordinate, then we fall into patterns of life that are not unlike substance addiction. As in all addiction, we are in denial about the

degree to which we are controlled by our god-substitutes. And inordinate love creates inordinate, uncontrollable anguish if anything goes wrong with the object of our greatest hopes.

As a pastor at my first church in Hopewell, Virginia, I found myself counselling two different women, both of whom were married, both of whom had husbands who were poor fathers, and both of whom had teenage sons who were beginning to get into trouble in school and with the law. Both of the women were angry at their husbands. I advised them and talked (among other things) about the problems of unresolved bitterness and the importance of forgiveness. Both women agreed and sought to forgive. However, the woman who had the worst husband and who was the least religious was able to forgive. The other woman was not. This puzzled me for months until one day the unforgiving woman blurted out, 'Well, if my son goes down the drain then my whole life will have been a failure!' She had centred her life on her son's happiness and success. That was why she couldn't forgive.[10]

In *Easter Everywhere: A Memoir*, Darcey Steinke recounts how she, the daughter of a Lutheran minister, left her Christian profession. Moving to New York City she entered a life of club-hopping and sexual obsession. She wrote several novels. She continued, however, to be extremely restless and unfulfilled. In the middle of the book she quotes from Simone Weil to summarise the main issue in her life. 'One has only the choice between God and idolatry,' Weil wrote. 'If one denies God . . . one is worshipping some things of this world in the belief that one sees them only as such, but in fact, though unknown to oneself imagining the attributes of Divinity in them.'[11]

A life not centred on God leads to emptiness. Building our lives on something besides God not only hurts us if we don't get the desires of our hearts, but also if we *do*. Few of us get all of our wildest dreams fulfilled in life, and therefore it is easy to live in the illusion that if you were as successful, wealthy, popular or beautiful as you wished, you'd finally be happy and at peace. That just isn't so. In a *Village Voice* column, Cynthia Heimel thought back on all the people she knew in New York City before they became famous movie stars. One worked behind the make-up counter at Macy's, one worked selling tickets at cinemas, and so on. When they became successful, every one of them became more angry, manic, unhappy and unstable than they had been when they were working hard to get to the top. Why? Heimel writes:

> *That giant thing they were striving for, that fame thing that was going to make everything OK, that was going to make their lives bearable, that was going to fill them with ha-ha-happiness* had happened, *and the next day they woke up and they were still* them. *The disillusionment turned them howling and insufferable.*[12]

## The Social Consequences of Sin

Sin does not only have an internal impact on us but also a devastating effect on the social fabric. In the wake of the Second World War the English writer Dorothy Sayers saw many British intellectual elites in despair about the direction of human society. In her 1947 book *Creed or Chaos?* she proposed that their hopelessness was largely due to their loss of belief in the Christian doctrine of 'original' sin, that is, humanity's inherent pride and self-centredness. 'The people who are most discouraged,' she wrote, 'are those who cling to an optimistic belief in the civilizing influence of progress and enlightenment.' To them, the genocide in totalitarian states and the greed and selfishness of capitalist society 'are not merely shocking and alarming. For them, these things are the utter negation of everything in which they have believed. It is as though the bottom had dropped out of their universe.' Christians, however, are accustomed to the idea that 'there is a deep interior dislocation in the very center of human personality'. She concluded:

> *The Christian dogma of the double nature in man – which asserts that man is disintegrated and necessarily imperfect in himself and all his works, yet closely related by a real unity of substance with an eternal perfection within and beyond him – makes the present parlous state of human society seem less hopeless and less irrational.*[13]

In *The Nature of True Virtue*, one of the most profound treatises on social ethics ever written, Jonathan Edwards lays out how sin destroys the social fabric. He argues that human society is deeply fragmented when anything but God is our highest love. If our highest goal in life is the good of our family, then, says Edwards, we will tend to care less for other families. If our highest goal is the good of our nation, tribe or race, then we will tend to be racist or nationalistic. If our ultimate goal in life is our own individual happiness, then we will put our own economic and power interests ahead of those of others. Edwards concludes that only if God is our *summum bonum*, our ultimate good and life centre, will we find our heart drawn out not only to people of all families, races and classes, but to the whole world in general.[14]

How does this destruction of social relationships flow from the internal effects of sin? If we get our very identity, our sense of worth, from our political position, then politics is not really about politics, it is about *us*. Through our cause we are getting a self, our worth. That means we *must* despise and demonise the opposition. If we get our identity from our ethnicity or socioeconomic status, then we *have* to feel superior to those of other classes and races. If you are profoundly proud of being an open-minded, tolerant soul, you will be extremely indignant toward people you think are bigots. If you are a very moral person, you will feel very superior to people you think are licentious. And so on.

There is no way out of this conundrum. The more we love and identify deeply with our family, our class, our race or our religion, the harder it is to not feel superior or even hostile to other religions, races, etc. So racism, classism and sexism are not matters of ignorance or a lack of education. Foucault and others in our time have shown that it is far harder than we think to have a self-identity that doesn't lead to exclusion. The real culture war is taking place inside our own disordered hearts, wracked by inordinate desires for things that control us, that lead us to feel superior and exclude those without them, and that fail to satisfy us even when we get them.

## The Cosmic Consequences of Sin

The Bible speaks even more comprehensively (and more mysteriously) about the effects of sin than we have indicated so far. The first and second chapters of Genesis show God speaking the world into being and, almost literally, getting his hands dirty. 'And God formed man from the dust of the ground and breathed into his nostrils the breath of life' (Genesis 2:7). The contrast with all other ancient creation accounts could not be greater.

In most ancient creation accounts, creation is the by-product of some kind of warfare or other act of violence. Virtually never is the creation deliberate and planned. Secular scientific accounts of the origin of things are, interestingly, almost identical to the older pagan ones. The physical shape of the world as well as the biological life is the product of violent forces.

Unique among the creation accounts, the Bible depicts a world that is brimming with dynamic, abundant forms of life that are perfectly interwoven, interdependent and mutually enhancing and enriching. The Creator's response to this is delight. He keeps repeating that it is all *good*. When he creates human beings he instructs them to continue to cultivate and draw out the vast resources of creation like a gardener does in a garden. 'Go keep this going,' the Creator seems to be saying in Genesis 1:28, 'Have a ball!'[15]

The Hebrew word for this perfect, harmonious interdependence among all parts of creation is called *shalom*. We translate it as 'peace', but the English word is basically negative, referring to the absence of trouble or hostility. The Hebrew word means much more than that. It means absolute wholeness – full, harmonious, joyful, flourishing life.

The devastating loss of *shalom* through sin is described in Genesis 3. We are told that as soon as we determined to serve ourselves instead of God – as soon as we abandoned living for and enjoying God as our highest good – the entire created world became broken. Human beings are so integral to the fabric of things that when human beings turned from God the entire warp and woof of the world unravelled. Disease, genetic disorders, famine, natural disasters, ageing and death itself are as much the result of sin as are oppression, war, crime and violence. We have lost God's *shalom* – physically, spiritually, socially, psychologically, culturally. Things now fall apart. In Romans 8, Paul says that the entire world is now 'in bondage to decay' and 'subject to futility' and will not be put right until we are put right.

## What Can Put It All Right?

At some point in most lives, we are confronted with the fact that we are not the persons we know we should be. Almost always our response is to 'turn over a new leaf' and try harder to live according to our principles. That ultimately will only lead us into a spiritual dead end.

In C. S. Lewis's essay 'Is Christianity Hard or Easy?' he depicts normal human striving:

> *The ordinary idea which we all have is that . . . we have a natural self with various desires and interests . . . and we know something called 'morality' or 'decent behaviour' has a claim on the self. . . . We are all hoping that when all the demands of morality and society have been met, the poor natural self will still have some chance, some time, to get on with its own life and do what it likes. In fact, we are very like an honest man paying his taxes. He pays them, but he does hope that there will be enough left over for him to live on.*

> *The Christian way is different – both harder and easier. Christ says, 'Give me ALL. I don't want just this much of your time and this much of your money and this much of your work – so that your natural self can have the rest. I want you. Not your things. I have come not to torture your natural self . . . I will give you a new self instead. Hand over the whole natural self – ALL the desires, not just the ones you think wicked but the ones you think innocent – the whole outfit. I will give you a new self instead.'*

Here Lewis works from Kierkegaard's definition of sin. Sin is not simply doing bad things, it is putting good things in the place of God. So the only solution is not simply to change our behaviour, but to reorient and centre the entire heart and life on God.

> *The almost impossibly hard thing is to hand over your whole self to Christ. But it is far easier than what we are all trying to do*

*instead. For what we are trying to do is remain what we call 'ourselves' – our personal happiness centred on money or pleasure or ambition – and hoping, despite this, to behave honestly and chastely and humbly. And that is exactly what Christ warned us you cannot do. If I am a grass field – all the cutting will keep the grass less but won't produce wheat. If I want wheat . . . I must be ploughed up and re-sown.*

Does that scare you? Does it sound stifling? Remember this – if you don't live for Jesus you will live for something else. If you live for career and you don't do well it may punish you all of your life, and you will feel like a failure. If you live for your children and they don't turn out all right you could be absolutely in torment because you feel worthless as a person.

If Jesus is your centre and Lord and you fail him, he will forgive you. Your career can't die for your sins. You might say, 'If I were a Christian I'd be going around pursued by guilt all the time!' But we *all* are being pursued by guilt because we must have an identity and there must be *some* standard to live up to by which we get that identity. Whatever you base your life on – you have to live up to *that*. Jesus is the one Lord you can live for who died for you – who breathed his last breath for you. Does that sound oppressive?

You may say, 'I see that Christianity might be just the thing for people who have had collapses in their lives. But what if I don't fail in my career and what if I have a *great* family?' As Augustine said, if there is a God who created you, then the deepest chambers of your soul simply cannot be filled up by anything less. That is how great the human soul is. If Jesus is the Creator-Lord, then by definition nothing could satisfy you like he can, even if you are successful. Even the most successful careers and families cannot give the significance, security and affirmation that the author of glory and love can.

Everybody has to live for something. Whatever that something is becomes 'Lord of your life', whether you think of it that way or not. Jesus is the only Lord who, if you receive him, will fulfil you completely, and, if you fail him, will forgive you eternally.

# ELEVEN

## RELIGION AND THE GOSPEL

*At the very moment of that vain-glorious thought, a qualm
came over me, a horrid nausea and the most dreadful shudder-
ing . . . I looked down . . . I was once more Edward Hyde.*

—Robert Louis Stevenson,
*The Strange Case of Dr Jekyll and Mr Hyde*

CHRISTIANITY teaches that our main problem is sin. What
then is the solution? Even if you accept the Christian diagno-
sis of the problem, there doesn't seem to be any particular reason
why one must look only to Christianity for the solution. You may
say, 'Fine, I understand that if you build your identity on anything
but God, it leads to breakdown. Why must the solution be Jesus
and Christianity? Why can't some other religion do as well, or just
my own personal faith in God?'

The answer to that is that there is a profound and fundamental
difference between the way that other religions tell us to seek salvation and the way described in the gospel of Jesus. All other major
faiths have founders who are teachers who show the way to salvation. Only Jesus claimed to actually *be* the way of salvation himself.
This difference is so great that, even though Christianity can certainly be called a religion in the broader sense, for the purposes of
discussion we will use the term 'religion' in this chapter to refer to

174

'salvation through moral effort' and 'gospel' to refer to 'salvation through grace'.[1]

## Two Forms of Self-Centredness

In Robert Louis Stevenson's *The Strange Case of Dr Jekyll and Mr Hyde*, Dr Jekyll comes to realise that he is 'an incongruous compound of good and evil'. His bad nature is holding his good nature back, he believes. He can aspire to do things, but he cannot follow through on them. Therefore he comes up with a potion that can separate out his two natures. His hope is that his good self, which will come out during the day, will be free from the influence of evil and will be able to realise its goals. However, when he takes the potion one night and his bad side comes out, he is far more evil than he expected. He describes his evil self using classic Christian categories:

> *I knew myself, at the first breath of this new life, to be more wicked, tenfold more wicked, sold a slave to my original evil; and the thought in that moment, braced and delighted me like wine. . . . [Edward Hyde's] every act and thought centred on self.*

Edward Hyde is so named not just because he is hideous but because he is hidden. He thinks solely of his own desires; he doesn't care in the slightest who he hurts in order to gratify himself. He kills if someone gets in his way. Stevenson is saying that even the best of people hide from themselves what is within – an enormous capacity for egotism, self-absorption and regard for your own interests over those of all others. Self-aggrandisement is at the foundation of so much of the misery of the world. It is the reason that the powerful and the rich are indifferent to the plight of the poor.

It is the reason for most of the violence, crime and warfare in the world. It is at the heart of most cases of family disintegration. We hide from ourselves our self-centred capacity for acts of evil, but situations arise that act as a 'potion', and out they come.

Once Jekyll realises that he has this capacity for evil acts, he decides to clamp down heavily on this terrible self-centredness and pride at the core of his being. In a sense, he 'gets religion'. He solemnly resolves not to take the potion any more. He devotes himself to charity and good works, partially as atonement for what Edward Hyde has done, and partially as an effort to simply smother his selfish nature with acts of unselfishness.

However, one day Dr Jekyll is sitting on a bench in Regent's Park, thinking about all the good he has been doing, and how much better a man he was, despite Edward Hyde, than the great majority of people.

> I resolved in my future conduct to redeem the past; and I can say with honesty that my resolve was fruitful of some good. You know how earnestly, in the last months of the last year, I laboured to relieve suffering; you know that much was done for others. . . . [But as] I smiled, comparing myself with other men, comparing my active goodwill with the lazy cruelty of their neglect . . . at the very moment of that vain-glorious thought, a qualm came over me, a horrid nausea and the most dreadful shuddering. . . . I looked down. . . . I was once more Edward Hyde.

This is a deadly turn of events. For the first time Jekyll becomes Hyde involuntarily, without the potion, and this is the beginning of the end. Unable to control his transformations any longer, Jekyll kills himself. Stevenson's insight here is, I think, profound. Why would Jekyll become Hyde without the potion? Like so many people, Jekyll knows he is a sinner, so he tries desperately to cover his sin with great

176

piles of good works. Yet his efforts do not actually shrivel his pride and self-centredness, they only aggravate it. They lead him to superiority, self-righteousness, pride and suddenly – look! Jekyll becomes Hyde, not in spite of his goodness, but because of his goodness.

Sin and evil are self-centredness and pride that lead to oppression against others, but there are two forms of this. One form is being very bad and breaking all the rules, and the other form is being very good and keeping all the rules and becoming self-righteous. There are two ways to be your own Saviour and Lord. The first is by saying, 'I am going to live my life the way *I* want.' The second is described by Flannery O'Connor, who wrote about one of her characters, Hazel Motes, that 'he knew that the best way to avoid Jesus was to avoid sin'.[2] If you are avoiding sin and living morally so that God will have to bless and save you, then ironically, you may be looking to Jesus as a teacher, model and helper but you are avoiding him as Saviour. You are trusting in your own goodness rather than in Jesus for your standing with God. You are trying to save yourself by following Jesus.

That, ironically, is a rejection of the gospel of Jesus. It is a Christianised form of religion. It is possible to avoid Jesus as Saviour as much by keeping all the biblical rules as by breaking them. Both religion (in which you build your identity on your moral achievements) and irreligion (in which you build your identity on some other secular pursuit or relationship) are, ultimately, spiritually identical courses to take. Both are 'sin'. Self-salvation through good works may produce a great deal of moral behaviour in your life, but inside you are filled with self-righteousness, cruelty and bigotry, and you are miserable. You are always comparing yourself to other people, and you are never sure you are being good enough. You cannot, therefore, deal with your hideousness and self-absorption through the moral law, by trying to be a good person through an act of the will. You need a complete transformation of the very motives of your heart.

The devil, if anything, prefers Pharisees – men and women who try to save themselves. They are more unhappy than either mature Christians *or* irreligious people, and they do a lot more spiritual damage.

## The Damage of Pharisaism

Why is Pharisaic religion so damaging? Recall the 'sickness unto death', the spiritual deep nausea we experience when we fail to build our identity on God. We struggle for a sense of worth, purpose and distinctiveness, but it is based on conditions that we can never achieve or maintain, and that are always slipping away from us. As Kierkegaard says, we have not become ourselves. This is experienced internally as anxiety, insecurity and anger. It leads us externally to marginalise, oppress and exclude others.

Despite all their legal righteousness, then, Pharisees have lives that are, if anything, *more* driven by the despair of sin. They build their sense of worth on their moral and spiritual performance, as a kind of résumé to present before God and the world. The moral and spiritual standards of all religions are very high, and Pharisees know deep down that they are not fully living up to those standards. They are not praying as often as they should. They are not loving and serving their neighbour as much as they should. They are not keeping their inner thoughts as pure as they should. The resulting internal anxiety, insecurity and irritability will often be much greater than anything experienced by the irreligious.

Richard Lovelace captures well another way that Pharisaic religion is so damaging:

*Many . . . draw their assurance of acceptance with God from their sincerity, their past experience of conversion, their recent religious performance or the relative infrequency of their con-*

*scious, wilful disobedience. . . . Their insecurity shows itself in*
*pride, a fierce, defensive assertion of their own righteousness,*
*and defensive criticism of others. They come naturally to hate*
*other cultural styles and other races in order to bolster their own*
*security and discharge their suppressed anger.*[3]

As Lovelace says, Pharisaic religion doesn't just damage the inner
soul, it also creates social strife. Pharisees need to shore up their
sense of righteousness, so they despise and attack all who don't
share their doctrinal beliefs and religious practices. Racism and cultural imperialism result. Churches that are filled with self-righteous,
exclusive, insecure, angry, moralistic people are extremely unattractive. Their public pronouncements are often highly judgemental, while internally such churches experience many bitter
conflicts, splits and divisions. When one of their leaders has a moral
lapse, the churches either rationalise it and denounce the leader's
critics, or else they scapegoat him. Millions of people raised in or
near these kinds of churches reject Christianity at an early age or in
college largely because of their experience. For the rest of their
lives, then, they are inoculated against Christianity. If you are
someone who has been disillusioned by such churches, when anyone recommends Christianity to you, you assume they are calling
you to adopt 'religion'. Pharisees and their unattractive lives leave
many people confused about the real nature of Christianity.

## The Difference of Grace

There is, then, a great gulf between the understanding that God
accepts us because of our efforts and the understanding that God
accepts us because of what Jesus has done. Religion operates on the
principle 'I obey – therefore I am accepted by God.' But the operating principle of the gospel is 'I am accepted by God through what

Christ has done – therefore I obey.' Two people living their lives on the basis of these two different principles may sit next to each other in the church pew. They both pray, give money generously and are loyal and faithful to their family and church, trying to live decent lives. However, they do so out of two radically different motivations, in two radically different spiritual identities, and the result is two radically different kinds of lives.

The primary difference is that of motivation. In religion, we try to obey the divine standards out of fear. We believe that if we don't obey we are going to lose God's blessing in this world and the next. In the gospel, the motivation is one of gratitude for the blessing we have already received because of Christ. While the moralist is forced into obedience, motivated by fear of rejection, a Christian rushes into obedience, motivated by a desire to please and resemble the one who gave his life for us.

Another difference has to do with our identity and self-regard. In a religious framework, if you feel you are living up to your chosen religious standards, then you feel superior and disdainful toward those who are not following in the true path. This is true whether your religion is of a more liberal variety (in which case you will feel superior to bigots and narrow-minded people) or of a more conservative variety (in which case you will feel superior to the less moral and devout). If you are not living up to your chosen standards, then you will be filled with a loathing toward yourself. You will feel far more guilt than if you had stayed away from God and religion altogether.

When my own personal grasp of the gospel was very weak, my self-view swung wildly between two poles. When I was performing up to my standards – in academic work, professional achievement or relationships – I felt confident but not humble. I was likely to be proud and unsympathetic to failing people. When I was not living up to standards, I felt humble but not confident, a failure. I discovered, however, that the gospel contained the resources to build a unique identity. In Christ I could know I was accepted by grace not only despite my flaws, but because I was willing to admit them. The Christian gospel is that I am so flawed that Jesus had to die for me, yet I am so loved and valued and that Jesus was glad to die for me. This leads to deep humility and deep confidence at the same time. It undermines both swaggering and snivelling. I cannot feel superior to anyone, and yet I have nothing to prove to anyone. I do not think more of myself nor less of myself. Instead, I think of myself less. I don't need to notice myself – how I'm doing, how I'm being regarded – so often.

Religion and the gospel also differ fundamentally in how they treat the Other – those who do not share one's own beliefs and practices. Postmodern thinkers understand that the self is formed and strengthened through the exclusion of the Other – those who do not have the values or traits on which I base my own significance. We define ourselves by pointing to those whom we are not. We bolster our sense of worth by devaluing those of other races, beliefs and traits.[4] This gospel identity gives us a new basis for harmonious and just social arrangements. A Christian's worth and value are not created by excluding anyone, but through the Lord who was excluded for me. His grace both humbles me more deeply than religion can (since I am too flawed to ever save myself through my own effort), yet it also affirms me more powerfully than religion can (since I can be absolutely certain of God's unconditional acceptance).

That means that I cannot despise those who do not believe as I do. Since I am not saved by my correct doctrine or practice, then this person before me, even with his or her wrong beliefs, might be morally superior to me in many ways. It also means I do not have to be intimidated by anyone. I am not so insecure that I fear the power or success or talent of people who are different from me. The gospel makes it possible for a person to escape oversensitivity, defensiveness and the need to criticise others. The Christian's identity is not based on the need to be perceived as a good person, but on God's valuing of you in Christ.

Religion and the gospel also lead to divergent ways of handling troubles and suffering. Moralistic religion leads its participants to the conviction that if they live an upstanding life, then God (and others) owe them respect and favour. They believe they deserve a decent, happy life. If, however, life begins to go wrong, moralists will experience debilitating anger. Either they will be furious with God (or 'the universe') because they feel that since they live better than others, they should have a better life. Or else they will be deeply angry at themselves, unable to shake the feeling that they have not lived as they should or kept up to standards. The gospel, however, makes it possible for someone to escape the spiral of bitterness, self-recrimination and despair when life goes wrong. They know that the basic premise of religion – that if you live a good life, things will go well for you – is wrong. Jesus was the most morally upright person who ever lived, yet he had a life filled with the experience of poverty, rejection, injustice and even torture.

## The Threat of Grace

When many first hear the distinction between religion and the gospel, they think that it just sounds too easy. 'Nice deal!' they may say. 'If that is Christianity, all I have to do is get a personal relationship to God and then do anything I want!' Those words, however, can only be spoken on the outside of an experience of radical grace. No one from the inside speaks like that. In fact, grace can be quite threatening.

Some years ago I met with a woman who began coming to church at Redeemer. She said that she had gone to church growing up and had never before heard a distinction drawn between the gospel and religion. She had always heard that God accepts us only if we are good enough. She said that the new message was scary. I asked her why it was scary, and she replied:

> *If I was saved by my good works then there would be a limit to what God could ask of me or put me through. I would be like a taxpayer with 'rights' – I would have done my duty and now I would deserve a certain quality of life. But if I am a sinner saved by sheer grace – then there's nothing he cannot ask of me.*

She understood the dynamic of grace and gratitude. If when you have lost all fear of punishment you also lose all incentive to live a good, unselfish life, then the only incentive you ever had to live a decent life was fear. This woman could see immediately that the wonderful-beyond-belief teaching of salvation by sheer grace had an edge to it. She knew that if she was a sinner saved by grace, she was (if anything) more subject to the sovereign Lordship of God. She knew that if Jesus really had done all this for her, she would not be her own. She would joyfully, gratefully belong to Jesus, who provided all this for her at infinite cost to himself.

From the outside that might sound coercive, like a grinding obligation. From the inside the motivation is all joy. Think of what happens when you fall in love. Your love makes you eager for acceptance from the beloved. You ask, 'Do you want to go out?' or maybe even, 'Will you marry me?' What happens when the answer is 'Yes'? Do you say, 'Great! I'm in! Now I can act any way I want'? Of course not. Now you don't even wait for the object of your affection to directly ask you to do something for them. You anticipate whatever pleases and delights them. There's no coercion or sense of obligation, yet your behaviour has been radically changed by the mind and heart of the person you love.

No one put this more vividly than Victor Hugo in *Les Misérables*. His main character, Jean Valjean, is a bitter ex-convict. He steals silver from a bishop who has already shown him kindness. He is caught by gendarmes, and is brought back under arrest to the bishop's home. In an act of radical grace the bishop gives Valjean the silver and releases him from arrest. This act of mercy shakes him to the core. In the following chapter Hugo spells out how threatening this grace was:

> *To this celestial kindness [of the bishop] he opposed pride, which is the fortress of evil within us. He was indistinctly conscious that the pardon of this priest was the greatest assault and the most formidable attack which had moved him yet; that his obduracy was finally settled if he resisted this clemency; that if he yielded, he should be obliged to renounce that hatred with which the actions of other men had filled his soul through so many years, and which pleased him; that this time it was necessary to conquer or to be conquered; and that a struggle, a colossal and final struggle, had been begun between his viciousness and the goodness of that man.*[5]

Valjean chooses to let grace have its way with him. He gives up his deep self-pity and bitterness and begins to live a life of graciousness toward others. He is changed at the root of his being.

The other main character in the novel is the police officer Javert, who has built his entire life on his understanding of rewards and punishments. He relentlessly and self-righteously pursues Valjean throughout the book, even though it is wrecking his own life. Finally, Javert falls into Valjean's hands. Instead of killing him, Valjean lets his enemy go. This act of radical grace is deeply troublesome to Javert. He realises that to appropriately respond to this gesture will require a complete change in his worldview. Rather than make that change, he throws himself into the Seine.

This may seem the greatest paradox of all. The most liberating act of free, unconditional grace demands that the recipient give up control of his or her life. Is that a contradiction? No, not if you remember the point of Chapters 3 and 9. We are not *in* control of our lives. We are all living for something and we are controlled by that, the true lord of our lives. If it is not God, it will endlessly oppress us. It is only *grace* that frees us from the slavery of self that lurks even in the middle of morality and religion. Grace is only a threat to the illusion that we are free, autonomous selves, living life as we choose.

The gospel makes it possible to have such a radically different life. Christians, however, often fail to make use of the resources of the gospel to live the lives they are capable of in Christ. It is critical for anyone reading this book to recognise this fundamental difference between the gospel and religion. Christianity's basic message differs *at root* with the assumptions of traditional religion. The founders of every other major religion essentially came as teachers, not as saviours. They came to say: 'Do this and you will find the divine.' But Jesus came essentially as a saviour rather than a teacher (though he was that as well). Jesus says: 'I am the divine come to *you*, to do what you could not do for yourselves.' The Christian message is that we are saved not by our record, but by Christ's record. So Christianity is not religion or irreligion. It is something else altogether.

# TWELVE

# THE (TRUE) STORY OF THE CROSS

*I could accept Jesus as a martyr, and embodiment of sacrifice, and a divine teacher. His death on the cross was a great example to the world, but that there was anything like a mysterious or miraculous virtue in it, my heart could not accept.*

—Gandhi, *An Autobiography*

*I would catch a glimpse of the cross – and suddenly my heart would stand still. In an instinctive, intuitive way I understood that something more important, more tumultuous, more passionate, was at issue than our good causes, however noble they might be. . . . I should have worn it. . . . It should have been my uniform, my language, my life. I shall have no excuse; I can't say I didn't know. I knew from the beginning, and turned away.*

—Malcolm Muggeridge, *Jesus Rediscovered*

THE primary symbol of Christianity has always been the cross. The death of Jesus for our sins is at the heart of the gospel, the good news. Increasingly, however, what the Christian church has considered good news is considered by the rest of our culture to be bad news.

In the Christian account, Jesus dies so that God can forgive sins. For many, that seems ludicrous or even sinister. 'Why would Jesus *have* to die?' is a question that I have heard from people in New York far more often than 'Does God exist?' 'Why couldn't God just forgive us?' they ask. 'The Christian God sounds like the vengeful gods of primitive times who needed to be appeased by human sacrifice.' Why can't God just accept everyone or at least those who are sorry for their wrongdoings? While the Christian doctrine of the cross confuses some people, it alarms others. Some liberal Protestant theologians reject the doctrine of the cross altogether because it looks to them like 'divine child abuse'.

Why, then, don't we just leave the cross out? Why not focus on the life of Jesus and his teachings rather than on his death? Why did Jesus have to die?

## The First Reason: Real Forgiveness Is Costly Suffering

Let's begin with a purely economic example. Imagine that someone borrows your car, and as he backs it out of the driveway he strikes a gate, knocking it down along with part of a wall. Your property insurance doesn't cover the gate and garden wall. What can you do? There are essentially two options. The first is to demand that he pay for the damages. The second is to refuse to let him pay anything. There may also be middle-of-the-road solutions in which you both share the payment. Notice that in every option the cost of the damage must be borne by *some*one. Either you or he absorbs the cost for the deed, but the debt does not somehow vanish into thin air. Forgiveness, in this illustration, means bearing the cost for his misdeed yourself.

Most of the wrongs done to us cannot be assessed in purely

economic terms. Someone may have robbed you of some happiness, reputation, opportunity or certain aspects of your freedom. No price tag can be put on such things, yet we still have a sense of violated justice that does not go away when the other person says, 'I'm really sorry.' When we are seriously wronged we have an indelible sense that the perpetrators have incurred a debt that must be dealt with. Once you have been wronged and you realise there is a just debt that can't simply be dismissed – there are only two things to do.

The first option is to seek ways to make the perpetrators suffer for what they have done. You can withhold relationship and actively initiate or passively wish for some kind of pain in their lives commensurate to what you experienced. There are many ways to do this. You can viciously confront them, saying things that hurt. You can go around to others to tarnish their reputation. If the perpetrators suffer, you may begin to feel a certain satisfaction, feeling that they are now paying off their debt.

There are some serious problems with this option, however. You may become harder and colder, more self-pitying, and therefore more self-absorbed. If the wrongdoer was a person of wealth or authority you may instinctively dislike and resist that sort of person for the rest of your life. If it was a person of the opposite sex or another race you might become permanently cynical and prejudiced against whole classes of people. In addition, the perpetrator and his friends and family often feel they have the right to respond to your payback in kind. Cycles of reaction and retaliation can go on for years. Evil has been done to you – yes. But when you try to get payment through revenge the evil does not disappear. Instead it spreads, and it spreads most tragically of all into you and your own character.

There is another option, however. You can forgive. Forgiveness means refusing to make them pay for what they did. However, to refrain from lashing out at someone when you want to do so with all your being is *agony*. It is a form of suffering. You not only suffer the original loss of happiness, reputation and opportunity, but now you forgo the consolation of inflicting the same on them. You are absorbing the debt, taking the cost of it completely on yourself instead of taking it out of the other person. It hurts terribly. Many people would say it feels like a kind of death.

Yes, but it is a death that leads to resurrection instead of the lifelong living death of bitterness and cynicism. As a pastor I have counselled many people about forgiveness, and I have found that if they do this – if they simply refuse to take vengeance on the wrongdoer in action and even in their inner fantasies – the anger slowly begins to subside. You are not giving it any fuel and so the resentment burns lower and lower. C. S. Lewis wrote in one of his *Letters to Malcolm* that 'last week, while at prayer, I suddenly discovered – or felt as if I did – that I had really forgiven someone I had been trying to forgive for over thirty years. Trying, and praying that I might.'[1] I remember once counselling a sixteen-year-old girl about the anger she felt towards her father. We weren't getting anywhere until I said to her, 'Your father has defeated you, as long as you hate him. You will stay trapped in your anger unless you forgive him thoroughly from the heart and begin to love him.' Something thawed in her when she realised that. She went through the suffering of costly forgiveness, which at first always feels far worse than bitterness, into eventual freedom. Forgiveness must be granted before it can be felt, but it does come eventually. It leads to a new peace, a resurrection. It is the only way to stop the spread of the evil.

When I counsel forgiveness to people who have been harmed, they often ask about the wrongdoers, 'Shouldn't they be held accountable?' I usually respond, 'Yes, but only if you forgive them.' There are many good reasons that we should want to confront wrongdoers. Wrongdoers have inflicted damage and, as in the example of the gate I presented earlier, it costs something to fix the damage. We should confront wrongdoers – to wake them up to their real character, to move them to repair their relationships, or to at least constrain them and protect others from being harmed by them in the future. Notice, however, that all those reasons for confrontation are reasons of love. The best way to love them and the other potential victims around them is to confront them in the hope that they will repent, change and make things right.

The desire for vengeance, however, is motivated not by goodwill but by ill will. You may say, 'I just want to hold them accountable,' but your real motivation may be simply to see them hurt. If you are not confronting them for their sake or for society's sake but for your own sake, just for payback, the chance of the wrongdoer ever coming to repentance is virtually nil. In such a case you, the confronter, will overreach, seeking not justice but revenge, not their change but their pain. Your demands will be excessive and your attitude abusive. He or she will rightly see the confrontation as intended simply to cause hurt. A cycle of retaliation will begin.

Only if you first seek inner forgiveness will your confrontation be temperate, wise and gracious. Only when you have lost the need to see the other person hurt will you have any chance of actually bringing about change, reconciliation and healing. You have to submit to the costly suffering and death of forgiveness if there is going to be any resurrection.

No one embodied the costliness of forgiveness any better than Dietrich Bonhoeffer, whose story I recounted in Chapter 4.[2] After Bonhoeffer returned to Germany to resist Hitler, he wrote in *The Cost of Discipleship* (1937) that true forgiveness is always a form of suffering.

*My brother's burden which I must bear is not only his outward lot, his natural characteristics and gifts, but quite literally his sin. And the only way to bear that sin is by forgiving it in the power of*

*the cross of Christ in which I now share. . . . Forgiveness is the*
*Christlike suffering which it is the Christian's duty to bear.*[3]

In April 1943 Bonhoeffer was arrested and imprisoned. He was
eventually moved to Flossenburg concentration camp and executed
just before the end of the Second World War.

How did Bonhoeffer live out his own words? His forgiveness
was costly suffering, because it actually confronted the hurt and
evil before him. His forgiveness was not what he called (in *The Cost
of Discipleship*) 'cheap grace'. He did not ignore or excuse sin. He
resisted it head on, even though it cost him everything. His forgiveness was also costly because he refused to hate. He passed through
the agonising process required to love your enemies, so his resistance to their evildoing was measured and courageous, not venom-
ous and cruel. The startling evidence for this is found in the letters
and papers that Bonhoeffer wrote while in prison. The lack of bitterness was remarkable.

*Please don't ever get anxious or worried about me, but don't*
*forget to pray for me – I'm sure you don't. I am so sure of God's*
*guiding hand that I hope I shall always be kept in that certainty.*
*You must never doubt that I'm travelling with gratitude and*
*cheerfulness along the road where I'm being led. My past life is*
*brim-full of God's goodness and my sins are covered by the forgiv-*
*ing love of Christ crucified. . . .*[4]

Here we see Bonhoeffer simply living out what Jesus had done for
him. Jesus bore his sins, bearing the cost of them. Now Bonhoeffer
is free to do the same for others. Bonhoeffer uses divine forgiveness
to help him understand human forgiveness. But let's now use Bonhoeffer's marvellous example of human forgiveness to understand
the divine.

## The Forgiveness of God

'Why did Jesus have to die? Couldn't God just forgive us?' This is what many ask, but now we can see that no one 'just' forgives, if the evil is serious. Forgiveness means bearing the cost instead of making the wrongdoer do it, so you can reach out in love to seek your enemy's renewal and change. Forgiveness means absorbing the debt of the sin yourself. Everyone who forgives great evil goes through a death into resurrection, and experiences nails, blood, sweat and tears.

Should it surprise us, then, that when God determined to forgive us rather than punish us for all the ways we have wronged him and one another, that he went to the cross in the person of Jesus Christ and died there? As Bonhoeffer says, everyone who forgives someone bears the other's sins. On the cross we see God doing visibly and cosmically what every human being must do to forgive someone, though on an infinitely greater scale. I would argue, of course, that human forgiveness works this way because we unavoidably reflect the image of our Creator. That is why we should not be surprised that if *we* sense that the only way to triumph over evil is to go through the suffering of forgiveness, that this would be far more true of God, whose just passion to defeat evil and loving desire to forgive others are both infinitely greater than ours.

It is crucial at this point to remember that the Christian faith has always understood that Jesus Christ is God.[5] God did not, then, inflict pain on someone else, but rather on the cross absorbed the pain, violence and evil of the world into himself. Therefore the God of the Bible is not like the primitive deities who demanded our blood for their wrath to be appeased. Rather, this is a God who becomes human and offers his own lifeblood in order to honour moral justice and merciful love so that some day he can destroy all evil without destroying us.

Therefore the cross is not simply a lovely example of sacrificial love. Throwing your life away needlessly is not admirable – it is wrong.[6] Jesus' death was only a good example if it was more than an example, if it was something absolutely necessary to rescue us. And it was. Why did Jesus *have* to die in order to forgive us? There was a debt to be paid – God himself paid it. There was a penalty to be borne – God himself bore it. Forgiveness is always a form of costly suffering.

We have seen how human forgiveness and its costliness sheds light on divine forgiveness. However, it is divine forgiveness that is the ultimate ground and resource for the human. Bonhoeffer repeatedly attested to this, claiming that it was Jesus' forgiveness of him on the cross that gave him such a security in God's love that he could live a life of sacrificial service to others.

## The Second Reason: Real Love Is a Personal Exchange

In the mid-nineties, a Protestant denomination held a theological conference in which one speaker said, 'I don't think we need a theory of atonement at all; I don't think we need folks hanging on crosses and blood dripping and weird stuff.'[7] Why can't we just concentrate on teaching about how God is a God of love? The answer is that if you take away the cross you don't *have* a God of love.

In the real world of relationships it is impossible to love people with a problem or a need without in some sense sharing or even changing places with them. All real life-changing love involves some form of this kind of exchange.

It requires very little of you to love a person who is pulled together and happy. Think, however, of emotionally wounded people. There is no way to listen and love people like that and stay completely emotionally intact yourself. It may be that they may feel

193

stronger and more affirmed as you talk, but that won't happen without you being quite emotionally drained yourself. It's them or you. To bring them up emotionally you must be willing to be drained emotionally.

Take another example. Imagine you come into contact with a man who is innocent, but who is being hunted down by secret agents or by the government or by some other powerful group. He reaches out to you for help. If you don't help him, he will probably die, but if you ally with him, you – who were perfectly safe and secure – will be in mortal danger. This is the stuff that movie plots are made of. Again, it's him or you. He will experience increased safety and security through your involvement, but only because you are willing to enter into his insecurity and vulnerability.

Consider parenting. Children come into the world in a condition of complete dependence. They cannot operate as self-sufficient, independent agents unless their parents give up much of their own independence and freedom for years. If you don't allow your children to hinder your freedom in work and play at all, and if you only get to your children when it doesn't inconvenience you, your children will grow up physically only. In all sorts of other ways they will remain emotionally needy, troubled and overdependent. The choice is clear. You can either sacrifice your freedom or theirs. It's them or you. To love your children well, you must decrease that they may increase. You must be willing to enter into the dependency they have so eventually they can experience the freedom and independence you have.

All life-changing love towards people with serious needs is a substitutional sacrifice. If you become personally involved with them, in some way, their weaknesses flow towards you as your strengths flow toward them. In *The Cross of Christ*, John Stott writes that substitution is at the heart of the Christian message:

194

*The essence of sin is we human beings substituting ourselves for God, while the essence of salvation is God substituting himself for us. We . . . put ourselves where only God deserves to be; God . . . puts himself where we deserve to be.*[8]

If that is true, how can God be a God of love if he does not become personally involved in suffering the same violence, oppression, grief, weakness and pain that we experience? The answer to that question is twofold. First, God can't. Second, only one major world religion even claims that God does.

## The Great Reversal

JoAnne Terrell wrote about how her mother was murdered by her mother's boyfriend. 'I had to find a connection between my mom's story and my story and Jesus' story,' she said. She found it in understanding the cross – namely, that Jesus did not only suffer for us but with us. He knew what it was like (literally) to be under the lash, and to refuse to be cowed by those in power, and to pay for it with his life. He voluntarily took his place beside those who were without power and suffering from injustice.[9] As John Stott wrote, 'I could never myself believe in God if it were not for the cross. In the real world of pain, how could one worship a God who was immune to it?'

Therefore the cross, when properly understood, cannot possibly be used to encourage the oppressed to simply accept violence. When Jesus suffered for us, he was honouring justice. But when Jesus suffered with us he was identifying with the oppressed of the world, not with their oppressors. All life-changing love entails an exchange, a reversal of places, but here is the Great Reversal. God, in the place of ultimate power, reverses places with the marginalised, the poor and the oppressed. The prophets always sang songs about God as one who has 'brought down rulers from their thrones but has lifted up the poor' (Luke 1:52), but never could they have imagined that God himself would come down off his ultimate throne and suffer with the oppressed so that they might be lifted up.

This pattern of the cross means that the world's glorification of power, might and status is exposed and defeated. On the cross Christ wins through losing, triumphs through defeat, achieves power through weakness and service, comes to wealth via giving all away. Jesus Christ turns the values of the world upside down. As N. T. Wright says:

> *The real enemy, after all, was not Rome but the powers of evil that stood behind human arrogance and violence. . . . [On the cross] the kingdom of God triumphed over the kingdoms of this world by refusing to join in their spiral of violence. [On the cross, Jesus] would love his enemies, turn the other cheek, go the second mile.*[10]

This upside-down pattern so contradicts the thinking and practice of the world that it creates an 'alternative kingdom', an alternative reality, a counterculture among those who have been transformed by it. In this peaceable kingdom there is a reversal of the values of the world with regard to power, recognition, status and wealth. In this new counterculture, Christians look at money as something to give away. They look at power as something to use strictly for service. Racial and class superiority, accrual of money and power at the expense of others, yearning for popularity and recognition, these normal marks of human life, are the opposite of the mindset of those who have understood and experienced the cross. Christ creates a whole new order of life. Those who are shaped by the great reversal of the cross no longer need self-justification through money, status, career, or pride of race and class. So the cross creates a counterculture in which sex, money and power cease to control us and are used in life-giving and community-building rather than destructive ways.

To understand why Jesus had to die it is important to remember both the result of the cross (costly forgiveness of sins) and the pattern of the cross (reversal of the world's values). On the cross neither justice nor mercy loses out – both are fulfilled at once. Jesus' death was necessary if God was going to take justice seriously and still love us. This same concern for both love and justice should mark all our relationships. We should never acquiesce in injustice. Jesus identified with the oppressed. Yet we should not try to overcome evil with evil. Jesus forgave his enemies and died for them.

Why then, did Jesus have to die? Even Jesus asked that question. In the Garden of Gethsemane he asked if there was any other way. There wasn't. There isn't. On the cross, in agony, he cried out the question, *'Why!?'* Why was he being forsaken?[11] Why was it all necessary? The answer of the Bible is – for us.

## The Story of the Cross

I have tried to explain what Jesus has done for us when he died. I've done so by distilling some principles. I can't do the doctrine of the cross full justice, however. I've heard that the great author Flannery O'Connor was once asked to put the meaning of one of her short stories 'in a nutshell'. She responded tartly that, if she could have put the meaning into a nutshell, she wouldn't have had to write the story. I've been trying to put the cross of Jesus in a nutshell because I think it is an important exercise. Nevertheless, an exposition like this chapter of mine can't convey all the life-changing power of the narrative arc itself.

The stories that always seem to move us most deeply are those in which someone faces irremediable loss or death in order to bring life to someone else. There is almost no popular movie, for example, that doesn't make this its main theme. One of my personal favourites is *Angels with Dirty Faces*. James Cagney plays Rocky Sullivan, a celebrity criminal who is the idol of all the young juvenile delinquents in the city. He is about to go to the electric chair. The night before his execution he is visited by his boyhood friend Jerry, played by Pat O'Brien, who is now a priest trying to save inner-city kids from a life of crime. Jerry makes a shocking request, but he says it is the only way that the kids he is working with can be turned away from the destructive path they've chosen.

*I want you to let them down. You see, you've been a hero to these kids, and hundreds of others, all through your life – and now you're gonna be a glorified hero in death, and I want to prevent that, Rocky. They've got to despise your memory. They've got to be ashamed of you.*

Rocky is incredulous.

*You asking me to pull an act, turn yellow, so those kids will think I'm no good. . . . You ask me to throw away the only thing I've got left. . . . You ask me to crawl on my belly – the last thing I do in life. . . . Nothing doing. You're asking too much. . . . You want to help those kids, you got to think about some other way.*

Jerry is calling Rocky to do the Great Reversal, the substitutionary sacrifice. If you hold on to your dignity, he says, they'll die in shame. If you die in shame, relinquish your glory, the boys' lives can be saved. It's the only way to release his boys from their hero worship. Rocky refuses. But the next morning he walks to the execution chamber. Suddenly he begins to cry out for mercy in cowardly hysterics, and dies in humiliation, making the ultimate sacrifice. Movie viewers are always stunned. I should know because every time I watch it I am shaken and it makes me want to live my life differently. Such is the life-affecting power of story.

Another great example of this kind of narrative is *A Tale of Two Cities*. Charles Darnay and Sydney Carton look very much alike, and they both love the same woman, Lucie Manette. Lucie chooses and marries Charles and they have a child. The setting of the story is the French Revolution, and Charles, who is a French aristocrat, is arrested, imprisoned and sentenced to die by guillotine.

At the end of the novel, Sydney, who is English, visits Charles the night before he is to be executed. He offers to exchange places with him. Charles refuses, but Sydney has him drugged and smuggles him away into a waiting carriage. Then Sydney takes Charles's place. Charles and his family escape afterward to England.

That night in the prison, a young seamstress who is also condemned to die comes up to Sydney and begins to converse with him, thinking him to be Charles Darnay. When she realises that it is not him, her eyes widen and she asks: 'Are you dying for him?' Sydney responds: 'And his wife and child. Hush! Yes.' The seamstress then confesses that she is terribly frightened and is not sure she will be able to face her death. She asks the brave stranger if he will hold her hand to the end. When the time comes, they go to death hand in hand. She finds herself composed, even comforted and hopeful, as long as she keeps her eyes on him.

The girl in the story was sinking under the weight of her trial. Her strength was giving out, but then she was smitten by the wonder of his substitutionary sacrifice, and it enabled her to face the ultimate test.

Moving? Yes, but the gospel goes one better.[12] I always found these stories of sacrifice very emotionally affecting. I came away from them resolving to live more courageously and unselfishly. I never did follow through on my resolutions, however. The stories moved my emotions and pricked my conscience, but my heart's basic patterns stayed intact. I was still driven by a need to prove myself to others, to win approval and acclaim, to control what people thought of me. As long as these fears and needs had such power over me, my intentions to change could not go very far.

The gospel, however, is not just a moving fictional story about someone else. It is a true story about *us*. We are actually in it. We are those delinquent boys, and to save us Jesus gave up something infinitely greater than human celebrity. Also, Jesus has come to us in our prison and despite our unwillingness to be saved has taken our place. The seamstress was moved by a sacrifice that wasn't even for her. How much more can we be empowered by the discovery that Jesus has given himself for us, has changed places with us?

I can only say that observing these stories from the outside stirred me, but when I realised I was actually inside Jesus' story (and he inside mine) it changed me. The fear and pride that captured my heart was finally dislodged. The fact that Jesus *had* to die for me humbled me out of my pride. The fact that Jesus was *glad* to die for me assured me out of my fear.

# THIRTEEN

## THE REALITY OF THE RESURRECTION

*My question – that which at the age of fifty brought me to the verge of suicide – was the simplest of questions, lying in the soul of every man . . . a question without an answer to which one cannot live. It was: 'What will come of what I am doing today or tomorrow? What will come of my whole life? Why should I live, why wish for anything, or do anything?' It can also be expressed thus: Is there any meaning in my life that the inevitable death awaiting me does not destroy?*

—Leo Tolstoy, *A Confession*

WHEN I was studying philosophy and religion in college, I was taught that the resurrection of Jesus was a major historical problem, no matter how you looked at it. Most modern historians made the philosophical assumption that miracles simply cannot happen, and that made the claim of the resurrection highly problematic. However, if you disbelieved the resurrection you then had the difficulty of explaining how the Christian church got started at all.

Several years ago I was diagnosed with thyroid cancer. It was treatable and was removed successfully with surgery and other therapy. However, to paraphrase Samuel Johnson, the 'cancer' word pronounced over you under any circumstances concentrates the mind

201

wonderfully. During my treatment I discovered N. T. Wright's *The Resurrection of the Son of God*, the latest historical scholarship on Jesus' resurrection. I read it with great attention. It became quite clear to me how much more than a historical, philosophical issue this was. It is that, but it is much more. If it happened, it changes our lives completely.

Sometimes people approach me and say, 'I really struggle with this aspect of Christian teaching. I like this part of Christian belief, but I don't think I can accept that part.' I usually respond: 'If Jesus rose from the dead, then you have to accept all he said; if he didn't rise from the dead, then why worry about any of what he said? The issue on which everything hangs is not whether or not you like his teaching but whether or not he rose from the dead.' That is how the first hearers felt who heard reports of the resurrection. They knew that if it was true it meant we can't live our lives any way we want. It also meant we don't have to be afraid of anything, not Roman swords, not cancer, nothing. If Jesus rose from the dead, it changes everything.

Did he? Let's look at the reasons and evidence, the arguments and counterarguments.

Most people think that, when it comes to Jesus' resurrection, the burden of proof is on believers to give evidence that it happened. That is not completely the case. The resurrection also puts a burden of proof on its non-believers. It is not enough to simply believe Jesus did not rise from the dead. You must then come up with a historically feasible alternate explanation for the birth of the church. You have to provide some other plausible account for how things began. Most people who don't believe the resurrection of Jesus really happened offer something like the following scenario for Christian beginnings.

People at that time, it is said, did not have our scientific knowledge about the world. They were credulous about magical and supernatural happenings. They could easily have fallen prey to reports of a risen Jesus, because they believed that resurrections from the dead were possible. Jesus' followers were heartbroken when he was killed. Since they believed he was the Messiah, they may have begun to sense that he was still with them, guiding them, living on in their hearts in spirit. Some may have even felt they had visions of him speaking to them. Over the decades these feelings of Jesus living on spiritually developed into stories that he had been raised physically. The resurrection accounts in the four Gospels were devised to bolster this belief.

The alternative account proposed in the preceding paragraph sounds plausible to the average contemporary person, but only because we are ignorant of the historical and cultural context.

## The Empty Tomb and the Witnesses

The first fallacy in the alternative account is the claim that the resurrection narratives in the Gospels of Matthew, Mark, Luke and John must have been developed later, long after the events themselves. It is argued that the two main features of these texts – the empty tomb and the eyewitnesses – were fabrications. That can't be true.

The first accounts of the empty tomb and the eyewitnesses are not found in the Gospels, but in the letters of Paul, which every historian agrees were written just fifteen to twenty years after the death of Jesus. One of the most interesting texts is 1 Corinthians 15:3-6:

> For what I received I passed on to you as of first importance: that Christ died for our sins according to the Scriptures, that he was buried, that he was raised on the third day according to the Scriptures, and that he appeared to

Peter, and then to the Twelve. After that, he appeared to
more than five hundred of the brothers at the same time,
most of whom are still living, though some have died.

Here Paul not only speaks of the empty tomb and resurrection on
the 'third day' (showing he is talking of a historical event, not a
symbol or metaphor) but he also lists the eyewitnesses. Paul indicates that the risen Jesus not only appeared to individuals and small
groups, but he also appeared to five hundred people at once, most
of whom were still alive at the time of his writing and could be
consulted for corroboration. Paul's letter was to a church, and
therefore it was a public document, written to be read aloud. Paul
was inviting anyone who doubted that Jesus had appeared to people
after his death to go and talk to the eyewitnesses if they wished. It
was a bold challenge and one that could easily be taken up, since
during the *pax Romana* travel around the Mediterranean was safe
and easy. Paul could not have made such a challenge if those eyewitnesses didn't exist.

Another important feature of this text is that Paul insists that he
was faithfully recounting the testimony that had been handed to
him. Critical scholars from the nineteenth and early twentieth centuries assumed the early Christians would have used a process for
transmitting popular folktales that altered tales in the telling, like a
cultural version of the children's game 'Chinese Whispers'. As I
noted in Chapter 6, however, more recent anthropological studies
show that ancient cultures clearly distinguish between fictional stories and historical accounts in transmission. Historical accounts
were not allowed to be changed.[1] That is what Paul is claiming, that
the reports of the resurrection he conveys were taken intact from
the mouths of the people who actually saw Jesus.

Additionally, the accounts of the resurrection in the Bible were
too problematic to be fabrications. Each Gospel states that the first

eyewitnesses to the resurrection were women. Women's low social status meant that their testimony was not admissible evidence in court. There was no possible advantage to the church to recount that all the first witnesses were women. It could only have undermined the credibility of the testimony. The only possible explanation for why women were depicted as meeting Jesus first is if they really had. N. T. Wright argues that there must have been enormous pressure on the early proclaimers of the Christian message to remove the women from the accounts. They felt they could not do so – the records were too well known.[2] The accounts of the first eyewitnesses of the resurrection would have been electrifying and life-changing, passed along and retold more than any other stories about the life of Jesus.

Also, as Wright argues, the empty tomb and the accounts of personal meetings with Jesus are even more historically certain when you realise they must be taken together. If there had been only an empty tomb and no sightings, no one would have concluded it was a resurrection. They would have assumed that the body had been stolen. Yet if there had been only eyewitness sightings of Jesus and no empty tomb, no one would have concluded it was a resurrection, because people's accounts of seeing departed loved ones happen all the time. Only if the two factors were both true together would anyone have concluded that Jesus was raised from the dead.[3]

Paul's letters show that Christians proclaimed Jesus' bodily resurrection from the very beginning. That meant the tomb *must* have been empty. No one in Jerusalem would have believed the preaching for a minute if the tomb was not empty. Sceptics could have easily produced Jesus' rotted corpse. Also, Paul could not be telling people in a public document that there were scores of eyewitnesses alive if there were not. We can't permit ourselves the luxury of thinking that the resurrection accounts were only fabricated years later. Whatever else happened, the tomb of Jesus must have really been empty and hundreds of witnesses must have claimed that they saw him bodily raised.

## Resurrection and Immortality

There is, therefore, very strong evidence that the tomb was empty and there were hundreds of people who claimed they saw the risen Christ. That much is 'historically secure', as Wright puts it. 'But surely', someone can respond, 'that doesn't prove Jesus was really resurrected. Surely the followers desperately wanted to believe that Jesus was raised from the dead. If anyone had stolen the body in order to make it look like he had been raised, many sincere people could have thought they'd seen him, and maybe a few others went along with saying so for a good cause.'

The assumption behind this very common hypothesis is a form of what C. S. Lewis has called 'chronological snobbery'. We imagine that we modern people take claims of a bodily resurrection with scepticism, while the ancients, full of credulity about the supernatural, would have immediately accepted it. That is not the case. To all the dominant worldviews of the time, an individual bodily resurrection was almost inconceivable.

N. T. Wright does an extensive survey of the non-Jewish thought of the first-century Mediterranean world, both east and west, and reveals that the universal view of the people of that time was that a bodily resurrection was impossible. Why? In Graeco-Roman thinking, the soul or spirit was good and the physical and material world was weak, corrupt and defiling. To them the physical, by definition, was always falling apart and therefore salvation was conceived as *liberation* from the body. In this worldview resurrection was not only impossible, but totally undesirable. No soul, having gotten free from its body, would ever want it back. Even those who believed in reincarnation understood that the return to embodied life meant that the soul was not yet out of its prison. The goal was to get free of the body for ever. Once your soul is free of its body, a return to re-embodied life was outlandish, unthinkable and impossible.[4]

The report of Jesus' resurrection would have also have been unthinkable to the Jews. Unlike the Greeks, the Jews saw the material and physical world as good. Death was not seen as liberation from the material world but as a tragedy. By Jesus' day many Jews had come to hope that some day in the future there would be a bodily resurrection of all the righteous, when God renewed the entire world and removed all suffering and death.[5] The resurrection, however, was merely one part of the complete renewal of the whole world, according to Jewish teaching. The idea of an individual being resurrected, in the middle of history, while the rest of the world continued on burdened by sickness, decay and death, was inconceivable. If someone had said to any first-century Jew, 'So-and-so has been resurrected from the dead!' the response would be, 'Are you crazy? How could that be? Has disease and death ended? Is true justice established in the world? Has the wolf lain down with the lamb? Ridiculous!' The very idea of an individual resurrection would have been as impossible to imagine to a Jew as to a Greek.

Over the years, sceptics about the resurrection have proposed that the followers of Jesus may have had hallucinations, that they may have imagined him appearing to them and speaking to them. This assumes that their master's resurrection was imaginable for his Jewish followers, that it was an option in their worldview. It was not. Others have put forth the conspiracy theory, that the disciples stole the body and claimed he was alive to others. This assumes that the disciples would expect other Jews to be open to the belief that an individual could be raised from the dead. But none of this is possible. The people of that time would have considered a bodily resurrection to be as impossible as the people of our own time, though for different reasons.

In the first century there were many other messianic movements whose would-be messiahs were executed. However,

> *In not one single case do we hear the slightest mention of the dis-*
> *appointed followers claiming that their hero had been raised*
> *from the dead. They knew better. Resurrection was not a private*
> *event. Jewish revolutionaries whose leader had been executed by*
> *the authorities, and who managed to escape arrest themselves,*
> *had two options: give up the revolution, or find another leader.*
> *Claiming that the original leader was alive again was simply*
> *not an option. Unless, of course, he was.*[6]

There were dozens of other messianic pretenders whose lives and careers ended the same way Jesus' did. Why would the disciples of Jesus have come to the conclusion that that his crucifixion had not been a defeat but a triumph – unless they had seen him risen from the dead?

## The Explosion of a New Worldview

After the death of Jesus the entire Christian community suddenly adopted a set of beliefs that were brand-new and until that point had been unthinkable. The first Christians had a resurrection-centred view of reality. They believed that the future resurrection had already begun in Jesus. They believed that Jesus had a transformed body that could walk through walls yet eat food. This was not simply a resuscitated body like the Jews envisioned, nor a solely spiritual existence like the Greeks imagined. Jesus' resurrection guaranteed our resurrection and brought some of that future new life into our hearts now.[7]

As N. T. Wright points out, every one of these beliefs was unique in the world up to that time, but in every other instance that we know of, such a massive shift in thinking at the worldview level only happens to a group of people over a period of time.[8] It ordinarily takes years of discussion and argument in which various thinkers and writers debate the 'nature of the resurrection' until one side wins. That is how culture and worldviews change.

However, the Christian view of resurrection, absolutely unprecedented in history, sprang up full-blown immediately after the death of Jesus. There was no process or development. His followers said that their beliefs did not come from debating and discussing. They were just telling others what they had seen themselves. No one has come up with any plausible alternative to this claim. Even if you propose the highly unlikely idea that one or two of Jesus' disciples did get the idea that he was raised from the dead on their own, they would never have got a movement of other Jews to believe it unless there were multiple, inexplicable, plausible, repeated encounters with Jesus.

The subsequent history of the church gets even more difficult to account for. How could a group of first-century Jews have come to worship a human being as divine? Eastern religions believe that God is an impersonal force that permeates all things. Therefore they can accept the idea that some human beings have more divine consciousness than others. Western religions believed that the various gods often took human guise. It was possible, therefore, that some human figure could really be Zeus or Hermes. Jews, however, believed in a single, transcendent, personal God. It was absolute blasphemy to propose that any human being should be worshipped. Yet hundreds of Jews began worshipping Jesus literally overnight. The hymn to Christ as God that Paul quotes in Philippians 2 is generally recognised to have been written just a few years after the crucifixion. What enormous event broke through all of that Jewish resistance? If they had seen him resurrected, that would account for it. What other historical answer can do so?

There is one more thing to keep in mind. As Pascal put it, 'I [believe] those witnesses that get their throats cut.' Virtually all the apostles and early Christian leaders died for their faith, and it is hard to believe that this kind of powerful self-sacrifice would be done to support a hoax.

It is not enough for the sceptic, then, to simply dismiss the Christian teaching about the resurrection of Jesus by saying, 'It just couldn't have happened.' He or she must face and answer all these historical questions: Why did Christianity emerge so rapidly, with such power? No other band of messianic followers in that era concluded their leader was raised from the dead – why did this group do so? No group of Jews ever worshipped a human being as God. What led them to do it? Jews did not believe in divine men or individual resurrections. What changed their worldview virtually overnight? How do you account for the hundreds of eyewitnesses to the resurrection who lived on for decades and publicly maintained their testimony, eventually giving their lives for their belief?

## The Challenge of the Resurrection

Nothing in history can be proven the way we can prove something in a laboratory. However, the resurrection of Jesus is a historical fact much more fully attested to than most other events of ancient history we take for granted. Every effort to account for the birth of the church apart from Jesus' resurrection flies in the face of what we know about first-century history and culture. If you don't short-circuit the process with the philosophical bias against the possibility of miracle, the resurrection of Jesus has the most evidence for it.

The problem is, however, that people *do* short-circuit the investigation. Instead of doing the work of answering these very tough historical questions and then following the answers where they lead, they bail out with the objection that miracles are impossible. N. T. Wright makes a scathing response:

> *The early Christians did not invent the empty tomb and the meetings or sightings of the risen Jesus. . . . Nobody was expecting this kind of thing; no kind of conversion experience would have invented it, no matter how guilty (or how forgiven) they felt, no matter how many hours they pored over the scriptures. To suggest otherwise is to stop doing history and enter into a fantasy world of our own.*[9]

I sympathise with the person who says, 'So what if I can't think of an alternate explanation? The resurrection just couldn't happen.' Let's not forget, however, that first-century people felt exactly the same way. They found the resurrection just as inconceivable as you do. The only way anyone embraced the resurrection back then was by letting the evidence challenge and change their worldview, their view of what was possible. They had just as much trouble with the claims of the resurrection as you, yet the evidence – both of the eyewitness accounts and the changed lives of Christ's followers – was overwhelming.

Each year at Easter I get to preach on the resurrection. In my sermon I always say to my sceptical, secular friends that, even if they can't believe in the resurrection, they should want it to be true. Most of them care deeply about justice for the poor, alleviating hunger and disease, and caring for the environment. Yet many of them believe that the material world was caused by accident and that the world and everything in it will eventually simply burn up in the death of the sun. They find it discouraging that so few people care about justice without realising that their own worldview undermines any motivation to make the world a better place. Why sacrifice for the needs of others if in the end nothing we do will make any difference? If the resurrection of Jesus happened, however, that means there's infinite hope and reason to pour ourselves out for the needs of the world. In a sermon, N. T. Wright said:

> *The message of the resurrection is that this world matters! That the injustices and pains of this present world must now be addressed with the news that healing, justice, and love have won . . . If Easter means Jesus Christ is only raised in a spiritual sense – [then] it is only about me, and finding a new dimension in my personal spiritual life. But if Jesus Christ is truly risen from the dead, Christianity becomes good news for the whole world – news which warms our hearts precisely because it isn't just about warming hearts. Easter means that in a world where injustice, violence and degradation are endemic, God is not prepared to tolerate such things – and that we will work and plan, with all the energy of God, to implement the victory of Jesus over them all. Take away Easter and Karl Marx was probably right to accuse Christianity of ignoring problems of the material world. Take it away and Freud was probably right to say Christianity is wish-fulfillment. Take it away and Nietzsche probably was right to say it was for wimps.*[10]

# FOURTEEN

## THE DANCE OF GOD

*In 1938 . . . I was suffering from splitting headaches; each sound hurt me like a blow. . . . I discovered the poem . . . called 'Love' [by George Herbert] which I learnt by heart. Often, at the culminating point of a violent headache, I made myself say it over, concentrating all my attention upon it and clinging with all my soul to the tenderness it enshrines. I used to think I was merely reciting it as a beautiful poem, but without my knowing it the recitation had the virtue of a prayer. It was during one of these recitations that Christ himself came down and took possession of me. In my arguments about the insolubility of the problem of God I had never foreseen the possibility of that, of a real contact, person to person, here below, between a human being and God.*

—Simone Weil, *Waiting for God*

I believe that Christianity makes the most sense out of our individual life stories and out of what we see in the world's history. In the last six chapters I have been arguing that the Christian understanding of where we came from, what's wrong with us, and how it can be fixed has greater power to explain what we see and experience than does any other competing account. It is time to draw together the various threads of the narrative we have been examining and view the story line of Christianity as a whole. The

Bible has often been summed up as a drama in four acts – creation, fall, redemption and restoration.

## The Divine Dance

Christianity, alone among the world faiths, teaches that God is triune. The doctrine of the Trinity is that God is one being who exists eternally in three persons: Father, Son and Holy Spirit. The Trinity means that God is, in essence, relational.

The Gospel writer John describes the Son as living from all eternity in the 'bosom of the Father' (John 1:18), an ancient metaphor for love and intimacy. Later in John's Gospel, Jesus, the Son, describes the Spirit as living to 'glorify' him (John 16:14). In turn, the Son glorifies the Father (17:4) and the Father, the Son (17:5). This has been going on for all eternity (17:5b).

What does the term 'glorify' mean? To glorify something or someone is to praise, enjoy and delight in them. When something is useful you are attracted to it for what it can bring you or do for you. But if it is beautiful, then you enjoy it simply for what it is. Just being in its presence is its own reward. To glorify someone is also to serve or defer to him or her. Instead of sacrificing their interests to make yourself happy, you sacrifice your interests to make them happy. Why? Your ultimate joy is to see them in joy.

What does it mean, then, that the Father, Son and Holy Spirit glorify one another? If we think of it graphically, we could say that self-centredness is to be stationary, static. In self-centredness we demand that others orbit around us. We will do things and give affection to others, as long as it helps us meet our personal goals and fulfils us.

The inner life of the triune God, however, is utterly different. The life of the Trinity is characterised not by self-centredness but by mutually self-giving love. When we delight and serve someone else, we enter into a dynamic orbit around him or her, we centre on the interests and desires of the other. That creates a dance, particularly if there are three persons, each of whom moves around the other two. So it is, the Bible tells us. Each of the divine persons centres upon the others. None demands that the others revolve around him. Each voluntarily circles the other two, pouring love, delight and adoration into them. Each person of the Trinity loves, adores, defers to and rejoices in the others. That creates a dynamic, pulsating dance of joy and love. The early leaders of the Greek church had a word for this – *perichoresis*. Notice the root of our word 'choreography' within it. It means literally to 'dance or flow around'.[1]

> *The Father . . . Son . . . and Holy Spirit glorify each other. . . . At the center of the universe, self-giving love is the dynamic currency of the Trinitarian life of God. The persons within God exalt, commune with, and defer to one another. . . . When early Greek Christians spoke of* perichoresis *in God they meant that each divine person harbors the others at the center of his being. In constant movement of overture and acceptance each person envelops and encircles the others.*[2]

> *In Christianity God is not an impersonal thing nor a static thing – not even just one person – but a dynamic pulsating activity, a life, a kind of drama, almost, if you will not think me irreverent, a kind of dance. . . . [The] pattern of this three-personal life is . . . the great fountain of energy and beauty spurting up at the very centre of reality.*[3]

The doctrine of the Trinity overloads our mental circuits. Despite its cognitive difficulty, however, this astonishing, dynamic conception of the triune God is bristling with profound, wonderful, life-shaping, world-changing implications.[4]

## The Dance of Love

If there is no God, then everything in and about us is the product of blind impersonal forces. The experience of love may feel significant, but evolutionary naturalists tell us that it is merely a biochemical state in the brain.

But what if there is a God? Does love fare any better? It depends on who you think God is. If God is unipersonal, then until God created other beings there was no love, since love is something that one person has for another. This means that a unipersonal God was power, sovereignty and greatness from all eternity, but not love. Love then is not of the essence of God, nor is it at the heart of the universe. Power is primary.

However, if God is triune, then loving relationships in community are the 'great fountain . . . at the center of reality'. When people say, 'God is love,' I think they mean that love is extremely important, or that God really wants us to love. But in the Christian conception, God really has love as his essence. If he was just one person he couldn't have been loving for all eternity. If he was only the impersonal all-soul of Eastern thought, he couldn't have been loving, for love is something persons do. Eastern religions believe the individual personality is an illusion, and therefore love is, too.[5] Chesterton wrote, 'For the Buddhist . . . personality is the fall of man, for the Christian it is the purpose of God, the whole point of his cosmic idea.'[6] It is the purpose of God because he is essentially, eternally, interpersonal love.

Ultimate reality is a community of persons who know and love one another. That is what the universe, God, history and life is all about. If you favour money, power and accomplishment over human relationships, you will dash yourself on the rocks of reality. When Jesus said you must lose yourself in service to find yourself

(Mark 8:35), he was recounting what the Father, Son and Holy Spirit have been doing throughout eternity. You will, then, never get a sense of self by standing still, as it were, and making everything revolve around your needs and interests. Unless you are willing to experience the loss of options and the individual limitation that comes from being in committed relationships, you will remain out of touch with your own nature and the nature of things.

In many other places in this volume, I've traced out how impossible it is to stay fully human if you refuse the cost of forgiveness, the substitutional exchange of love, and the confinements of community. I quoted C. S. Lewis saying that the only place besides heaven that is free from the pain and suffering of relationships is hell.

Why is this? Because, according to the Bible, this world was not created by a God who is only an individual, nor is it the emanation of an impersonal force. It is not the product of power struggles between personal deities nor of random, violent, accidental natural forces. Christians reject these other creation accounts, which refuse to give love primacy. We believe the world was made by a God who is a community of persons who have loved each other for all eternity. You were made for mutually self-giving, other-directed love. Self-centredness destroys the fabric of what God has made.

## The Dance of Creation

Jonathan Edwards, in reflecting on the interior life of the triune God, concluded that God is infinitely happy. Within God is a community of persons pouring glorifying, joyful love into one another. Think about this pattern in our own experience. Imagine there is someone you admire more than anyone else in the world. You would do anything for him or her. Now imagine you discover that this person feels exactly the same about you, and you enter into either a lifetime friendship or a romantic relationship and marriage. Sound like heaven? Yes, because it comes from heaven – that is what God has known within himself but in depths and degrees that are infinite and unimaginable. That is why God is infinitely happy, because there is an 'other-orientation' at the heart of his being, because he does not seek his own glory but the glory of others.[7]

'But wait,' you say. 'On nearly every page of the Bible God calls us to glorify, praise and serve him. How can you say he doesn't seek his own glory?' Yes he does ask us to obey him unconditionally, to glorify, praise and centre our lives around him. But now, I hope, you finally see why he does that. He wants our joy! He has infinite happiness not through self-centredness, but through self-giving, other-centred love. And the only way we, who have been created in his image, can have this same joy, is if we centre our entire lives around him instead of ourselves.

Why would a God like this create a world of beings like us? On the basis of biblical passages such as John 17:20-24, Jonathan Edwards reasoned it out. Historian George Marsden summarises Edwards's idea:

*Why would such an infinitely good, perfect, and eternal being create? . . . Here Edwards drew on the Christian Trinitarian conception of God as essentially interpersonal. . . . The ultimate reason that God creates, said Edwards, is not to remedy some lack in God, but to extend that perfect internal communication of the triune God's goodness and love. . . . God's joy and happiness and delight in divine perfections is expressed externally by communicating that happiness and delight to created beings. . . . The universe is an explosion of God's glory. Perfect goodness, beauty, and love radiate from God and draw creatures to ever increasingly share in the Godhead's joy and delight. . . . The ulti-*

*mate end of creation, then, is union in love between God and loving creatures.*[8]

God did not create us to get the cosmic, infinite joy of mutual love and glorification, but to share it. We were made to join in the dance. If we will centre our lives on him, serving him not out of self-interest, but just for the sake of who he is, for the sake of his beauty and glory, we will enter the dance and share in the joy and love he lives in. We were designed, then, not just for belief in God in some general way, nor for a vague kind of inspiration or spirituality. We were made to centre our lives upon him, to make the purpose and passion of our lives knowing, serving, delighting and resembling him. This growth in happiness will go on eternally, increasing unimaginably (1 Corinthians 2:7-10).

This leads to a uniquely positive view of the material world. The world is not, as other creation accounts would have it, an illusion, the result of a battle among the gods, nor the accidental outcome of natural forces. It was made in joy and therefore is good in and of itself. The universe is understood as a dance of beings united by energies binding yet distinct, like planets orbiting stars, like tides and seasons, 'like atoms in a molecule, like the tones in a chord, like the living organisms on this earth, like the mother with the baby stirring in her body'.[9] The love of the inner life of the Trinity is written all through it. Creation is a dance!

## Losing the Dance

The story of the Bible begins with the dance of creation, but in Genesis 3 we read of the Fall. God tells Adam and Eve that they must not eat of one tree on penalty of death. But what would be so bad about eating of this tree? No answer is forthcoming. However, if we comply with God's directions only when it fits in with our goals and interests, then we are trying to get God to orbit around us. God becomes the means to an end, not an end in himself. God, then, is saying to humanity something like, 'Obey me about the tree just because you love me. Just for my sake.'

And we failed. We became stationary, self-centred. And according to Genesis 3, when our relationship with God unravelled, all our other relationships disintegrated as well. Self-centredness creates psychological alienation. Nothing makes us more miserable than self-absorption, the endless, unsmiling concentration on our needs, wants, treatment, ego and record. In addition, self-centredness leads to social disintegration. It is at the root of the breakdown in relationships between nations, races and classes, and individuals. Finally, in some mysterious way, humanity's refusal to serve God has led to our alienation from the natural world as well.

We lost the dance. The dance of joyful, mutually self-giving relationships is impossible in a world in which everyone is stationary, trying to get everything else to orbit around them.

However, God does not leave us there. The Son of God was born into the world to begin a new humanity, a new community of people who could lose their self-centredness, begin a God-centred life, and, as a result, slowly but surely have all other relationships put right as well. Paul calls Jesus 'the last Adam'. As the first Adam was tested in the Garden of Eden, the last Adam (Jesus) was tested in the Garden of Gethsemane. The first Adam knew that he would live if he obeyed God about the tree. But he didn't. The last Adam was also tested by what Paul called a 'tree', the cross. Jesus knew that he would be crushed if he obeyed his Father. And he still did.

Why did Jesus die for us? What was Jesus getting out of it? Remember, he already had a community of joy, glory and love. He didn't need us. So what benefit did he derive from this? Not a thing. And that means that when he came into the world and died on the cross to deal with our sins, he was circling and serving *us*.

'I have given them the glory that you gave me' (John 17). He began to do with us what he had been doing with the Father and the Spirit from all eternity. He centres upon us, loving us without benefit to himself.

## Returning to the Dance

If the beauty of what Jesus did moves you, that is the first step toward getting out of your own self-centredness and fear into a trust relationship with him. When Jesus died for you he was, as it were, inviting you into the dance. He invites you to begin centring everything in your life on him, even as he has given himself for you.

If you respond to him, all your relationships will begin to heal. As I noted in Chapter 9, sin is centring your identity on anything but God. We give ourselves only to relationships and pursuits that build us up and bolster our efforts at self-justification and self-creation. But this also leads us to disdain and look down on those who do not have the same accomplishments or identity-markers.

However, when we discern Jesus moving toward us and encircling us with an infinite, self-giving love, we are invited to put our lives on a whole new foundation. We can make him the new centre of our lives and stop trying to be our own Saviour and Lord. We can accept both his challenge to recognise ourselves as sinners in need of his salvation, and his renewing love as the new basis of our identity. Then we don't need to prove ourselves to others. We won't need to use others to bolster our fragile sense of pride and self-worth. And we will be enabled to move out toward others as Jesus has moved toward us.

*In self-giving, if anywhere, we touch a rhythm not only of all creation but of all being. For the Eternal Word also gives himself in sacrifice. When he was crucified he 'did that in the wild weather of his outlying provinces which He had done at home in glory and gladness' from before the foundation of the world. . . . From the highest to the lowest, self exists to be abdicated and, by that abdication, it becomes more truly self, to be thereupon yet the more abdicated, and so forever. This is not a . . . law which we can escape. . . . What is outside the system of self-giving is . . . simply and solely Hell . . . that fierce imprisonment in the self. . . . Self-giving is absolute reality.*[10]

## The Future of the Dance

How, then, will the story of human history end? At the end of the final book of the Bible, we see the very opposite of what other religions predict. We do not see the illusion of the world melt away nor do we see spiritual souls escaping the physical world into heaven. Rather, we see heaven *descending* into our world to unite with it and purify it of all its brokenness and imperfection. It will be a 'new heavens and new earth'. The prophet Isaiah depicts this as a new Garden of Eden, in which there is again absolute harmony of humanity with nature and the end of injury, disease and death, along with the end of all racial animosity and war. There will be no more poor, slaves, criminals or broken-hearted mourners.

This all follows from what we know about creation as a dance. The Trinity virtually 'rejoiced' the world into being. Out of delight God created a universe of beings to step into his joy, and the new-made stars sang of it. Even now creation continually tells of God's glory and looks to him, it 'shouts for joy and sings' (Psalms 65:12-13). God moves toward his world in care and love. He is committed to every part of his creation, loving it and upholding it. And though sin and evil have marred the world, so it is just a shadow of its true self, at the end of time, nature will be restored to its full glory and we with it. 'Creation itself will be liberated from its bondage to decay and brought into the glorious freedom of the children of God' (Romans 8:21). The whole world will be healed as it is drawn into the fullness of God's glory. Evil will be destroyed and all the potentialities in creation, latent until that moment, will explode into fullness and beauty. Compared to what we will be then, we are now mere vegetables. Even the trees will sing and make music before the face of the returning King, who, by his presence, always turns mourning into dancing.

Because creation was made in the image of a God who is equally one and many, the human race will finally be reunited and yet our racial and cultural diversity will remain intact in the renewed world. The human race finally lives together in peace and interdependence. Glory to God in the highest goes with peace on earth.

## The Christian Life

How do we respond to this? When we look at the whole scope of this story line, we see clearly that Christianity is not only about getting one's individual sins forgiven so we can go to heaven. That is an important *means* of God's salvation, but not the final end or purpose of it. The purpose of Jesus' coming is to put the whole world right, to renew and restore the creation, not to escape it. It is not just to bring personal forgiveness and peace, but also justice and *shalom* to the world. God created both body and soul, and the resurrection of Jesus shows that he is going to redeem both body and soul. The work of the Spirit of God is not only to save souls but also to care and cultivate the face of the earth, the material world.

It is hard to overemphasise the uniqueness of this vision. Outside of the Bible, no other major religious faith holds out any hope or even interest in the restoration of perfect *shalom*, justice and wholeness in this material world. Vinoth Ramachandra, a Sri Lankan

223

Christian writer, can see this very clearly. All other religions, he says, offer as salvation some form of liberation from ordinary humanness. Salvation is seen as escape from the shackles of individuality and physical embodiment into some kind of transcendent spiritual existence.

> *[Biblical] salvation lies not in an escape from this world but in the transformation of this world. . . . You will not find hope for the world in any of the religious systems or philosophies of humankind. . . . The Biblical vision is unique. That is why when some say there is salvation in other faiths too, I ask them – 'What salvation are you talking about?' No faith holds out a promise of eternal salvation for the world – the ordinary world – that the cross and resurrection of Jesus do.*[11]

What does it mean, then, to become part of God's work in the world? What does it mean to live a Christian life? One way to answer that question is to look back into the life of the Trinity and the original creation. God made us to ever increasingly share in his own joy and delight in the same way he has joy and delight within himself. We share his joy first as we give him glory (worshipping and serving him rather than ourselves); second, as we honour and serve the dignity of other human beings made in the image of God's glory; and third, as we cherish his derivative glory in the world of nature, which also reflects it. We glorify and enjoy him only as we worship him, serve the human community, and care for the created environment.

Another way to look at the Christian life, however, is to see it from the perspective of the final restoration. The world and our hearts are broken. Jesus' life, death and resurrection was an infinitely costly rescue operation to restore justice to the oppressed and marginalised, physical wholeness to the diseased and dying, community to the isolated and lonely, and spiritual joy and connection to those alienated from God. To be a Christian today is to become part of that same operation, with the expectation of suffering and hardship *and* the joyful assurance of eventual success.

The story of the gospel makes sense of moral obligation and our belief in the reality of justice, so Christians do restorative and redistributive justice wherever they can. The story of the gospel makes sense of our indelible religiousness, so Christians do evangelism, pointing the way to forgiveness and reconciliation with God through Jesus. The gospel makes sense of our profoundly relational character, so Christians work sacrificially to strengthen human communities around them as well as the Christian community, the church. The gospel story also makes sense of our delight in the presence of beauty, so Christians become stewards of the material world, from those who cultivate the natural creation through science and gardening to those who give themselves to artistic endeavours, all knowing why these things are necessary for human flourishing. The skies and trees 'sing' of the glory of God, and by caring for them and celebrating them we free their voices to praise him and delight us. In short, the Christian life means not only building up the Christian community through encouraging people to faith in Christ, but building up the human community through deeds of justice and service.

Christians, then, are the true 'revolutionaries' who work for justice and truth, and we labour in expectation of a perfect world in which:

> He will wipe every tear from their eyes. There will be no more death or mourning or crying or pain, for the old order of things is passed away. (Revelation 21:4)

And when we get there, we will say, *I've come home at last! This is my real country! I belong here. This is the land I've been looking for all my life, though I never knew it!* And it will by no means be the end of our story. In fact, as C. S. Lewis put it, all the adventures we have ever had will end up being only 'the cover and the title page'. Finally we will begin 'Chapter One of the Great Story, which no one on earth has read; which goes on forever; in which every chapter is better than the one before.'[12]

# Epilogue
## Where Do We Go from Here?

*To know oneself, is above all, to know what one lacks. It is to measure oneself against the Truth, and not the other way around.*
—Flannery O'Connor, 'The Fiction Writer and His Country'

*And then the heart of Eowyn changed, or else at last she understood it.*
—J. R. R. Tolkien, *The Return of the King*

IT is possible though by no means certain that Christianity may be more plausible to you now that you've read this book. You may have been personally moved by some of the descriptions of our world's need, your own condition, and Christ's mission in the world. What if you are ready to explore what it means to put your faith in Christ? Where do you go from here?

## Examining Your Motives

Motivations are nearly always mixed. If you wait until your motives are pure and unselfish before you do something, you will wait forever. Nevertheless, it is important to ask what is primarily moving you toward an action, especially when it comes to faith commitment. For example, you may be at a time of great difficulty and

227

need. You are sharply conscious, maybe for the first time in your life, that you need God and some kind of spiritual help in order to make it. There's nothing mistaken about that, but it would be very easy in that condition to approach God as a means to an end. Are you getting into Christianity to serve God, or to get God to serve you? The latter is a kind of shamanism, an effort to get control of God through your prayers and practices. It is using God rather than trusting him.

We have to recognise that virtually all of us begin our journey towards God because we want something from him. However, we must come to grips with the fact that we owe him our entire lives just because of what he has done for us already. He is our Creator, and for that fact alone we owe him everything. However, he is also our Redeemer, who rescued us at infinite cost to himself. Any heart that has come to its senses wants to surrender to Someone who not only is all-powerful but has proved that he will sacrifice anything for our good.

We usually begin the journey toward God thinking, 'What do I have to do to get this or that from him?' but eventually we have to begin thinking, 'What do I have to do to get him?' If you don't make that transition, you will never actually meet the real God, but will only end up believing in some caricature version of him.

## Counting the Cost

A Christian is, literally, 'Christ's one', someone who is not just vaguely influenced by Christian teaching, but who has switched his or her most fundamental allegiance to Jesus. Christians understand the all-or-nothing choice that is forced upon us by the magnitude of Jesus' claims.

From the earliest days, the confession of Christians was *Christos Kurios* – 'Jesus is Lord'. In the historical context, in which it was required to say *Kaiser Kurios*, 'Caesar is Lord', this confession meant that Jesus was the supreme power. He was not just a divine angelic being, but, as an early Christian hymn put it, he had 'the name above every name' (Philippians 2:9). In him 'All the fullness of the Godhead dwells bodily' (Colossians 2:9).

This is an enormous claim, but there is a certain logic to it. One of the most recent people to note this logic is Bono, the lead singer of U2, in a conversation with Michka Assayas:

Assayas: *Christ has his rank among the world's great thinkers. But Son of God, isn't that far-fetched?*

Bono: *No, it's not far-fetched to me. Look, the secular response to the Christ story always goes like this: He was a great prophet, obviously a very interesting guy, had a lot to say along the lines of other great prophets, be they Elijah, Muhammad, Buddha, or Confucius. But actually Christ doesn't allow you that. He doesn't let you off that hook. Christ says, No. I'm not saying I'm a teacher, don't call me teacher. I'm not saying I'm a prophet. I'm saying: 'I'm the Messiah.' I'm saying: 'I am God incarnate.' And people say: No, no, please, just be a prophet. A prophet we can take. You're a bit eccentric. We've had John the Baptist eating locusts and wild honey, we can handle that. But don't mention the 'M' word! Because, you know, we're gonna have to crucify you. And he goes: No, no, I know you're expecting me to come back with an army and set you free from these creeps, but actually I am the Messiah. At this point, everyone starts staring at their shoes, and says: Oh, my God, he's gonna keep saying this. So what you're left with is either Christ was who He said He was – the Messiah – or a complete nutcase. I mean, we're talking nutcase on the level of Charles Manson. . . . I'm not joking here. The idea that the entire course of civilisation for over half of the globe could have its*

229

*fate changed and turned upside-down by a nutcase, for me that's far-fetched . . .*

Bono is describing how Jesus' statements about himself force us all into an all-or-nothing choice. He asks how likely it is that a mentally deranged man on the order of Charles Manson or David Koresh could have produced the kind of impact on his followers and on the world that he has. However, if Jesus was not a lunatic, then our only alternative is to accept his claims and centre our entire lives around him. The one thing we have no right to do is to respond to him mildly.

Flannery O'Connor makes the same point in 'A Good Man Is Hard to Find'. The Misfit is a bandit who apprehends a family in a rural area in the South. The head of the family, the grandmother, tries to talk him out of killing her by chattering on about prayer and church and Jesus, but the Misfit responds:

*Jesus . . . thrown everything off balance. If He did what He said, then it's nothing for you to do but throw away everything and follow Him, and if He didn't, then it's nothing for you to do but enjoy the few minutes you got left the best way you can by killing somebody or burning down his house or doing some other meanness to him. No pleasure but meanness.*

O'Connor once commented about this encounter saying that the Misfit indeed understood the all-or-nothing implications of Jesus. 'The story is a duel of sorts between the grandmother and her superficial beliefs and the Misfit's more profoundly felt involvement with Christ's action, which set the world off balance for him.'[1] O'Connor felt this pressure personally. There was no use just saying you believed in Jesus unless you let that change your life and affect your view of everything. 'Redemption is meaningless unless there is

230

a cause for it in the actual life we live,' she wrote in an essay, 'I see from the standpoint of Christian orthodoxy. This means that for me the meaning of life is centred in our redemption by Christ and what I see in the world I see in its relation to that.'[2]

Bono and O'Connor are extremely different personalities, and yet both of them have personally felt the radical implications of Jesus' claims. Christians are people who let the reality of Jesus change everything about who they are, how they see, and how they live.

## Taking Inventory

Perhaps these challenges from Bono and O'Connor make you gulp. What if you are increasingly respectful of and interested in Christianity but you are not yet ready to make such a big commitment? You may sense that there are still barriers between you and Christian faith.

If that is your situation don't simply put things on hold, hoping that somehow your feelings will change and somehow the barriers will melt away. Take an inventory in order to discern the specific reasons for your reservations. Here is a possible set of questions to help you in this process.

- **Content issues:** Are there any parts of the Christian message – creation, sin, Jesus as God, cross, resurrection – that you don't understand or agree with?
- **Coherence issues:** Are there still doubts and objections to the Christian faith that you cannot resolve?
- **Cost issues:** Do you perceive that a move into full Christian faith will cost you something dear? What fears do you have about commitment?

You can use an outline like this to analyse and identify your barriers to full commitment, but don't trust yourself to do this on your own. Almost anything – from a new language to a new skill – is best learned in a community of others who are at various stages in their own pilgrimage. Spend time in a Christian church, in its worship and in friendship with its members, to talk with Christians and to hear how they have handled these doubts themselves.

Most important of all, remember that becoming a Christian is not simply a matter of ticking off a list of things to believe and do. At the end of Matthew 11, Jesus calls us to 'Come to me, all you who are weary and heavy laden and I will give you rest. . . . Take my yoke upon you, and learn of me. . . . For my yoke is easy and my burden is light.' A man once said to a pastor that he would be happy to believe in Christianity if the cleric could only give him a watertight argument for its truth. The pastor replied, 'What if God hasn't given us a watertight argument, but rather a watertight person?'[3] Jesus is saying 'I am that person. Come to *me*. Look at who I am. Look at my cross. Look at my resurrection. No one could have made this up! Come to me, and you will find rest for your souls.'

Ultimately faith and certainty grows as we get to know more about Jesus, who he is, and what he did.

There's one more barrier that many people feel at this point but it may not be as hard to deal with as you think. New York City is filled with people who were raised and baptised in various churches but who abandoned their faith in their teens and college and have not thought much about it for years. Then something brings them up short and they find themselves in spiritual search mode. They work through the basics of the Christian faith and it seems to them they had never really understood it before. Their question to me as a pastor is, 'I don't really know if I am a Christian or not. Am I returning to my faith or finding it for the first time?' The answer is simple – I can't tell, and it doesn't matter. If you want to either connect to God or reconnect to God, you have to do the same two things. What are those two things?

## Making the Move

The first thing you have to do is repent. That's not a very elegant sounding word but there is no getting around it. The repentance that begins a new relationship with God is not primarily a matter of drawing up lists of specific sins you are sorry for and want to change. Don't get me wrong: if you are exploiting the poor or cheating on your spouse, and you want to put your faith in Christ, then by all means stop doing those things. A Christian should love the poor and be faithful to his or her marriage vows. But those behavioural changes alone will not make you a Christian. Lots of people in the world are socially and personally ethical but do not have a relationship with God through Jesus Christ. Repentance is not *less* than being sorry for individual sins, but it means much more.

The repentance that really changes your heart and your relationship with God begins when you recognise that your main sin, the sin under the rest of your sins, is your self-salvation project. As we saw in Chapters 9 and 10, in both our bad deeds *and* in our good deeds we are seeking to be our own Saviours and Lords. We have alternative trusts and 'gods', even though we do not call them that. We try to prove ourselves by our moral goodness or through achievement or family or career. Even diligent involvement in church and religion may need to be repented of once we understand that it was all a way to put God and others in our debt.

Repentance, then, is confessing the things besides God himself that you have been relying on for your hope, significance and security. That means we should repent not only for things we have done wrong (like cheating or lying), but also for the motivations beneath our good works.

The second thing you have to do is believe in Christ. Belief in Christ has a definite content to it. We must believe he was who he said he was, that we require salvation, that on the cross he secured that salvation, that he rose from the dead. However, while life-changing Christian faith is not *less* than believing these things with your intellect, it is much more.

The faith that changes the life and connects to God is best conveyed by the word 'trust'. Imagine you are on a high cliff and you lose your footing and begin to fall. Just beside you as you fall is a branch sticking out of the very edge of the cliff. It is your only hope and it is more than strong enough to support your weight. How can it save you? If your mind is filled with intellectual certainty that the branch can support you, but you don't actually reach out and grab it, you are lost. If your mind is instead filled with doubts and uncertainty that the branch can hold you, but you reach out and grab it anyway, you will be saved. Why? It is not the strength of your faith but the object of your faith that actually saves you. Strong faith in a weak branch is fatally inferior to weak faith in a strong branch.

This means you don't have to wait for all doubts and fears to go away to take hold of Christ. Don't make the mistake of thinking that you have to banish all misgivings in order to meet God. That would turn your faith into one more way to be your own Saviour. Working on the quality and purity of your commitment would become a way to merit salvation and put God in your debt. It is not the depth and purity of your heart but the work of Jesus Christ on our behalf that saves us.

Faith, then, begins as you recognise and reject your alternative trusts and gods and turn instead to the Father, asking for a relationship to him on the basis of what Jesus has done, not on the basis of your moral effort or achievements. Several young adults of my acquaintance made their move of faith this way. They prayed:

*Father, I've always believed in you and Jesus Christ, but my heart's most fundamental trust was elsewhere – in my own competence and decency. This has only got me into trouble. As far as I know my own heart, today I give it to you, I transfer my trust to you, and ask that you would receive and accept me not for anything I have done but because of everything Christ has done for me.*

This begins a lifelong process in which, through steady change in every area of life, the gospel story shapes us more and more.

## Committing to Community

When people ask me, 'How can I actually become a Christian?' I usually say, 'It takes two things, and a third.' The two things – repentance and faith – I have just laid out. There is another crucial aspect, however. Why not just say that there are actually three things, then? I would prefer to say 'two and a third' because the third is not so much a third thing as it is the way you do the first two.

Becoming a Christian always has both an individual and a corporate aspect. People in Western cultures underestimate the degree to which they are the product not of their personal choices but of their families, communities and cultures. Therefore, repentance and faith must be done both individually and communally. We do them when we personally approach God in prayer (as in the previous examples), and also when we publicly identify with Christ by becoming part of the church.

The Gospel of Luke tells us that Jesus was crucified between two robbers who were also being executed. One hurled abuse at Jesus, but the second said to the first, 'We are punished justly, for we are getting what our deeds deserve. But this man has done nothing wrong.' Under the circumstances this was remarkable insight. The thief perceived that Jesus was innocent, dying for the

THE REASON FOR GOD

guilty. Then he turned and said, 'Jesus, remember me when you come into your kingdom.' He was putting all his trust and hope in Jesus, that he would be bringing about a future kingdom, a new heaven and new earth. The moment he put his trust in Christ, Jesus assured him, 'I tell you the truth, today you will be with me in paradise' (Luke 23:41-43).

I recount this because this incident makes it clear that a person can be assured of belonging to Christ the very moment he or she makes that personal heart transaction with God. Nevertheless, everything in the New Testament indicates that Christians should confirm and seal that personal commitment through public, communal action in baptism and becoming part of the church. Hearts are unruly things, and to be sure that we have put our heart-trust in Jesus rather than in other things, we need to follow through and join a body of believers.

I realise that so many people's main problem with Christianity has far more to do with the church than with Jesus. They don't want to be told that to become a Christian and live a Christian life they need to find a church they can thrive in. They've had too many bad experiences with churches. I fully understand. I will grant that, on the whole, churchgoers may be weaker psychologically and morally than non-churchgoers. That should be no more surprising than the fact that people sitting in a doctor's office are on the whole sicker than those who are not there. Churches rightly draw a higher proportion of needy people. They also have a great number of people whose lives have been completely turned around and filled by the joy of Christ.

The church of Jesus Christ is therefore like the ocean. It is enormous and diverse. Like the ocean there are warm and clear spots and deadly cold spots, places you can enter easily without danger and places where it will immediately whisk you away and kill you. I realise how risky it is to tell my readers that they should seek out a church. I don't do it lightly, and I urge them to do so with the utmost care. But there is no alternative. You can't live the Christian life without a band of Christian friends, without a family of believers in which you find a place.

## The Trauma of Grace

When people ask, 'How do I become a Christian?' it is important to give a concrete answer. It is also dangerous to give the impression that finding God is basically a technique, something that is basically up to us. Certainly we should be very active in seeking God, and Jesus himself called us to 'ask, seek, knock' in order to find him. Yet those who enter a relationship with God inevitably look back and recognise that God's grace had sought *them* out, breaking them open to new realities. In some way that you would never expect, the reality of your own fallen nature and God's radical grace breaks through. You realise that your very efforts to be good or happy or authentic have been part of the problem. The penny drops and you see things differently, but you never know how this is going to happen. I could show this in a hundred famous spiritual biographies, such as those of St Paul, Augustine, Martin Luther, John Wesley, or in a thousand testimonies of life change in my own congregation. But my favourite example of the trauma of grace is the one depicted by Flannery O'Connor in her short story 'Revelation'.

The story begins in a doctor's office, where Mrs Turpin and her husband, Claud, are waiting with others for their appointments. Mrs Turpin spends her time sizing up and feeling superior to virtually all the types of people – the races, classes, body types and temperaments – represented by those in the room. She is very smug and self-righteous, but in a very believable way. O'Connor skilfully depicts Mrs Turpin's judgemental thought processes about others in a way that is uncomfortably familiar.

She begins a conversation with another woman who is there with her daughter, a girl named Mary Grace, who is reading a book. As she talks, Mrs Turpin's enormous self-satisfaction and condescension toward others comes out. Mary Grace, though saying nothing, scowls and grimaces as the woman blathers on and on. Finally, Mrs Turpin exclaims:

> *If it's one thing I am, it's grateful. When I think who all I could have been besides myself and what all I got, I just feel like shouting, 'Thank you, Jesus, for making everything the way it is!' It could have been different! . . . Oh thank you, Jesus, thank you!*

At that very moment, Mary Grace explodes. She heaves the book she is reading (entitled *Human Development*) at Mrs Turpin, hitting her in the eye. She crashes across a table, puts her fingers around her throat, and begins to choke her. Mary Grace then has an epileptic fit, and as others restrain her the stunned Mrs Turpin leans over her. ' "What have you got to say to me?" she asked hoarsely and held her breath, waiting, as for a revelation.' At one level, she is asking for an apology, but at another level she begins to realise that the girl is a messenger of God's grace. Mary Grace looks up and says, 'Go back to hell where you came from, you old wart hog!'

The revelation had reached its target, but Mrs Turpin now has to change her worldview in accordance with it. Later that day she is alone with her thoughts out by her own hog pen. 'What do you send a message like that for?' she snarled at God. 'How am I a hog and me both? How am I saved and from hell too?' Centuries before, Martin Luther had learned, in no less a traumatic way, that God saves by grace, not by good works. He realised that a Christian is *simul iustus et peccator* (simultaneously just and accepted – in Christ, by his grace alone) and yet *peccator*, a sinner. Saved and a warthog from hell at the same time.

However, Mrs Turpin, like Martin Luther, resists the revelation of God's grace at first. 'Why me?' she rumbled. 'It's no trash around here, black or white, that I haven't given to. And break my back to the bone every day working. And do for the church. If you like trash better, go get yourself some trash then. . . . Exactly how am I like them? . . . I could quit working and take it easy and be filthy,' she growled. 'Lounge about the sidewalks all day drinking root beer. Dip snuff and spit in every puddle and have it all over my face. I could be nasty.' A final surge of fury shakes her and she cries out to God, '*Who do you think you are?*'

At that moment the sun sets and she sees a purple streak in the sky.

*A visionary light settled in her eyes. She saw . . . a vast swinging bridge extending upward from the earth through a field of living fire. Upon it a vast horde of souls were rumbling toward heaven. There were whole companies of . . . trash . . . and battalions of freaks and lunatics shouting and clapping and leaping like frogs. [But at the] end was a tribe of people whom she recognized at once as those who, like herself and Claud, had always had a little of everything and the God-given wit to use it right. . . . They were marching behind the others with great dignity, accountable as they had always been for good order and common sense and respectable behavior. They alone were on key. Yet she could see by their shocked and altered faces that even their virtues were being burned away. . . . In a moment the vision faded. . . . In the woods around her the invisible cricket choruses had struck up, but what she heard were the voices of the souls climbing upward into the starry field and shouting hallelujah.*[4]

What a radical idea! The 'freaks and lunatics' going to heaven before the morally upright tribe? But Jesus said the same thing, when he announced to the shocked religious leaders of his day, 'I tell you the truth, the tax collectors and the prostitutes are entering the kingdom of God ahead of you' (Matthew 21:31).

WHAT IF YOU HAVE REACHED the end of this book and, as the result of reading it, you wish you could have faith but you don't? The writer Joseph Epstein once admitted that he envied people with the kind of intelligent, deep faith that can see them through the darkest crises. In particular, he was amazed at how Flannery O'Connor's Christian faith enabled her to face an early death due to lupus without complaint or fear. But, he concluded, 'Faith envy is envy, alas, about which one can do nothing but quietly harbor it.'[5] I appreciate Epstein's respect for the mystery of faith. It is not something you can create in yourself through a technique. However, is there really nothing to do?

During a dark time in her life, a woman in my congregation complained that she had prayed over and over, 'God, help me find you,' but had got nowhere. A Christian friend suggested to her that she might change her prayer to, 'God, come and find me. After all, you are the Good Shepherd who goes looking for the lost sheep.' She concluded when she was recounting this to me, 'The only reason I can tell you this story is – he did.'

# Acknowledgements

I want to thank the people and leaders of Redeemer Presbyterian Church, and especially the many enquirers, strugglers and critics I have met there over the years. This book is nothing but the record of what I've learned from them. Thanks to Jill Lamar for her long-time encouragement and support for my writing. Also, thanks to David McCormick, a great agent, Brian Tart, an awesome editor, Nathaniel Calhoun, Jennifer Samuels, David Negrin, Lynn Land, Jim and Susie Lane, Janice Worth, and Nicole Diamond-Austin, the Round Robin women and their spouses, and my three sons – David, Michael and Jonathan – for lending so much support and so many great suggestions as I wrote this over the last four years.

I also owe a deeper sort of acknowledgement to the three people to whom I am most indebted for the fundamental shape of my Christian faith. They are, in order, my wife, Kathy, the British author C. S. Lewis, and the American theologian Jonathan Edwards.

Lewis's words appear in nearly every chapter. It would be wrong not to admit how much of what I think about faith comes from him. Edwards' words appear more seldom, because he has contributed more to the underlying structure of what could be called my 'theology'. Nevertheless, Lewis's and Edwards' thoughts agree and converge in this book in surprising ways. For example, Chapter 13 on the Dance of God is as indebted to one as to the other.

My wife, Kathy, never gets footnoted, yet she is the main author of the faith and thought of *this* author. She put me on to Lewis, to Edwards and Reformed theology, and to the importance of prayer, social justice and the city. When you are that foundational to someone's world- and life-view, you get mentioned in the acknowledgements, but not in the footnotes. The main reason I am putting this book into print is because she likes it. 'The praise of the praiseworthy is above all rewards.'

# Notes

## Introduction

1 See the report 'One in Three Adults Is Unchurched' (March 28, 2005) at the George Barna Group. In Europe, the number of people not attending church has plunged even more precipitously, with British church attendance somewhere in between. See Grace Davie, 'Europe: The Exception that Proves the Rule?' in Peter L. Berger, ed., *The Desecularization of the World: Resurgent Religion and World Politics* (Eerdmans, 1999) and Peter Brierly, *The Tide Is Running Out* (Christian Research, 2000).

2 Ross Douthat, 'Crises of Faith', *The Atlantic Monthly*, July/August 2007.

3 George Marsden, *The Soul of the American University: From Protestant Establishment to Established Non-belief* (Oxford University Press, 1999).

4 Source: Peter Berger at the Pew Forum Faith Angle Conference, 'Religion in a Globalizing World', December 4, 2006, Key West, Florida. Transcript accessed at http://pewforum.org/events/index.php?Event ID=136. See also Douthat, 'Crises of Faith', *The Atlantic Monthly* (July/August 2007). Douthat picks up on the same data that Berger notes, showing that contrary to widespread impressions, Europe is gradually growing more religious while America is becoming more deeply divided between the religious and the secular. Both

these trends, he says, mean ongoing cultural and political conflict and extremism on both sides.

5 'Defending the Faith', by Douglas Groothuis, *Books and Culture* (July/August 2003): 12. See Quentin Smith, 'The Metaphilosophy of Naturalism', *Philo* 4, no. 2 at www.philoonline.org/library/smith_4_2.htm. Today the Society of Christian Philosophers (founded in 1978) includes more than 10 per cent of all the teachers and professors of philosophy in the country. For more on this see K. Clark, *Philosophers Who Believe* (Oxford University Press).

6 'One University Under God?' *The Chronicle of Higher Education: Careers*, January 7, 2005.

7 For a good overview, read the entire transcript of the Peter Berger–led Pew Forum referenced above.

8 'A New Jerusalem', *The Economist*, September 21, 2006.

9 It is often agreed that a 'fact' is either a) something that is self-evident to virtually everyone (e.g., 'There's a rock in the road') or b) something that is not self-evident to the senses but can be proved scientifically. If we hold to something that can't be demonstrated in either of those ways then it is a 'belief' or an act of faith.

10 For a good short summary of why we are all 'believers', see Christian Smith, 'Believing Animals', *Moral Believing Animals: Human Personhood and Culture* (Oxford University Press, 2003).

11 Each Easter at Redeemer we ask members to share the personal accounts of their faith journeys. These are a selection from Easter 2006. Used with permission.

## ONE—There Can't Be Just *One* True Religion

1 The quotes at the beginning of each chapter are taken from an e-mail survey of young New Yorkers in their mid-twenties who were asked to articulate their main doubts and objections to Christianity. I've changed the names. Thanks to Nicole Diamond-Austin for the idea and the execution of the survey.

2 The recent wave of bestselling anti-religion books by Richard

Dawkins, Sam Harris, Daniel Dennett and Christopher Hitchens do not recommend that religion be outlawed, but only because they don't think that strategy is workable. Their main hope is for religion to be so strongly condemned, ridiculed and formally privatised that it becomes weakened and marginalised.

3 Alister McGrath, *The Twilight of Atheism: The Rise and Fall of Disbelief in the Modern World* (Oxford University Press, 2004), p. 230. See also pp. 187, 235.

4 Many prominent thinkers in the mid-twentieth century believed that by the time their grandchildren were their age most religions would have waned or died out. As an example, an anthropologist could write in 1966: *'The evolutionary future of religion is extinction. . . . Belief in supernatural powers is doomed to die out, all over the world, as the result of the increasing adequacy and diffusion of scientific knowledge.'* A. F. C. Wallace, *Religion: An Anthropological View* (Random House, 1966), p. 265.

5 For some account of how sociologists have backed away from the secularisation thesis, see Peter L. Berger, ed., *The Desecularization of the World: Resurgent Religion and World Politics* (Eerdmans, 1999).

6 On the growth of Christianity in the non-Western world, see Philip Jenkins, *The Next Christendom* (Oxford University Press, 2002) and Lamin Sanneh, *Whose Religion Is Christianity?* (Eerdmans, 2003).

7 Joe Klein, 'Because I Promised and You Seemed So Darn Curious . . .' on the *Time* magazine blog, March 7, 2007. Accessed that date at http://time-blog.com/swampland/2007/03/because_i_promised_ and_you_see.html.

8 Lesslie Newbigin, *The Gospel in a Pluralist Society* (Eerdmans, 1989), pp. 9–10, 170.

9 Peter Berger, *A Rumor of Angels: Modern Society and the Rediscovery of the Supernatural* (Doubleday, 1969), p. 40.

10 There are many sophisticated critiques that demonstrate the self-refuting nature of relativism. Just one example is H. Siegel, *Relativism Refuted: A Critique of Contemporary Epistemological Relativism* (Dordrecht: D. Reidel, 1987). There is a very influential view that

claims 'truth' only exists within a particular framework of beliefs and that each is of equal value because there is no framework-transcending criterion by which to adjudicate between all the truth-claims. A more postmodern version of this claim is the assertion that reality is 'language-ridden' and every truth-claim is nothing but the insights of a particular linguistic community. But, as Siegel points out, to say that all reality accounts are language-ridden and relative to their own linguistic communities is itself a universal account of the working of language across all communities and therefore is a claim about the human condition as such. The relativists' own view of things does not give them the right to speak like that. They do the very thing they forbid other communities to do. 'Thus . . . relativism cannot proclaim itself, or even recognize itself, without defeating itself' (p. 43).

11 Alvin Plantinga, 'A Defense of Religious Exclusivism', in *The Analytic Theist*, ed. James F. Sennett (Eerdmans, 1998), p. 205.

12 John Hick, *The Myth of God Incarnate* (Westminster, 1977) and *An Interpretation of Religion* (Yale University Press, 1989). For a much more extensive answer to Hick than I give here see Peter Van Inwagen, 'Non Est Hick', in *The Rationality of Belief and the Plurality of Faith*, ed. T. Senor (Cornell University Press, 1995).

13 A sophisticated presentation of this point is found in Stanley Fish's 'The Trouble with Tolerance' in the November 10, 2006, issue of the *Chronicle of Higher Education*. This is a review of Wendy Brown's *Regulating Aversion: Tolerance in the Age of Identity and Empire* (Princeton University Press, 2006). Her point (and Fish's) is that the Western idea of 'tolerance for all views' is itself a very particular set of assumptions about reality that is then used as a criterion to determine who society will tolerate and who it won't. Fish says that our society has its own set of holy, unquestionable beliefs, like 'the sanctity of choice'. Brown and Fish argue that many historic, traditional beliefs have only become 'intolerant' in our society because of the new construction our liberal Western society puts upon them. 'It assumes that people do things not because of what they believe, but because they are Jews, Muslims, blacks or

gays . . . they are immune to rational appeal.' Therefore any religion that values its own truth ahead of tolerance is considered 'over-attached' to their culture and incapable of being rational. 'Once a group has rejected tolerance as a guiding principle and opted instead for the cultural imperatives of the church or tribe, it becomes a candidate for intolerance that will be performed in the name of tolerance.'

14  C. John Sommerville, *The Decline of the Secular University* (Oxford University Press, 2006), p. 63.

15  Mark Lilla, 'Getting Religion: My Long-lost Years as a Teenage Evangelical', in *New York Times Magazine* September 18, 2005, p. 95.

16  Robert Audi, 'The Separation of Church and State and the Obligations of Citizenship', *Philosophy and Public Affairs* 18 (1989): 296; John Rawls, *Political Liberalism* (Columbia University Press, 1993), pp. 212–254.

17  On February 28, 2007, this document could be accessed at http://www.cfidc.org/declaration.html.

18  Richard Rorty, 'Religion as a Conversation-Stopper', *Philosophy and Social Hope* (Penguin, 1999), pp. 168–169.

19  See Richard Rorty, *Consequences of Pragmatism* (University of Minnesota Press, 1982) pp. 166–67.

20  Stephen L. Carter, *The Dissent of the Governed* (Harvard University Press, 1999), p. 90.

21  For example, Linda Hirshman makes a case against women staying out of the marketplace to raise children at home. She insists that it is wrong for women to do that even if it is their free, voluntary choice. *'The family – with its repetitious, socially invisible, physical tasks – is a necessary part of life, but it allows fewer opportunities for full human flourishing than public spheres like the market or the government. This less-flourishing sphere is not the natural or moral responsibility only of women. . . . Women assigning it to themselves is . . . unjust.'* ('Homeward Bound', in *The American Prospect* 16, no. 12 (December 2005). Notice her argument is based on an

assessment of 'human flourishing' that could never be empirically proven. It is rooted in views of human dignity and society that on the surface seem secular but are certainly unproveable, controversial and ultimately based on worldview faith-assumptions. David Brooks takes issue with Hirshman: '[She asserts] that high-paying jobs lead to more human flourishing than parenthood. Look back over your life. Which memories do you cherish more, those with your family or those at the office?' See 'The Year of Domesticity', *New York Times*, January 1, 2006.

22  Gary Rosen, 'Narrowing the Religion Gap?', *New York Times Sunday Magazine*, February 18, 2007.

23  This interchange is adapted from C. John Sommerville, 'The Exhaustion of Secularism', *The Chronicle Review* (June 9, 2006).

24  Michael J. Perry, *Under God? Religious Faith and Liberal Democracy* (Cambridge University Press, 2003), p. 44. Nevertheless, Perry rightly argues that religiously grounded public discourse in a liberal democracy must be 'deliberative', not just 'dogmatic'. That is, speakers must be willing to be criticised, to answer criticism, to deliberate and debate and seek to make one's case as plausible to the other side as possible.

25  See Perry's Chapter 3: 'Why Political Reliance on Religiously Grounded Morality Is Not Illegitimate in a Liberal Democracy' in *Under God?* above.

26  See John Witte, Jr, 'God's Joust, God's Justice: An Illustration from the History of Marriage Law', in *Christian Perspectives on Legal Thought*, M. McConnell, R. Cochran, A. Carmella, eds. (Yale University Press, 2001), pp. 406–425.

27  Stanley Fish, 'Our Faith in Letting It All Hang Out', *New York Times*, February 12, 2006.

28  Miroslav Volf, 'Soft Difference: Theological Reflections on the Relation Between Church and Culture in 1 Peter', *Ex Auditu* 10 (1994): 15–30.

29  See C. S. Lewis's appendix, 'Illustrations of the Tao' in *The Abolition of Man* (Macmillan, 1947). Lewis's point is that there is sig-

nificant overlap among the religions with regard to ethics – how we are supposed to live in the world. The sharp differences between religions come in another area – 'soteriology'. Religions differ in their directions for how to connect to God and get the spiritual power to live in the prescribed way.

30 This statement may surprise many readers who have heard that older religions and paganism were more positive towards women than Christianity was. It was extremely common in the Graeco-Roman world to throw out new female infants to die from exposure, because of the low status of women in society. The church forbade its members to do so. Graeco-Roman society saw no value in an unmarried woman, and therefore it was illegal for a widow to go more than two years without remarrying. But Christianity was the first religion to not force widows to marry. They were supported financially and honoured within the community so that they were not under great pressure to remarry if they didn't want to. Pagan widows lost all control of their husband's estate when they remarried but the church allowed widows to maintain their husband's estate. Finally, Christians did not believe in cohabitation. If a Christian man wanted to live with a woman he had to marry her, and this gave women far greater security. Also, the pagan double standard of allowing married men to have extramarital sex and mistresses was forbidden. In all these ways Christian women enjoyed far greater security and equality than did women in the surrounding culture. See Rodney Stark, *The Rise of Christianity* (Harper, 1996), Chapter 5: 'The Role of Women in Christian Growth'.

31 A great summary of why Christianity triumphed over the older paganism through its practices of compassion and justice is found in Rodney Stark, *The Rise of Christianity* (Harper, 1996), Chapters 4, 6, 7.

## TWO—How Could a Good God Allow Suffering?

1 This argument was put in its most classic form by David Hume in *Dialogues Concerning Natural Religion*, ed. Richard Popkin

(Hackett, 1980). 'Epicurus' old questions are yet unanswered. Is [God] willing to prevent evil but not able? Then he is impotent. Is he able but not willing? Then he is malevolent. Is he both able *and* willing? From whence then is evil?' (p. 63).

2  Ron Rosenbaum, 'Disaster Ignites Debate: Was God in the Tsunami?', *New York Observer*, January 10, 2005. Of course Mackie was only articulating a very ancient question, from Epicurus through David Hume. See note 1 above.

3  W. P. Alston, 'The Inductive Argument from Evil and the Human Cognitive Condition', *Philosophical Perspectives* 5:30–67. See also *The Evidential Argument from Evil*, Daniel Howard-Snyder, ed., (Indiana University Press, 1996) for an extensive survey of the a-theological argument from evil.

4  The summary of Mackie's argument is based on that of Daniel Howard-Snyder in his 'God, Evil, and Suffering', in *Reason for the Hope Within*, ed. M. J. Murray (Eerdmans, 1999), p. 84. The Howard-Snyder article is an excellent summary article in its own right, and shows why there are not currently confident assertions among philosophers that evil and suffering disprove the existence of God. Indeed, the book by Mackie (1982) may be the last significant work to do so.

5  The 'no-see-um' argument and related issues on the problem of evil are treated in Alvin Plantinga, *Warranted Christian Belief* (Oxford, 2000), pp. 466–67. See also Alvin Plantinga, 'A Christian Life Partly Lived' in *Philosophers Who Believe*, ed. Kelly James Clark (IVP, 1993), p. 72.

6  C. S. Lewis, *Mere Christianity* (Macmillan, 1960), p. 31.

7  Alvin Plantinga, 'A Christian Life Partly Lived', *Philosophers Who Believe*, ed. Kelly James Clark (IVP, 1993), p. 73.

8  William Lane, *The Gospel According to Mark* (Eerdmans, 1974), p. 516.

9  Ibid, p. 573.

10  Jonathan Edwards concludes: 'The sufferings which Christ endured in his body on the cross . . . were yet the least part of his last

sufferings. . . . If it had been only the sufferings which he endured in his body, though they were very dreadful, we cannot conceive that the mere anticipation of them would have such an effect on Christ. Many of the martyrs have endured as severe tortures in their bodies as Christ did . . . yet their souls have not been so overwhelmed.' See 'Christ's Agony', *The Works of Jonathan Edwards*, vol. 2, E. Hickman, ed. (Banner of Truth, 1972).

11 In the history of theology there has been much debate over whether an infinite, eternal God can actually have 'passions' and experience joy and pain and grief. One side argues the 'impassibility' of God and insists all such biblical language is merely metaphorical. Others, like Jürgen Moltmann (*The Crucified God*) argue strongly for the 'passibility' of God. A balanced view of this is provided by Don Carson, in *The Difficult Doctrine of the Love of God* (IVP, 2000), pp. 66–73. Carson argues that God does suffer grief and pain, but guards this position with careful qualifications and balancing assertions.

12 *Essais* (Gallimard, 1965), p. 444. Translated and quoted by Bruce Ward in 'Prometheus or Cain? Albert Camus's Account of the Western Quest for Justice', *Faith and Philosophy* (April 1991): 213.

13 J. R. R. Tolkien, 'The Field of Cormallen', *The Return of the King* (various editions).

14 This may be the reason George MacDonald can say: 'We do not know how much of the pleasures even of life we owe to the intermingled sorrows. Joy [alone] cannot unfold the deepest truths, although deepest truth must be the deepest joy.' *Phantastes: A Faerie Romance* (Eerdmans, 1981), p. 67.

15 Fyodor Dostoevsky, *The Brothers Karamazov*, Chapter 34. I think it should be stated that Dostoevsky does not say it will be possible to justify the evil itself. Evil may be used by God to bring about even greater good than if it had not occurred, but it nonetheless remains evil, and therefore inexcusable and unjustifiable in itself.

16 C. S. Lewis, *The Great Divorce* (Macmillan, 1946), p. 64.

THREE—**Christianity Is a Straitjacket**

1 M. Scott Peck, *The People of the Lie: The Hope for Healing Human Evil* (Simon and Schuster, 1983), Chapter 4, p. 168. Peck uses Charlene as an example of the mental un-health that engulfs a person who has nothing in his or her life more important than the fulfilment of individual needs and wants. *'Mental health requires that the human will submit itself to something higher than itself. To function decently in this world we must submit ourselves to some principle that takes precedence over what we want at any given moment.'* p. 162.

2 Emma Goldman, 'The Failure of Christianity', first published in 1913, in Goldman's *Mother Earth* journal. Found at http://dwardmac.pitzer .edu/Anarchist_Archives/goldman/failureofchristianity.html accessed on December 26, 2005.

3 This is from the famous 'Sweet Mystery of Life' statement in the Supreme Court's *Planned Parenthood v. Casey* ruling: *'At the heart of liberty is the right to define one's own concept of existence, of meaning of the universe, and the mystery of human life.'* Notice that the statement does not say we are just free to 'discover' truth for ourselves but rather to 'define' and create it.

4 From David Friend and the editors of *Life*, *The Meaning of Life: Reflections in Words and Pictures on Why We Are Here* (Little, Brown, 1991), p. 33.

5 From 'Truth and Power', in Michel Foucault, *Power/Knowledge: Selected Interviews and Other Writing 1972–1977*, ed. Colin Gordon (Pantheon, 1980), p. 131.

6 C. S. Lewis, *The Abolition of Man* (Collins, 1978), p. 48.

7 Emily Eakin, 'The Latest Theory Is That Theory Doesn't Matter', *New York Times*, April 19, 2003, and 'The Theory of Everything, RIP', *New York Times*, October 17, 2004. See also Dinitia Smith, 'Cultural Theorists, Start Your Epitaphs', *New York Times*, January 3, 2004.

8 G. K. Chesterton, in *Orthodoxy: The Romance of Faith* (Doubleday, 1990), pp. 33, 41–42.

9 For a good summary of the faith-commitments underlying any 'liberal democracy' see Michael J. Perry, *Under God?*, p. 36. See also Stanley Fish's November 10, 2006, *Chronicle of Higher Education* article, 'The Trouble with Tolerance'.

10 Alasdair MacIntyre, *After Virtue: A Study in Moral Theory*, 2nd ed. (University of Notre Dame Press, 1984), and *Whose Justice? Which Rationality?* (University of Notre Dame Press, 1988).

11 On this subject there are many good books. Among them are Stephen L. Carter, *The Dissent of the Governed* (Harvard University Press, 1999), p. 90. See also Alasdair MacIntyre, *Whose Justice? Which Rationality?* (Duckworth, 1987). Richard John Neuhaus, *The Naked Public Square: Religion and Democracy in America*, 2nd ed. (Eerdmans, 1986), and Wilfred McClay, 'Two Kinds of Secularism', *The Wilson Quarterly* (Summer 2000). A sophisticated dialogue on this subject can be found in R. Audi and N. Wolterstorff, *Religion in the Public Square: The Place of Religious Convictions in Political Debate* (Rowman and Littlefield, 1997). See Chapter 8 for more on the worldview soil that human rights need in order to grow.

12 Michel Foucault has pointed out that the Western society's emphasis on individual rights and 'inclusion' of minorities, women, *et al* is accompanied by a 'shadow narrative' of exclusion. How do we regard those who don't accept the Western concepts of individual rights and privacy? Foucault points out that those who question modernity's views of rights and reason are stigmatised not as 'immoral' or 'heretical' (as in medieval times) but now as 'irrational' and 'uncivilised'. For a good summary of Foucault's critique of so-called Western 'inclusiveness' see Miroslav Volf, *Exclusion and Embrace: A Theological Exploration of Identity, Otherness, and Reconciliation* (Abingdon, 1996), pp. 58–64.

13 'Radical indeterminacy . . . is a correlate of a consistent drive toward inclusion that levels all boundaries that divide. [But does this] . . . not undermine from within the idea of inclusion, however? Without boundaries we will be able to know only what we are

fighting against but not what we are fighting for. Intelligent struggle against exclusion demands categories and normative criteria that enable us to distinguish between repressive . . . practices . . . and nonrepressive ones. . . . 'No boundaries' means . . . neither happiness nor pleasure, neither freedom nor justice, could be identified.' Volf, *Exclusion and Embrace*, p. 61.

14 An obvious example was the remark by Jerry Falwell on Pat Robertson's *The 700 Club* in the wake of the 9–11 attacks. 'I really believe that the pagans, and the abortionists, and the feminists, and the gays and the lesbians who are actively trying to make that an alternative lifestyle, the ACLU, People for the American Way, all of them who have tried to secularize America. I point the finger in their face and say "you helped this happen".' The widespread outcry and complaints from within the church forced Falwell to retract his statement within hours. (See http://archives.cnn.com/2001/US/09/14/Falwell.apology. Last accessed March 5, 2007.)

15 Lamin Sanneh, *Whose Religion Is Christianity?* (Eerdmans, 2003), p. 15.

16 Philip Jenkins, *The Next Christendom: The Coming of Global Christianity* (Oxford University Press, 2002), p. 56.

17 Ibid., p. 70.

18 David Aikman, *Jesus in Beijing: How Christianity Is Transforming China and Changing the Global Balance of Power* (Regnery, 2003), p. 285.

19 Sanneh attributes this to Christianity's 'translatability'. A Gambian and former Muslim, he contrasts Christianity with Islam, which insists that the true Qu'ran cannot really be translated. To truly hear God's word, you must learn Arabic. But to privilege one language is to privilege one culture, because the key words in any language have a meaning rooted in a culture's traditions and thought-forms. In contrast to Islam, Christianity (according to the book of Acts) was born in the miracle of Pentecost in which every hearer heard the gospel in their own language. So no one language or culture is privileged over any other. The Bible is translated into

every culture and language. See Lamin Sanneh, 'Translatability in Islam and Christianity, with Special Reference to Africa', *Translating the Message: The Missionary Impact on Culture* (Orbis, 1987), p. 211ff.

20 Lamin Sanneh, *Whose Religion Is Christianity?* (Eerdmans, 2003), p. 43.

21 Ibid., pp. 43–44, 69–70.

22 Sanneh and Andrew F. Walls do not deny that missionaries from one culture (e.g., European) usually impose their own culture's form of Christianity on the new converts. But when converts get to read the Bible in their own language, they come to see things in the Word that the missionaries 'played down' (like exorcisms) and other things they 'played up' in accordance with their own cultural perspectives and biases. This may lead to a time of *over*-reaction against the missionaries' form of faith. Eventually the converts come to terms with their own cultures and traditions – rejecting parts of it, affirming parts of it, and modifying parts of it all in light of their reading of the Scriptures.

23 From R. Niebuhr, 'Humour and Faith', *The Essential Reinhold Niebuhr*, R. M. Brown, ed. (Yale University Press, 1986), p. 49ff. Quoted in Sommerville, *The Decline of the Secular University*, p. 129.

24 Andrew F. Walls, 'The Expansion of Christianity: An Interview with Andrew Walls', *Christian Century*, August 2–9, 2000, p. 792.

25 'Christianity is the religion of over two thousand different language groups in the world. More people pray and worship in more languages than in any other religion in the world. . . . Obviously these facts of cultural and linguistic pioneering conflict with the reputation of Christianity as one colossal act of cultural intolerance. This has produced a deep Christendom guilt complex, against which all evidence seems unavailing. It is important, however, to get people to budge, because the default Christianity they now practice is a worn-out cultural fragment of something much greater and fresher.' Sanneh, *Whose Religion Is Christianity?*, pp. 69–70.

26 This term comes from A. J. Conyers, 'Can Postmodernism Be Used as a Template for Christian Theology?', *Christian Scholar's Review* 33 (Spring 2004): 3.

27 Kevin Vanhoozer, 'Pilgrim's Digress: Christian Thinking on and About the Post/Modern Way', in *Christianity and the Postmodern Turn*, ed. Myron B. Penner (Brazos, 2005), p. 74.

28 Quoted in John Stott, *The Contemporary Christian* (IVP, 1992). The interview's English translation appeared in the *Guardian Weekly*, June 23, 1985.

29 C. S. Lewis, *The Four Loves* (Harcourt, 1960), p. 123.

30 The unnamed 'old author' is quoted in C. S. Lewis, *The Four Loves* (Harcourt, 1988), p. 140.

## FOUR—The Church Is Responsible for So Much Injustice

1 Mark Lilla, 'Getting Religion: My Long-lost Years as a Teenage Evangelical', in the *New York Times Magazine*, September 18, 2005, p. 94–95.

2 'If what you want is an argument against Christianity . . . you can easily find some stupid and unsatisfactory Christian and say . . . "So there's your boasted new man! Give me the old kind." But if once you have begun to see that Christianity is on other grounds probable, you will know in your heart that this is only evading the issue. What can you ever really know of other people's souls – of their temptations, their opportunities, their struggles? One soul in the whole creation you do know: and it is the only one whose fate is placed in your hands. If there is a God, you are, in a sense, alone with Him. You cannot put Him off with speculations about your next-door neighbours or memories of what you have read in books. What will all that chatter and hearsay count when the anaesthetic fog we call "nature" or "the real world" fades away and the Divine Presence in which you have always stood becomes palpable, immediate, and unavoidable?' C. S. Lewis, *Mere Christianity* (Macmillan, 1965), p. 168.

3 Christopher Hitchens, *God Is Not Great: How Religion Poisons Everything* (Hachette, 2007), pp. 35–36.

4 Some secular thinkers today insist that every religion has the seeds for oppression within it. This view, however, fails to take into consideration the enormous differences between religious faiths in their views of conversion. Buddhism and Christianity, for example, require a profound inner transformation based on personal decision. Coerced compliance with external rules is seen as spiritually deadly. These faiths, then, are much more likely to seek a society that values religious freedom, so that individuals can learn the truth and give themselves to it freely. Max Weber and others have demonstrated that Christian doctrine, particularly in its Protestant form, provides a basis for individual rights and freedom that is conducive for the growth of both democracy and capitalism. Other philosophies and faiths put much less value on individual freedom of choice. The difference between Christianity and Islam on the meaning of conversion is a case in point. Christian conversion involves coming from only 'knowing about' God to 'knowing God' personally. Most Muslims would consider it presumptuous to speak of knowing God intimately and personally. A child growing up in a Christian home may nonetheless speak of his or her conversion at age ten or fifteen or twenty. A child growing up in a Muslim home would never speak of being converted to Islam. This difference in understanding means that Christians see little value in putting social pressure on people to convert or to maintain their Christian profession. Islam, however, sees no problem with applying legal and social pressure to keep citizens aligned with Muslim commitments. (Thanks to Don Carson for this insight.)

5 Alister McGrath, *The Dawkins Delusion? Atheist Fundamentalism and the Denial of the Divine* (Inter-Varsity Press, 2007), p. 81.

6 Merold Westphal, *Suspicion and Faith: The Religious Uses of Modern Atheism* (Eerdmans, 1993), Chapters 32–34. See page 203: 'I would like to . . . accuse Marx of plagiarism. His critique of capitalism is, in essence, the biblical concern for widows and orphans, stripped of its theological foundation and applied to the conditions of modernity.'

7 Westphal, *Suspicion and Faith*, p. 205.

8 See Proverbs 14:31; 19:17; Matthew 25:31–46. Calvin's remark is from his commentary on Habbakuk 2:6 and is quoted in Westphal, *Suspicion and Faith*, p. 200.

9 C. John Sommerville, *The Decline of the Secular University* (Oxford University Press, 2006), p. 63.

10 Ibid., pp. 69–70.

11 Ibid., p. 70.

12 Rodney Stark, *For the Glory of God: How Monotheism Led to Reformations, Science, Witch-Hunts, and the End of Slavery* (Princeton University Press, 2004), p. 291. See pp. 338–53 for an overview of abolition movements.

13 See Deuteronomy 24:7 and 1 Timothy 1:9–11, which forbid kidnapping. Many people (both inside the Christian church and outside) assume that the Bible supports slavery. For more on this see Chapter 6.

14 See Mark Noll's *The Civil War as a Theological Crisis* (University of North Carolina Press, 2006) for an extensive discussion of how Christians debated slavery through different interpretations of the Scripture. Noll's book demonstrates how some church leaders used texts in the Bible regarding slavery to justify the slave trade. But they were blind to the stark differences between African chattel slavery and the bond-service and indentured servanthood treated in the Bible.

15 Stark, *For the Glory of God* (Princeton, 2004), pp. 350ff.

16 David L. Chappell, *A Stone of Hope: Prophetic Religion and the Death of Jim Crow* (University of North Carolina Press, 2003).

17 A narrative of the Catholic Church's resistance to Communism in the 1970s and 1980s is given in Chapter 17 in 'Between Two Crosses', in Charles Colson and Ellen Vaughn, *The Body* (Thomas Nelson, 2003).

18 Dietrich Bonhoeffer, *Letters and Papers from Prison: Enlarged Edition*, Eberhard Bethge, ed. (Macmillan, 1971), p. 418.

FIVE—**How Can a Loving God Send People to Hell?**

1 May 23, 2005, Pew Forum's biannual Faith Angle conference on religion, politics and public life in Key West, Florida. As of September 5, 2005, the transcript was found at http://pewforum.org/events/index.php?Event ID=80.

2 Robert Bellah, *et al.*, *Habits of the Heart: Individualism and Commitment in American Life*, 1st ed., (University of California Press, 1985), p. 228.

3 From C. S. Lewis, *The Abolition of Man* (Collins, 1978), p. 46. On this subject see also Lewis, *English Literature in the Sixteenth Century, Excluding Drama* in the Oxford History of English Literature series (Oxford University Press, 1953), pp. 13–14.

4 Lewis, *Abolition of Man*, p. 46.

5 Alan Jacobs, in his biography of Lewis, notes that he took pains to insist that he had no quarrel with the scientific method per se. That method actually assumes the uniformity of nature, and many scholars have pointed out that it was the Christian worldview that provided this. But Lewis is pointing out that modern science was born with 'dreams of power'. See Jacobs, *The Narnian: The Life and Imagination of C. S. Lewis* (Harper San Francisco, 2005), pp. 184–187.

6 Rebecca Pippert, *Hope Has Its Reasons* (Harper, 1990), Chapter 4, 'What Kind of God Gets Angry?'

7 Miroslav Volf, *Exclusion and Embrace: A Theological Exploration of Identity, Otherness, and Reconciliation* (Abingdon, 1996), pp. 303–304.

8 Volf, *Exclusion and Embrace*, p. 303.

9 Czeslaw Milosz, 'The Discreet Charm of Nihilism', *New York Review of Books*, November 19, 1998.

10 All descriptions and depictions of heaven and hell in the Bible are symbolic and metaphorical. Each metaphor suggests one aspect of the experience of hell. (For example, 'fire' tells us of the disintegration, while 'darkness' tells us of the isolation.) Having said that does not at all imply that heaven or hell *themselves* are 'metaphors'.

They are very much realities. Jesus ascended (with his physical body, mind you) into heaven. The Bible clearly proposes that heaven and hell are actual realities, but also indicates that all language about them is allusive, metaphorical and partial.

11 For more on the likeness of sin to addiction, see Cornelius Plantinga, *Not the Way It's Supposed to Be: A Breviary of Sin* (Eerdmans, 1995), Chapter 8, 'The Tragedy of Addiction'.

12 This is a compilation of quotes from three Lewis sources: *Mere Christianity* (Macmillan, 1964), p. 59; *The Great Divorce* (Macmillan, 1963), pp. 71–72; 'The Trouble with X', in *God in the Dock: Essays on Theology and Ethics* (Eerdmans, 1970), p. 155.

13 From C. S. Lewis, *The Problem of Pain* (Macmillan, 1961), p. 116; *The Great Divorce* (Macmillan, 1963), p. 69.

## six—Science Has Disproved Christianity

1 Richard Dawkins, *The Blind Watchmaker* (W. W. Norton, 1986), p. 6.

2 Richard Dawkins, *The God Delusion* (Boston: Houghton Mifflin, 2006), p. 100.

3 Van Harvey, for example, says that defences of miraculous events can never be taken seriously by the critical historian, because such thinking violates *'what we now call the common-sense view of the world'*. Van Harvey, *The Historian and Believer* (Macmillan, 1966), p. 68. See also his essay, 'New Testament Scholarship and Christian Belief' in *Jesus in History and Myth*, R. Joseph Hoffman and Gerald A. Larue, eds. (Prometheus, 1986).

4 John Macquarrie, *Principles of Christian Theology* (Scribner, 1977), p. 248, quoted in Plantinga, *Warranted Christian Belief*, p. 394.

5 Plantinga, *Warranted Christian Belief*, p. 406. Plantinga cites an important article by the philosopher William Alston, who argues that one can perfectly well do science even if one thinks God has done and even sometimes still does miracles. See 'Divine Action: Shadow or Substance?' in *The God Who Acts: Philosophical and*

Notes

*Theological Explorations*, Thomas F. Tracy, ed. (Pennsylvania State University Press, 1994), pp. 49–50.

6 See John Paul II's Message to the Pontifical Academy of Sciences, October 22, 1996, 'Magisterium Is Concerned with the Question of Evolution for It Involves Conception of Man'.

7 Francis Collins, *The Language of God: A Scientist Presents Evidence for Belief* (Free Press, 2006). Another example of a leading scientist who believes in a God-designed universe yet rejects both Intelligent Design and evolution as materialist philosophy is Harvard astronomer Owen Gingerich, who wrote *God's Universe* (Belknap Press, 2006).

8 Ian Barbour, *When Science Meets Religion: Enemies, Strangers, or Partners?* (Harper, 2000). Barbour argues that while Christians use all of these models, what he calls 'integration' is the best. See Chapter 4 on 'Evolution and Continuing Creation'.

9 Christian Smith, ed., *The Secular Revolution: Power, Interests, and Conflict in the Secularization of American Public Life* (University of California Press, 2003).

10 Ibid., pp. 1–12. See also Alister McGrath's chapter, 'Warfare: The Natural Sciences and the Advancement of Atheism', *The Twilight of Atheism* (Oxford University Press, 2002), and Rodney Stark's chapter, 'God's Handiwork: The Religious Origins of Science', in *For the Glory of God* (Princeton University Press, 2004).

11 Edward Larson and Larry Witham, 'Scientists Are Still Keeping the Faith', *Nature* (April 3, 1997). See also Stark, *To the Glory of God*, pp. 192–97.

12 Edward Larson and Larry Witham, 'Leading Scientists Still Reject God', *Nature* 394, no. 6691 (1998): 313.

13 Alister McGrath, *The Dawkins Delusion?*, p. 44.

14 From Stephen Jay Gould, 'Impeaching a Self-Appointed Judge', *Scientific American* 267, no. 1 (1992). Quoted in Alister McGrath, *The Dawkins Delusion?* (Inter-Varsity, 2007), p. 34.

15 Thomas Nagel, 'The Fear of Religion', *The New Republic* (October 23, 2006).

16 Stark, *For the Glory of God*, pp. 192–97.

17  See Gordon Wenham, *Genesis 1–15* (Word, 1987).

18  Despite widespread impressions to the contrary, both inside and outside the church, modern Creation Science was not the traditional response of conservative and evangelical Protestants in the nineteenth century when Darwin's theory first became known. There was widespread acceptance of the fact that Genesis 1 may have been speaking of long ages rather than literal days. R. A. Torrey, the fundamentalist editor of *The Fundamentals* (published from 1910–1915, which gave definition to the term 'fundamentalist'), said that it was possible *'to believe thoroughly in the infallibility of the Bible and still be an evolutionist of a certain type'* (quoted in Mark Noll, *Evangelical American Christianity: An Introduction* [Blackwells, 2001], p. 171). The man who defined the doctrine of biblical inerrancy, B. B. Warfield of Princeton (d. 1921), believed that God may have used something like evolution to bring about life-forms. The best account of the rise of modern Creation Science is by Ronald L. Numbers, *The Creationists: the Evolution of Scientific Creationism* (Knopf, 1992). See also Mark Noll, *The Scandal of the Evangelical Mind* (Eerdmans, 1994), 'Thinking About Science', and Mark Noll and David Livingstone, *B. B. Warfield on Evolution, Scripture, and Science* (Baker, 2000).

19  David Atkinson, *The Message of Genesis 1–11* (IVP, 1990), p. 31.

SEVEN—**You Can't Take the Bible Literally**

1  Quoted in a review of *Christ the Lord: Out of Egypt* by George Sim Johnston in *The Wall Street Journal*, November 12–13, 2005.

2  For example, the famous argument for the divinity of Christ – 'Liar, Lunatic, or Lord?' – does not work unless it can be shown that Jesus really claimed to be divine. C. S. Lewis put this argument in its classic form: 'A man who was merely a man and said the sort of things Jesus said would not be a great moral teacher. He would either be a lunatic – on the level with a man who says he is a poached egg – or he would be the devil of hell. You must take your choice. Either this was, and is,

the Son of God, or else a madman or something worse. You can shut Him up for a fool or you can fall at His feet and call Him Lord and God. But let us not come with any patronising nonsense about His being a great human teacher. He has not left that open to us.' (*Mere Christianity*, Book 2, Chapter 3.) The problem with this argument is that it assumes that the biblical accounts of Jesus' words are accurate. That requires the establishment that the Bible is historically reliable, at least in general. A better statement of the argument would be: Jesus is either 'Liar, Lunatic, Legend, or Lord'. Until you show that the picture of Christ in the Bible is not totally legendary, the famous argument is not effective.

3 The Jesus Seminar uses the 'double dissimilarity criteria' as a way of evaluating the historical validity of a biblical text. That is, they claim that we can only be sure a passage in the Gospel is historically genuine if its teaching could not possibly have come either from first-century Judaism or from the early church. It must, therefore, contradict what we know about the dominant beliefs of first-century Judaism or Christianity. (Otherwise we can't be sure that that passage wasn't created to support the dominant belief.) But this criteria assumes that Jesus could not have been affected by his Jewish heritage *and* that he could have left no mark on his followers. Because of the unlikeliness of this, more and more biblical scholars are sharply criticising the work of the Jesus Seminar as unnecessarily negative and biased against the Gospels.

4 I am not here trying to argue for the complete trustworthiness of the Bible, only that its portrayal of the life and teaching of Jesus is historically accurate. If it is, then we can draw conclusions about who Jesus is from the information we read there. If eventually we put our faith in Jesus, then his view of the Bible will become ours. Speaking personally, I take the whole Bible to be reliable not because I can somehow 'prove' it all to be factual. I accept it because I believe in Jesus and that was his view of the Bible.

5 A scholarly but readable response to the *The Da Vinci Code* is Ben Witherington, *The Gospel Code* (IVP, 2004). Witherington's

refutation of the historical assumptions behind *The Da Vinci Code* is devastating.

6 There is a large and growing body of top-flight scholarship that argues for the historical reliability of the Gospels. For a more detailed case than we can possibly conduct here, consult the following important books: Richard Bauckham, *Jesus and the Eyewitnesses* (Eerdmans, 2006), N. T. Wright, *Jesus and the Victory of God* (Fortress, 1998) and *The Resurrection of the Son of God* (Fortress, 2003), C. Blomberg, *The Historical Reliability of the Gospels* (IVP, 1987), and *The Historical Reliability of John's Gospel* (IVP, 2002), as well as the more popular and older F. F. Bruce, *The New Testament Documents: Are They Reliable?* (Eerdmans, reissued 2003 with a foreword by N. T. Wright). Much of the most sceptical criticism of the Bible purports to be based in rigorous historical research, but it is heavily influenced by philosophical presuppositions (i.e., alternative beliefs). For an analysis of these philosophical underpinnings, see C. Stephen Evans, *The Historical Christ and the Jesus of Faith* (Oxford University Press, 1996), and Alvin Plantinga, 'Two (or More) Kinds of Scripture Scholarship', *Warranted Christian Belief* (Oxford University Press, 2002).

7 Virtually all historians agree on this today. In the eighteenth and early nineteenth centuries, scholars in Europe were deeply influenced by the rationalism of the Enlightenment and therefore came to the biblical texts with the premise that the miraculous elements in the Gospels must have been added much later to original 'factual' accounts. Since they knew that legendary accounts of historical events had to be formulated a long time after the events, they posited that the Gospels were written at least a hundred years or more after Jesus' death. But over the last century manuscript evidence has forced even the most critical scholars to conclude that they were all written much sooner. For an accessible account of how to date the various New Testament documents (including the Gospels) see F. F. Bruce, *The New Testament Documents: Are They Reliable?*, with a new foreword by the prominent scholar N. T. Wright. Also see Paul Barnett, *The New Testament*. Most would say Mark was written in

the seventies, Matthew and Luke in the eighties, and John in the nineties. This makes sense, in that they would have been written down at the time that the apostles and other eyewitnesses were beginning to die, but at a time in which many were still available to be consulted. (See the claim of Luke in Luke 1:1-4.)

8  Richard Bauckham, *Jesus and the Eyewitnesses*, Chapters 2, 3 and 6. Furthermore, in Chapter 4, Bauckham does an exhaustive analysis of the names of the figures in the Gospel stories. He concludes that they reflect the types of names of Jews in Palestine before the destruction of Jerusalem in 70 A.D., and not the sharply different kinds of proper names Jews had in the diaspora after 70 A.D. The conclusion is that it is highly unlikely that the Gospel stories originated in later Christian communities outside of Palestine.

9  N. T. Wright, *Simply Christian* (Harper, 2006), p. 97.

10  Gopnik adds: 'There are no new beliefs, no new arguments, and certainly no new evidence in the papyrus that would cause anyone to doubt who did not doubt before.' He is talking about the Gnostic text *The Gospel of Judas*. See 'Jesus Laughed', *The New Yorker*, April 17, 2006.

11  For more on the formation of the New Testament canon, see Bruce M. Metzger, *The Canon of the New Testament: Its Origin, Development, and Significance* (Oxford University Press, 1987). For a briefer survey see David G. Dunbar, 'The Biblical Canon', in *Hermeneutic, Authority, and Canon*, D. Carson and J. Woodbridge, eds. (Zondervan, 1986).

12  C. John Sommerville, *The Decline of the Secular University*, pp. 105–106.

13  We will pay more attention to this feature of the Gospel narratives in Chapter 12.

14  Bauckham, *Eyewitnesses*, pp. 170–78.

15  Wright, *Simply Christian*, p. 97.

16  C. S. Lewis, *Christian Reflections*, Walter Hooper, ed. (Eerdmans, 1967), p. 155.

17  Bauckham, *Eyewitnesses*, pp. 324–346.

18 Ibid., p. 273.

19 David Van Biema, 'Rewriting the Gospels', *Time*, March 7, 2007.

20 Vincent Taylor, *The Formation of the Gospel Tradition* 2nd ed. (Macmillan, 1935), p. 41. Also quoted and commented on in Bauckham, p. 7.

21 In his book Bauckham calls for New Testament scholarship to make a clean break with the older, very sceptical approach to the Bible called 'form criticism' and connected especially to Rudolph Bultmann. Whether this is going to happen soon or not is a matter of opinion. But books by the likes of Bauckham and Wright are opening the door for many younger scholars who are more open to the evidence that the Bible can be trusted. For an interesting account of the historical origins of sceptical biblical criticism, see Hans Frei, *The Eclipse of Biblical Narrative* (Yale University Press, 1974). For an introduction on how recent scholarship has grown much less sceptical about the Gospels' historicity than the older scholarship, see Craig Blomberg, 'Where Do We Start Studying Jesus?' in *Jesus Under Fire: Modern Scholarship Reinvents the Historical Jesus*, M. J. Wilkins and J. P. Moreland, eds. (Zondervan, 1995). The best one-volume account of recent Jesus scholarship is B. Witherington, *The Jesus Quest*, 2nd ed. (IVP, 1997). An interesting example of how much more respectful of the Bible scholarship is getting is John P. Meier, the author of the massive trilogy, *A Marginal Jew: Rethinking the Historical Jesus.* He is a moderate, middle-of-the-road scholar who rejects some biblical texts as historically dubious. Yet he makes a rather devastating critique of the older scepticism and shows that all the basic lines of the traditional view of Jesus' words and deeds can be believed on the basis of thorough historical research.

22 See Murray J. Harris, *Slave of Christ: A New Testament Metaphor for Total Devotion to Christ* (IVP, 1999), pp. 44, 70. Also see Andrew Lincoln, *Ephesians*, Word Bible Commentary, 1990, pp. 416–17: 'Modern readers [of the Bible] need to free themselves from a number of assumptions about first-century slavery, including the assumptions that there was a wide separation between the status of

slave and freedperson . . . and that all who were enslaved were trying to free themselves from this bondage. . . . There was a broad continuum of statuses between slave and free in both Roman and Greek society. Slaves of Greek owners could own property, including their own slaves, and could obtain permission to take other employment in addition to their duties as slaves. . . . It was frequently in the owner's interest to manumit them, since their labor could be obtained more cheaply if they were freedpersons. . . . Though there were undoubtedly far too many cases of cruelty, brutality, and injustice, there was no general climate of unrest among slaves.'

23 'Although it has been fashionable to deny it, antislavery doctrines began to appear in Christian theology soon after the decline of Rome and were accompanied by the eventual disappearance of slavery in all but the fringes of Christian Europe. When Europeans subsequently instituted slavery in the New World, they did so over strenuous papal opposition, a fact that was conveniently 'lost' from history until recently. Finally, the abolition of New World slavery was initiated and achieved by Christian activists. . . . Slavery was once nearly universal to all societies able to afford it, and only in the West did significant moral opposition ever arise and lead to abolition' (Rodney Stark, *For the Glory of God*, Princeton University Press, 2004, p. 291).

## Intermission

1 Dawkins, *The God Delusion*, p. 31ff.

2 For a non-technical introduction to the difference between strong and critical rationalism, see Victor Reppert, *C. S. Lewis's Dangerous Idea* (Inter-Varsity, 2003), pp. 30–44.

3 W. K. Clifford's famous essay on this subject was 'The Ethics of Belief', in which he said: 'It is wrong always, everywhere, and for anyone, to believe anything upon insufficient [empirical] evidence.' A. J. Ayer's most well-known text was *Language, Truth, and Logic*.

4 See Reppert for examples.

5  Alasdair MacIntyre's *Whose Justice? Which Rationality?* (Notre Dame University Press, 1988) provocatively and convincingly shows how there are several different 'traditions' of rationality in the West alone – the Aristotelian, the Augustinian/Thomistic, Common Sense realism. Each of them has logic and reason operating within different fundamental assumptions about things like human nature, the relationship of reason to emotion and will, the relationship of the individual to social context and tradition, and so on. A 'rational' argument is defined as consistency within the whole set of beliefs of a particular tradition. There may be plenty of overlap between these rationalities, and some arguments could be considered convincing in more than one of these traditions. But it is doubtful (to MacIntyre, impossible) that there is any one argument about the being of God that would be completely convincing to every one in every rational tradition.

6  One of the best critiques of the Enlightenment view of strong rationalism is *Faith and Rationality: On Reason and Belief in God*, A. Plantinga and N. Wolterstorff, eds. (Notre Dame University Press, 1983). The Enlightenment view has been called classic or Cartesian 'foundationalism', and that approach has been almost universally abandoned among philosophers. See also Nicholas Wolterstorff, *Reason Within the Bounds of Religion* (Eerdmans, 1984).

7  Thomas Nagel, *The Last Word* (Oxford University Press: 1997), p. 130.

8  Terry Eagleton, 'Lunging, Flailing, Mispunching': a Review of Richard Dawkins' *The God Delusion* in *London Review of Books*, vol. 28, no. 20, October 19, 2006.

9  For a sophisticated case, see H. Siegel, *Relativism Refuted: A Critique of Contemporary Epistemological Relativism* (D. Reidel, 1987). Relativists insist that 'truth' is only true within one's own framework of beliefs, and that each framework is of equal validity with all the others. Relativists say there is no framework-transcending criterion by which to adjudicate between all the truth-claims. But as Siegel points out, the relativists' claim that all frameworks (not just

their own) are equal is itself a framework-transcendent criterion of truth. With such a claim they move out of their own framework and evaluate others with their own – which is the very thing they deny to others. *'Thus . . . relativism cannot proclaim itself, or even recognize itself, without defeating itself'* (p. 43).

10 A readable treatment of critical rationalism is in Reppert, *C. S. Lewis's Dangerous Idea*, p. 36ff.

11 From *A Devil's Chaplain* (Weidenfield and Nicolson, 2003), p. 81. Quoted in A. McGrath, *The Dawkins Delusion* (Inter-Varsity, 2007), p. 100 n16.

12 'The basic structure of my argument is this. Scientists, historians, and detectives observe data and proceed thence to some theory about what best explains the occurrence of these data. We can analyze the criteria which they use in reaching a conclusion that a certain theory is better supported by the data than a different theory. . . . Using those same criteria, we find that the view that there is a God explains *everything* we observe, not just some narrow range of data.' Richard Swinburne, *Is There a God?* (Oxford University Press, 1996), p. 2.

13 C. S. Lewis, 'Is Theology Poetry?', *The Weight of Glory and Other Addresses* (HarperCollins, 1980), p. 140.

### EIGHT—The Clues of God

1 A survey can be found in Alvin Plantinga's lecture notes, 'Two Dozen (or so) Theistic Arguments', available at http://www.homestead.com/philofreligion/files/Theisticarguments.html and many other places on the Internet. See also the summary of William C. Davis, 'Theistic Arguments', in Murray, *Reason for the Hope Within* (Eerdmans, 1999).

2 Stephen Hawking and Robert Penrose, *The Nature of Time and Space* (Princeton University Press, 1996), p. 20.

3 In an interview on Salon.com, http://www.salon.com/books/int/2006/08/07/collins/index2.html, last accessed on March 9, 2007.

4 Found at http://www.truthdig.com/report/page2/20060815_
sam_harris_language_ignorance/, last accessed on March 9, 2007.

5 For a short summary of this argument see Robin Collins, 'A Scientific Argument for the Existence of God: The Fine-Tuning Design Argument', *Reason for the Hope Within*, Michael J. Murray, ed. (Eerdmans, 1999).

6 In an interview on Salon.com, http://www.salon.com/books/int/ 2006/08/07/collins/index2.html, last accessed March 9, 2007.

7 Quoted in Francis Collins, *The Language of God: A Scientist Presents Evidence for Belief* (Free Press, 2006), p. 75.

8 See Richard Dawkins, *The God Delusion* (Houghton Mifflin, 2006), p. 107.

9 From Alvin Plantinga, 'Dennett's Dangerous Idea', in *Books and Culture* (May–June 1996): 35.

10 Recounted in Collins, 'A Scientific Argument', p. 77.

11 See 'Science Gets Strange' in C. John Sommerville, *The Decline of the Secular University* (Oxford University Press, 2006). See also Diogenes Allen, *Christian Belief in a Post-Modern World* (John Knox, 1989).

12 Arthur Danto, 'Pas de Deux, en Masse: Shirin Neshat's *Rapture*', *The Nation*, June 28, 1999.

13 From Leonard Bernstein's *The Joy of Music* (Simon and Schuster, 2004), p. 105.

14 Quoted by Robin Marantz Henig in her article 'Why Do We Believe?' in *The New York Times Magazine*, March 4, 2007, p. 58.

15 The classic statement of this argument is found in the chapter on 'Hope' in C. S. Lewis, *Mere Christianity* (Macmillan).

16 N. T. Wright points out that the Christian view of beauty is not the same as the Platonic. Plato and the Greek philosophers believed that all earthly experiences of beauty point us away from this material, shadow world into the eternal spiritual world of ultimate reality. But the biblical vision of salvation is for a new heaven and new Earth. Our unfulfilled longings are not just for a spiritual, eternal world, but for *this* world, put right and made

perfect (see Wright, *Simply Christian*, pp. 44–45). This is an important point, because C. S. Lewis's famous 'argument from desire' in his *Mere Christianity* follows the Platonic model a bit too closely.

17 Quoted in Leon Wieseltier, 'The God Genome', *New York Times Book Review*, February 19, 2006.

18 *The New York Times Magazine*, March 4, 2007.

19 Henig, 'Why Do We Believe?', p. 43.

20 Ibid., p. 58.

21 Dawkins, *The God Delusion*, p. 367ff, 'Our brains themselves are evolved organs . . . evolved to help us survive.'

22 Henig, p. 7.

23 In his foreword to Richard Dawkins' *The Selfish Gene*, Robert Trivers noted Dawkins' emphasis on the role of deception in animal life, and added if indeed 'deceit is fundamental to animal communication, then there must be strong selection to spot deception and this ought, in turn, to select for a degree of self-deception, rendering some facts and motives unconscious so as not to betray – by the subtle signs of self-knowledge – the deception being practiced'. Therefore, 'the conventional view that natural selection favors nervous systems which produce ever more accurate images of the world must be a very naïve view of mental evolution.' Quote from Robert Wright, *The Moral Animal* (Pantheon, 1994), pp. 263–64. Cognitive psychologist Justin Barrett writes: 'Some cognitive scientists assume that because our brains and their functions have been 'designed' by natural selection we can trust them to tell us the truth; such an assumption is epistemologically dubious. Just because we can successfully survive and reproduce in no way ensures that our minds as a whole tell us the truth about anything – especially when it comes to sophisticated thinking . . . what a completely naturalistic view of the human mind may safely embrace is that our minds were good for survival *in the past*.' Justin L. Barrett, *Why Would Anyone Believe in God?* (AltaMira Press, 2004), p. 19.

24 Patricia S. Churchland, 'Epistemology in the Age of Neuroscience', *Journal of Philosophy* (October 1987), p. 548. Quoted in Plantinga, *Warrant and Proper Function* (Oxford University Press, 2000), p. 218.

25 Nagel, *The Last Word*, pp. 134–35.

26 Quoted in Alvin Plantinga, 'Is Naturalism Irrational?' in *Warrant and Proper Function* (Oxford University Press, 2000), p. 219.

27 For the full argument, see A. Plantinga, Chapters 11 and 12 in *Warrant and Proper Function* (Oxford University Press, 2000).

28 From Alvin Plantinga's review of Richard Dawkins' *The God Delusion* in *Books and Culture* (March/April 2007): 24.

29 Wieseltier's review, 'The God Genome', appeared in the *New York Times*, February 19, 2006.

30 C. S. Lewis, 'On Living in an Atomic Age', in *Present Concerns* (Collins, 1986), p. 76.

NINE—**The Knowledge of God**

1 Quoted in Michael J. Perry, *Toward a Theory of Human Rights: Religion, Law, Courts* (Cambridge University Press, 2007), p. 28.

2 Christian Smith, *Moral Believing Animals: Human Personhood and Culture* (Oxford University Press, 2003), p. 8.

3 Works that try to explain our sense of moral obligation as a product of natural selection include Edward O. Wilson, *On Human Nature* (Harvard University Press, 1978) and 'The Biological Basis for Morality' in *Atlantic Monthly*, April 1998; Richard Dawkins, *The Selfish Gene* (Oxford University Press, 1976) and Robert Wright, *The Moral Animal: Evolutionary Psychology and Everyday Life* (Pantheon, 1994). For some fairly scathing critiques of this approach see Philip Kitcher, *Vaulting Ambition: Sociobiology and the Quest for Human Nature* (MIT Press, 1985); Hilary Rose and Steven Rose, *Alas, Poor Darwin: Arguments Against Evolutionary Psychology* (Harmony, 2000); John Dupre, *Human Nature and the Limits of Science* (Oxford University Press, 2001).

4 Francis Collins, *The Language of God*, p. 28, where he debunks a sometimes-used example of the sterile worker ant who sacrificially toils to create an environment for mother ants to have more of their siblings. 'But "ant altruism" is readily explained in evolutionary terms by the fact that the genes motivating the sterile worker ants are exactly the same ones that will be passed on by their mother to the siblings they are helping to create. That unusually direct DNA connection does not apply to more complex populations, where evolutionists almost universally agree that selection operates on the individual, not the population.' See also George Williams, *Adaptation and Natural Selection*, reprint ed., (Princeton University Press, 1996), who argues that group selection does not occur.

5 'If (as we are supposing) Nature . . . is the only thing in the universe, then . . . We never think a thought because it is true, only because blind Nature forces us to think it. We never do an act because it is right, only because Nature forces us to do it. . . . [But] really, this . . . conclusion is unbelievable. For one thing, it is only through trusting our own minds that we have come to know Nature herself . . . then the sciences themselves would be chance arrangements of atoms and we should have no reason for believing in them . . . they are only the way in which anthropoids of our species feel when the atoms under our own skulls get in certain states – those states being produced by causes quite irrational, unhuman, non-moral. . . . There is only one way to avoid this deadlock. We must go back to a much earlier view. We must accept that we are free spirits, free and rational beings, at present happening an irrational universe, and must draw the conclusion that we are not derived from it.' (C. S. Lewis, 'On Living in an Atomic Age' in *Present Concerns*).

6 'Cultural Relativism and Universal Human Rights' by Carolyn Fleuhr-Lobban, *The Chronicle of Higher Education*, June 9, 1995. This article was cited and used to make a similar argument in George M. Marsden's *The Outrageous Idea of Christian Scholarship* (Oxford University Press, 1997), p. 86.

7 Quoted in Michael J. Perry, *Toward a Theory of Human Rights: Religion, Law, Courts* (Cambridge University Press, 2007), p. 3.

8 Ibid., p. 6.

9 Chapter 1 of Alan M. Dershowitz, *Shouting Fire: Civil Liberties in a Turbulent Age* (Little, Brown, 2002).

10 Ibid., p. 15.

11 Quoted in Perry, p. 20.

12 Perry, p. 21.

13 See Sartre's famous essay, 'Existentialism Is a Humanism'. 'God does not exist, and . . . it is necessary to draw the consequences of his absence right to the end. . . . There can no longer be any good a priori, since there is no infinite and perfect consciousness to think it. It is nowhere written that "the good" exists, that one must be honest or must not lie, since we are now upon the plane where there are only men. Dostoevsky once wrote: "If God did not exist, everything would be permitted". . . . Everything is indeed permitted if God does not exist, and man is in consequence forlorn, for he cannot find anything to depend upon either within or outside himself.' This essay can be found in *Existentialism from Dostoyevsky to Sartre*, ed. Walter Kaufman (Meridian, 1989). It can be found on-line at http://www.marxists.org/reference/archive/sartre/works/exist/sartre.htm as of March 17, 2007.

14 Perry, *Toward a Theory of Human Rights*, p. xi.

15 Ibid., p. 23. Another recent book on this subject is E. Bucar and B. Barnett, eds., *Does Human Rights Need God?* (Eerdmans, 2005).

16 Arthur Allen Leff, 'Unspeakable Ethics, Unnatural Law', *Duke Law Journal* (December 1979).

17 F. Nietzsche, *Thus Spoke Zarathustra*, part IV, 'On the Higher Man', near the end of section I.

18 Raimond Gaita, *A Common Humanity: Thinking About Love and Truth and Justice.* (Quoted in Michael J. Perry, *Toward a Theory of Human Rights*, pp. 7 and 17–18.)

19 From Chapter 10, 'Fecundity', in Annie Dillard, *Pilgrim at Tinker Creek* (HarperCollins, 1974).

20 Quoted in Peter C. Moore, *One Lord, One Faith* (Thomas Nelson, 1994), p. 128.

21 C. S. Lewis, 'On Living in an Atomic Age' (1948), reprinted in the volume *Present Concerns*, pp. 73–80.

## TEN—The Problem of Sin

1 Barbara B. Taylor, *Speaking of Sin: The Lost Language of Salvation* (Cowley, 2000), pp. 57–67.

2 Andrew Delbanco, *The Real American Dream: A Meditation on Hope* (Harvard University Press, 2000), p. 25.

3 Søren Kierkegaard, *The Sickness Unto Death: A Christian Psychological Exposition for Edification and Awakening* (Penguin, 1989), pp. 111, 113.

4 Ernest Becker, *The Denial of Death* (Free Press, 1973), pp. 3, 7.

5 Ibid., p. 160.

6 Ibid., p. 109.

7 Ibid., p. 166. It is important to note that Becker was not trying to promote faith. He was an atheist, so that was not his agenda.

8 If we use Kierkegaard's definition we can categorise various 'god-substitutes' and the particular kinds of brokenness and damage that each one brings into a life. So we could discern some of the following:

- If you centre your life and identity on your spouse or partner, you will be emotionally dependent, jealous and controlling. The other person's problems will be overwhelming to you.
- If you centre your life and identity on your family and children, you will try to live your life through your children until they resent you or have no self of their own. At worst, you may abuse them when they displease you.
- If you centre your life and identity on your work and career, you will be a driven workaholic and a boring, shallow person.

At worst you will lose family and friends and, if your career goes poorly, develop deep depression.

- If you centre your life and identity on money and possessions, you'll be eaten up by worry or jealousy about money. You'll be willing to do unethical things to maintain your lifestyle, which will eventually blow up your life.

- If you centre your life and identity on pleasure, gratification and comfort, you will find yourself getting addicted to something. You will become chained to the 'escape strategies' by which you avoid the hardness of life.

- If you centre your life and identity on relationships and approval, you will be constantly overly hurt by criticism and thus always losing friends. You will fear confronting others and therefore will be a useless friend.

- If you centre your life and identity on a 'noble cause', you will divide the world into 'good' and 'bad' and demonise your opponents. Ironically, you will be controlled by your enemies. Without them, you have no purpose.

- If you centre your life and identity on religion and morality, you will, if you are living up to your moral standards, be proud, self-righteous and cruel. If you don't live up to your standards, your guilt will be utterly devastating.

9  Thomas C. Oden, *Two Worlds: Notes on the Death of Modernity in America and Russia* (IVP, 1992), Chapter 6.

10 It is important to remember that when you forgive a person that does not mean that you don't hold them accountable for what they have done. It is not an either/or situation – you must do both. When the women were counselled to forgive that does not mean they were advised to simply allow their husbands' behaviour to continue without confrontation. This is spelled out in more detail in Chapter 11.

11 Darcey Steinke, *Easter Everywhere: A Memoir* (Bloomsbury, 2007), p. 114.

12 Cynthia Heimel, 'Tongue in Chic' column, in *The Village Voice*, January 2, 1990, pp. 38–40.

13 Dorothy L. Sayers, *Creed or Chaos?* (Harcourt and Brace, 1949), pp. 38–39.

14 By far the best edition of this remarkable treatise is printed in Paul Ramsay, *The Works of Jonathan Edwards: Ethical Writings*, vol. 8 (Yale University Press, 1989). The introductory notes by Ramsay are very important.

15 Debra Rienstra, *So Much More: An Invitation to Christian Spirituality* (Jossey-Bass, 2005), p. 41.

## ELEVEN—Religion and the Gospel

1 In the broader sense, religion is any belief system of ultimate values that shapes our pursuit of a particular kind of life in the world. This is the reason that it is quite fair to call secularism a religion, and Christianity as well. However, virtually all religions require to one degree or another a form of self-salvation through merit. They require that people approach God and become worthy through various rites, observances and behaviours. This is also what most people think of when they think of religion, and in this sense Christianity as presented in the New Testament is radically distinct. That is why for the purposes of this chapter we will speak of Christianity as distinct from 'religion'.

2 Flannery O'Connor, *Wise Blood: Three by Flannery O'Connor* (Signet, 1962), p. 16.

3 Richard Lovelace, *The Dynamics of Spiritual Life* (IVP, 1979), pp. 212ff.

4 On how self is created by exclusion – Miroslav Volf, *Exclusion and Embrace* (Abingdon, 1996).

5 Victor Hugo, *Les Miserables*, Book One, Chapter 13, 'Little Gervais'.

## TWELVE—The (True) Story of the Cross

1 C. S. Lewis, *Letters to Malcolm: Chiefly on Prayer* (Harcourt Brace, and World, 1964), p. 106.

2 For a full discussion of Bonhoeffer's example of forgiveness, see Chapter 1, 'The Cost of Forgiveness: Dietrich Bonhoeffer and the Reclamation of a Christian Vision and Practice', in L. Gregory Jones, *Embodying Forgiveness: A Theological Analysis* (Eerdmans, 1995).

3 Dietrich Bonhoeffer, *The Cost of Discipleship* (Macmillan, 1967), p. 100.

4 Eberhard Bethge, Dietrich Bonhoeffer, eds. *Letters and Papers from Prison*, abridged (London: SCM Press, 1953), p. 144.

5 The charge that the cross is 'divine child abuse' seems to assume that the Father in heaven is the real God and Jesus is just some other kind of divine being who is being killed. This fails to do justice to the Christian doctrine of the Trinity. Christians believe that though the Father and the Son are distinct persons, they share the same being and substance, so that when Jesus bore the cost of forgiveness it was God doing so. For more on the Trinity see Chapter 13.

6 An illustration is in order. Imagine that you are walking along a river with a friend, and your friend suddenly says to you, 'I want to show you how much I love you!' and with that he throws himself into the river and drowns. Would you say in response, 'How he loved me!' No, of course not. You'd wonder about your friend's mental state. But what if you were walking along a river with a friend and you fell into the river by accident, and you can't swim. What if he dived in after you and pushed you to safety but was himself drawn under by the current and drowned. *Then* you would respond, 'Behold, how he loved me!' The example of Jesus is a bad example if it is *only* an example. If there was no peril to save us from – if we were not lost apart from the ransom of his death – then the model of his sacrificial love is not moving and life-changing; it is crazy. Unless Jesus died as our substitute, he can't die as a moving example of sacrificial love.

7 Quoted in David Van Biema, 'Why Did Jesus Have to Die?' *Time*, April 12, 2004, p. 59.

8 John Stott, *The Cross of Christ* (Inter-Varsity Press, 1986), p. 160.

9 JoAnne Terrell's story is recounted in Van Biema, 'Why Did Jesus Have to Die?', p. 61. The John Stott quote is found on the same page.

10 N. T. Wright, *Simply Christian* (Harper, 2006), p. 110.

11 Matthew 27:45–46.

12 'The Gospels contain . . . a story of a larger kind which embraces all the essence of [other] stories. But *this* story has entered history and the primary world . . . [T]his story is supreme; and it is true.' J. R. R. Tolkien, 'On Fairy Stories', in *The Tolkien Reader* (Del Rey, 1986).

## THIRTEEN—The Reality of the Resurrection

1 Bauckham, *Eyewitnesses*, p. 273.

2 N. T. Wright, *The Resurrection of the Son of God* (Fortress, 2003), p. 608.

3 Ibid., pp. 686, 688.

4 It is common for people to claim that the idea of 'dying and rising gods' was found in religions all over the ancient Near East. Yes, those myths existed, but even if you suppose Jesus' Jewish followers knew those pagan legends (which is not at all certain) nobody even in the pagan religions believed that resurrection happened to individual human beings. See N. T. Wright, *Simply Christian*, p. 113, and his extensive research on dying and-rising-god myths in *Resurrection of the Son of God*.

5 Wright, *The Resurrection of the Son of God* (Fortress, 2003), pp. 200–206.

6 Wright, *Who Was Jesus?* (Eerdmans, 1993), p. 63.

7 Wright, *The Resurrection of the Son of God* (Fortress, 2003), pp. 578–83.

8 Ibid., p. 552.

9 Ibid., p. 707 and n. 63.

10 N. T. Wright, *For All God's Worth: True Worship and the Calling of the Church* (Eerdmans, 1997), pp. 65–66.

FOURTEEN—**The Dance of God**

1  Hilary of Poitiers, in *Concerning the Trinity* (3:1), says each person of the Trinity 'reciprocally contains the others, so that one permanently envelopes and is permanently enveloped by, the others whom he yet envelopes'. See also Robert Letham on Tom Torrance: *The Holy Trinity: In Scripture, History, Theology, and Worship* (Presbyterian and Reformed, 2004), pp. 265, 373. '"Perichoresis" involves mutual movement as well as mutual indwelling. It is the eternal movement of Love or the Communion of Love which the Holy Trinity is ever within himself.'

2  Cornelius Plantinga, *Engaging God's World: A Christian Vision of Faith, Learning, and Living* (Eerdmans, 2002).

3  C. S. Lewis, 'The Good Infection', in *Mere Christianity*.

4  There are many very profound implications of Trinitarian thought that have been traced out by thinkers over the centuries. The ancient problem of the One and the Many – from Plato and Aristotle through to Modernity and Postmodernity – has bedevilled philosophers for centuries. Is unity more important than particularity, or vice versa? Is the individual more important than the group, or vice versa? Are universals more important than particularities and contexts, or vice versa? Cultures have had to choose between absolutism and relativism, between individualism and collectivism. But if God is triune and is as much a unity as a diversity, then Trinitarian philosophical thought should not fit on the spectrum between absolutism and relativism, nor should its social thought fit on a spectrum between collectivism and individualism. Neither the individual nor the family/tribe should be the ultimate social unit. Neither legalism nor relativism should characterise the moral philosophy. For some extremely stimulating reflections on the promise of Trinitarian thought, see the works of Colin Gunton, particularly *The One, the Three, and the Many (Bampton Lectures)* (Cambridge University Press, 1993); *The Triune Creator: A Historical and Systematic Study* (Eerdmans, 1998); and *The Promise of Trinitarian Theology* (T.&T. Clark, 2004).

5  Consider the statement of Lee Kuan Yew, Minister Mentor of Singapore, on the controversy over the judicial caning of Michael Fay in 1994. To Western journalists he said, 'To us in Asia, an individual is an ant. To you, he's a child of God. It is an amazing concept.' Quoted in Daniel C. Dennett, *Darwin's Dangerous Idea: Evolution and the Meaning of Life* (1995), p. 474.

6  G. K. Chesterton, *Orthodoxy* (Dodd, Mead, 1959), p. 245. Quoted in Rienstra, *So Much More*, p. 37.

7  'What we have, then, is a picture of God whose love, even before the creation of anything, is other-oriented. . . . There has always been an other-orientation in the very nature of God. . . . We are the friends of God by virtue of the intra-Trinitarian love of God that so worked out in the fullness of time that the plan of redemption, conceived in the mind of God in eternity past, has exploded into our space-time history at exactly the right moment.' D. A. Carson, *The Difficult Doctrine of the Love of God* (IVP/UK, 2000), pp. 44–45.

8  George Marsden, *Jonathan Edwards: A Life* (Yale University Press, 2003), pp. 462–63.

9  Rienstra, *So Much More*, p. 38.

10  C. S. Lewis, *The Problem of Pain* (Macmillan, 1961), p. 140.

11  Vinoth Ramachandra, *The Scandal of Jesus* (IVP, 2001).

12  C. S. Lewis, *The Last Battle* (Collier, 1970), pp. 171, 184.

## Epilogue

1  'Letter to Mr.–', *Flannery O'Connor: Collected Works* (Library of America, 1988), p. 1148.

2  'The Fiction Writer and His Country'. *Flannery O'Connor: Collected Works* (Library of America, 1988), pp. 804–805.

3  From a sermon by Dick Lucas, Matthew 11.

4  Quotes from 'Revelation' in *Three by Flannery O'Connor* (Penguin, 1983).

5  Joseph Epstein, 'The Green Eyed Monster: Envy Is Nothing to Be Jealous Of ', *Washington Monthly*, July/August 2003.

# INDEX

# About the Author

Timothy Keller was born and raised in Pennsylvania, and educated at Bucknell University, Gordon-Conwell Theological Seminary and Westminster Theological Seminary. However, he learned the most from his nine years as a pastor of West Hopewell Presbyterian Church in the small blue-collar town of Hopewell, Virginia. The congregation there loved him, suffered through his earliest days as a pastor, and taught an overeducated, egg-headed Northerner to be CLEAR. His second church was Redeemer Presbyterian Church, in Manhattan, which he started in 1989 with his wife, Kathy, and their three young sons. Today Redeemer has nearly six thousand regular attendees at five services, a host of daughter churches, and is planting churches in large cities throughout the world.